Metaphorical Theology

Metaphorical Theology

Models of God in Religious Language

SALLIE McFAGUE

FORTRESS PRESS   PHILADELPHIA

To Elizabeth and John

Library of Congress Cataloging in Publication Data

McFague, Sallie.
  Metaphorical theology.
    1. Christianity and language. 2. God—Knowableness.
I. Title.
BR115.L25M345 1982   201'.4   82-7246
ISBN 0–8006–1687–1   AACR2

Printed in the United States of America   1-1687

00 99   8 9 10 11 12 13 14 15 16

Contents

Preface   vii

Preface to the Second Printing   x

1 Toward a Metaphorical Theology   1
   The Problem of Religious Language   1
   The Idolatry of Religious Language   4
   The Irrelevance of Religious Language   7
   Can Religious Language Be Revitalized?   10
   Metaphorical Theology   14

2 Metaphor, Parable, and Scripture   31
   Metaphor   32
   Parable   42
   Scripture   54

3 Models in Science   67
   Models in the Social Sciences and Technology   67
   Natural Science, the Humanities, and the
     Imagination   75
   Paradigms   79
   Types of Models and Two Views of Models in
     Science   83
   Central Insights from Scientific Models
     Pertinent to Theology   90

4 Models in Theology   103
   Differences Between Scientific and Theological
     Models   103
   Parable, Paradigm, and Root-Metaphor in
     Christianity   108
   Creeds: Models or Dogmas?   111
   Models and Concepts   117

The Truth of Theological Models 131
Criteria for Theological Models 137

5 God the Father: Model or Idol? 145
Patriarchy in Perspective 147
Revolutionary Feminist Theology: A New Paradigm
and a New Model 152
Reformist Feminist Theology: The Search for New
Models 164
God the Friend 177

Conclusion 193

Notes 195

Index of Authors 223

Preface

The present essay is a sequel to my book *Speaking in Parables: A Study in Metaphor and Theology* (Philadelphia: Fortress Press, 1975). The earlier work focused on primary religious language: on the images, parables, metaphors, and stories that make up our most immediate expressions of religious reality. It also stressed some of the forms which emerged from these initial expressions in the Christian tradition—poetry, novels, and autobiographies. In part, the book attempted to suggest a variety of reflective forms other than constructive theology as genuine Christian literature in light of what appeared to me to be an improper primacy of theological reflection over other forms. The value of the book, in retrospect, was its recognition of the importance in religion of imagistic language as the base and funding for conceptual, theological language; however, I did not attend to the movement from the one language to the other. The present book attempts to make up for that lack.

The way in which I interpret what Robert Funk calls the tortuous route between the parables of Jesus and systematic theology is necessarily a limited, biased, and finally personal way. That is to say, it is but *one* way within a tradition that allows for other ways and it is a way influenced by my own tradition of Protestantism as well as by my own sensibility and personal faith. I believe it is a way, as I will try to show, that is both contemporary and Christian—but surely, not the only contemporary or Christian way. David Tracy, in his recent book *The Analogical Imagination: Christian Theology and the Culture of Pluralism* (New York: Crossroad, 1981), has done a great service by emphasizing the ecumenical, pluralistic character of theological reflection, not only within the Christian tradition, but also as that tradition enters into serious conversation with other major religious traditions. For too long, he says, theology has been done as if only one way were possible or right. The great theologians of whatever religious or theological persuasion know better; for one of the distinctive marks of their work is humility and a sense of limitation in the face of the awesomeness if not absurdity of their task—speaking of God. Our age, which has pressed home the lessons of historical relativity and pluralism, has also become aware of the relativity and pluralism of theology's resources: Scripture and tradition. Different perspectives and interpretations are not necessarily incorrect because they are different: limitation and variety are endemic to theological reflection given its subject matter—the meaning of human life in light of the transforming activity of God. In short, there is no *one* way to express this event as there can be no *one* perspective from which to approach it. Each theologian can only try to identify as clearly as possible the perspective from which she or he reflects, the tradition out of which he or she comes, and the sensibility which prompts one chosen perspective rather than another. Then, in conversation with other perspectives, the inadequacies, limitations, and possible errors can be mitigated.

In other words, no one writes the full, complete theology. As Tracy rightly points out, each theology is an intensification of a particular, concrete tradition and sensibility. It *should* be thus, as long as other ways are kept in view and the limitations of one's own way acknowledged. The present essay is such a limited attempt. It comes out of a post-Enlightenment, Protestant, feminist perspective, a perspective which I would characterize as skeptical, relativistic, prophetic, and iconoclastic. It is more aware of the discontinuities between God and the world than of the continuities. It seeks a way of believing in a nonbelieving time by asserting no more than the evidence supports rather than what the tradition has proclaimed. For instance, I have not found it possible as a contemporary Christian to support an incarnational christology or a canonical Scripture; nevertheless, I have found it possible to support a "parabolic" christology and Scripture as the Christian "classic." Both notions are in keeping, I believe, with the Protestant sensibility and both, I also believe, are legitimate interpretations of the evidence. Neither, however, is the only option open to Christians. I present them, as well as arguments on other matters, with intensity, conviction, and without constant qualification, for such qualification enervates arguments attempting to show legitimacy and appropriateness. Yet I am well aware that my perspective is not shared by many others—it may not be necessary for them or possible for them.

I have written this book as part of the "conversation" that is theology. I have done so in a somewhat single-minded way, attempting to see what "a metaphorical perspective" would produce if argued as consistently and thoroughly as is possible. In part, it is a "thought experiment": What would the relations between religious and theological language look like if seen in the light of the way metaphors become models, in light of the relativity and openness of metaphorical thinking, and in light of the intrinsic iconoclastic and transformative character of metaphorical thought? Would such a way of dealing with the tortuous route from Jesus' parables to systematic thought be both contemporary and Christian? Would it avoid the idolatry and literalism that has plagued much religious language and would it prove a way to make religious language more relevant to people excluded from traditional religious language? These are some of the questions which I have tried to deal with in my "thought experiment."

I am grateful for many helpful comments and suggestions from persons who read all or part of this book during various stages of its composition: Ian Barbour, Martha Crunkleton, F. W. Dillistone, Fiona Fredenburgh, Mary Lee Kelly, Mary Ann Tolbert, and Maurice Wiles. I wish to thank John Hollar of Fortress Press for his several suggestions for revision and his careful editing of the manuscript. I am also indebted to the Association of Theological Schools and to the National Endowment for the Humanities for grants enabling me to work on the book for a year in Oxford, England. Finally, I thank my mother, Jessie McFague, for typing the final manuscript.

Preface to the Second Printing

In his presidential address to the American Academy of Religion in 1982, Gordon Kaufman called upon theologians and students of religion in the Judeo-Christian tradition "to enter into the most radical kind of deconstruction and reconstruction of the traditions we have inherited, including especially their most central and precious symbols, *God* and *Jesus Christ* and *Torah*."* In that address Kaufman states that, in view of the unprecedented possibility that we may well annihilate not just ourselves but life as such on our planet, the traditional symbolism of the Judeo-Christian tradition may be not merely irrelevant but harmful. Consider, he suggests, the implications of dependence on an almighty, patriarchal God to save humanity and the earth from nuclear disaster. The traditional imagery for God, Kaufman claims, tends to support either militarism or escapism, but not the one thing needful—human responsibility for the fate of the earth.

The deconstruction and reconstruction of models by which we understand the relationship between God and the world is, in my opinion, one of the most serious tasks facing contemporary theology. The nuclear threat provides the most extreme reason for engaging in that enterprise but certainly not the only one. In many ways the traditional imagery is anachronistic and not in keeping with the contemporary cultural sensibility which can be characterized as "post-modern." The Enlightenment was the "first watershed," thrusting us into the modern world. Many now see us entering the "second watershed," which is distinguished by a set of assumptions different from those of modernity. These assumptions include a greater appreciation for nature; a recognition of the importance of language to human existence; a chastened admiration for technology; an acceptance of the challenge that other religious options present to the Judeo-Christian tradition; an apocalyptic sensibility; a sense of the displacement of the white, Western male and the rise of those dispossessed due to gender, race,

---

* Subsequently published as an article, "Nuclear Eschatology and the Study of Religion," *Journal of the American Academy of Religion* 51 (1983): 13.

or class; and, perhaps most significantly, a growing awareness of the radical interdependence of life at all levels and in every imaginable way. Theological work, as is true of all constructive work, must, I believe, take place within the post-modern context if it is to address the pressing issues of our time.

In the closing chapter of *Metaphorical Theology*, I attempt a "thought-experiment" with the model of God as friend. This experiment has generated a good deal of interest, in part, I believe, because this model provides a way of interpreting our relationship with God that is consonant with the post-modern sensibility and supports human responsibility for our world. Much more of this kind of theological work needs to be done, for it is only as the basic metaphors in which we imagine the relationship between God and the world change that our way of being in the world will change as well. If we are to have a nuclear-free world in which all beings live in mutuality and interdependence, we must begin to think of God and the world with models that support that vision. Some of these will be anthropomorphic models such as God as lover, mother, healer, liberator; others will be from the natural world; still others will be nonmaterial and abstract in character. *Metaphorical Theology* provides the theoretical context, I believe, for such work to take place, but it is only a beginning.

The difficulty of this project must not be underestimated. Mark Kline Taylor made a sobering comment on this point in a review of *Metaphorical Theology*: "McFague . . . must show how language has its power to revitalize when faced by the entrenched distortions of economic and social privilege."* As the deconstructionists, most notably Michel Foucault, have shown us, language is controlled by those in power and those who would change it have a formidable task. Some would say, Foucault among them, that only a revolution—reversing the "insiders" and the "outsiders"—will bring such change about. The powerless become the powerful and vice versa. Perhaps that is the only way. But models of God as mother, lover, friend, and healer suggest a different vision of existence. It is one of mutuality, nurture, self-sacrifice, fidelity, and care for the oppressed and vulnerable. In such a vision, delight in the other, not domination of the other, is central. If such a vision of an alternative way of being in the world is to be effective, it must take place not only within the academy but also and primarily among ordinary people who will begin to talk to and about God with new metaphors and models. Is such change possible? We are just beginning the serious deconstruction and reconstruction of religious lan-

---

Theology Today 40/4 (1984): 472.

guage and one aspect of that task is a "thought-experiment" to probe the implications of alternative models. Whether these models can gain acceptance and thus make a difference in both the ways we think about God and act in the world is not known. The "entrenched distortions of economic and social privilege" present a formidable opponent. But the pressures to change our orientation are becoming enormous, and as more and more people, both lay and academic, become concerned, genuine transformation is seen not as a desired, but as a necessary, dimension of the future.

Sallie McFague
May 29, 1984

1 Toward a Metaphorical Theology

There is a God. There is no God. Where is the problem? I am quite sure that there is a God in the sense that I am sure my love is no illusion. I am quite sure there is no God in the sense that I am sure there is nothing which resembles what I can conceive when I say that word.[1]

Simone Weil, in her book *Waiting for God*, states the problem of religious language in the classic way. As a religious person, she is certain that her love for God is not an illusion, but she is equally certain that none of her conceptions of the divine resembles God. Her comments are in the great tradition of deeply religious people, and especially the mystics of all religious traditions, who feel conviction at the level of experience, at the level of worship, but great uncertainty at the level of words adequate to express the reality of God.

Augustine, the great Bishop of Hippo, notes that even the person who says the most about God is but "dumb," and yet, he adds, our only alternatives are to speak in halting, inadequate words or to remain silent. The Judeo-Christian tradition, more than many other religious traditions, has chosen not to remain silent. In fact, this tradition and especially Christianity, and within Christianity especially Protestantism, has focused on and at times been obsessed by words, both "the Word of God" and human words about God.

The Problem of Religious Language

Increasingly, however, religious language is a problem for us, a problem of a somewhat different kind than the classical one. For most of us, it is not a question of being sure of God while being unsure of our language about God. Rather, we are unsure both at the experiential and the expressive levels. We are unsure at the experiential level because we are, even the most religious of us, secular in ways our foremothers and forefathers were not. We do not live in a sacramental universe in which the things of this world, its joys and catastrophes, harvests and famines, births and deaths, are understood as connected to and permeated by divine power and love. Our experience, our daily experience, is for the most part non-religious. Most of us go through the days accepting our fortunes and explaining our world without direct reference to God. If we experience God at all it tends to be at a private level and in a sporadic way; the natural and public events of our world do not stand for or image God.

Certainly we cannot return to the time of the sacramental universe; but apart from a *religious context* of some kind, religious language becomes both idolatrous and irrelevant. It becomes *idolatrous* because without a sense of awe, wonder, and mystery, we forget the inevitable distance between our words and the divine reality. It becomes *irrelevant* because without a sense of the immanence of the divine in our lives, we find language about God empty and meaningless. It is no accident, then, that the mystics in all religious traditions have been the most perceptive on the question of religious language. Aware as they are of the transcendence of God, they have not been inclined to identify our words with God; in fact, their tendency is more often to refuse any similarity between our words and the divine reality. Simone Weil stands foursquare in this tradition when she says there is "nothing" which resembles her thoughts about God. The mystics, however, have also been the most imaginative and free in their language about God, finding all sorts of language relevant. As Augustine notes, we must use all the best images available to us in order to say *something* about the divine. The mystics have also not restricted their language about God to biblical or traditional imagery, for the experience of God, the certainty and the immediacy of it, has been the basis for new and powerful religious language.

The *primary context*, then, for any discussion of religious language is worship. Unless one has a sense of the mystery surrounding existence, of the profound inadequacy of all our thoughts and words, one will most likely identify God with our words: God *becomes* father, mother, lover, friend. Unless one has a sense of the nearness of God, the overwhelming sense of the way God pervades and permeates our very being, one will not find religious images significant: the power of the images for God of father, mother, lover, friend will not be appreciated. Apart from a religious context, religious language will inevitably go awry either in the direction of idolatry or irrelevancy or both.

There is, however, another critical context for religious language, one that has not been as central in the classical tradition and that does not surface in the quotation by Weil. In the broadest sense, we could call this the *interpretive context*. It is the context that recognizes that we who attempt to speak about God are social, cultural, and historical beings with particular perspectives influenced by a wide range of factors. The interpretive context within religious faiths has usually been limited to the "tradition," meaning the church or another institution which has set the interpretive precedents for what is proper (orthodox) or improper (heretical) religious language. In the last two hundred years, however, the interpretive context has increased greatly as people have realized the relativity of perspectives. With the introduction of historical criticism of religious texts, we became aware of the relativity of the words and images in sacred Scriptures, that these texts were written by limited people who expressed their experiences of divine reality in the manners and mores of their historical times.

Most recently, we have become conscious, by deepening our awareness of the *plurality* of perspectives, of dimensions of interpretation which had been largely submerged. That is to say, it is not only our time and place in history that influences our religious language, but also our class, race, and sex; our nationality, education, and family background; our interests, prejudices, and concerns. We have become aware, for instance, of the varying interests that determined the perspectives of New Testament writers. They not only saw their religious experience through the glasses of first-century Palestine but also through the refractions provided by their own individual histories and concerns. Consciousness of the relativity and plurality of interpretations forces us to recognize that religious language is not just the halting attempts by "Christians" to say something appropriate about God, but is the halting attempts by specific individuals: by Paul, a first-century convert from Judaism, who had great empathy with the problems of Jewish Christians but little sympathy for women or slave Christians; by Julian of Norwich, a medieval woman mystic, who spoke of "our tender Mother Jesus"; by Reinhold Niebuhr, a twentieth-century preacher from Detroit, whose experience with American capitalism caused him to see human sinfulness as the basis for political "realism"; by Mary Daly, a twentieth-century, Catholic-educated feminist, who sees the history of the world's religions as an exercise in misogyny. If we lose sight of the relativity and plurality of the interpretive context, our religious language will, as with the loss of the religious context, become idolatrous or irrelevant. It will become idolatrous, for we will absolutize one tradition of images for God; it will become irrelevant, for the experiences of many people will not be included within the canonized tradition.

The issues that emerge, then, from both the worship and the interpretive contexts of religious language, are *idolatry* and *irrelevance*: either we take our language about God literally or we find it meaningless. Another way to phrase these issues is to ask the questions: How does religious language refer to God and which religious images are central? Is there a way of speaking of religious language as referring to God without identifying it with the divine? Are there images which are central to a religious tradition *and* are there revolutionary possibilities within that tradition aiding new images to emerge? These are very complex questions, for they focus on the heart of language—its truth and its meaning. Does religious language refer to anything; if so, to what and how? Does religious language mean anything; if so, what and to whom? Our route to suggesting modest answers to these questions will be slow and indirect, as I believe is appropriate to the subject matter; but a beginning can be made by illustrating the issues of idolatry and irrelevance, truth and meaning, through contemporary movements within our culture that find them especially problematic.

The Idolatry of Religious Language

On the issue of the truth of religious language, there are continuing, powerful, conservative religious movements which insist on the literal reference of language to God. Religious conservatism is a widespread tendency within contemporary culture, not restricted to groups which call themselves "evangelicals" or "fundamentalists." This tendency is linked with fear of relativizing Scripture through historical criticism and a refusal to accept a plurality of interpretive perspectives. The Bible, says this movement, *is* the Word of God; the Bible is inerrant or divinely inspired; the words and images of the Bible are the authoritative and appropriate words and images for God. The Bible is a sacred text, different from all other texts, and not relative and pluralistic as are all other human products. The Bible becomes an idol: the fallible, human words of Scripture are understood as referring correctly and literally to God. Even where these sentiments are not expressed clearly or in such extreme fashion, religious literalism remains a powerful current in our society. And it does not stem only from a fear of relativism and plurality. It also derives from the understanding of what counts as "true" in our culture. What is "true" in our positivistic, scientifically oriented society is what corresponds with "reality," with the "facts." Translated into artistic terms, this means realistic art; the "true" painting or sculpture is a copy of what it represents. Translated into religious terms, "true" religious language is also a copy of what it represents; in other words, a literal or realistic representation of God's nature. If the Bible says that God is "father" then God is literally, really, "father"; the word "father" and the associations of that word truly refer to God's nature. In the same way that the law of gravity refers to the way things really are in the world, so "father" refers to the way God really is.

But there is, I believe, an even deeper reason why religious literalism runs rampant in our time. It is not only that many people have lost the practice of religious contemplation and prayer, which alone is sufficient to keep literalism at bay, or that positivistic scientism has injected a narrow view of truth into our culture. While both are true, it is also the case that we do not think in symbols in the way our forebears did. That is to say, we do not see the things of this world as standing for something else; they are simply what they are. A symbolic sensibility, on the contrary, sees multilayered realities, with the literal level suggestive of meanings beyond itself. While it may have been more justified for people in earlier times to be biblical literalists since they were less conscious of relativity, as symbolic thinkers, they were *not* literalists. From the third century on, the "fourfold method of exegesis"—in which three levels of interpretation followed the literal level—permitted and encouraged the exercise of the imagination in the interpretation of Scripture. While many of the "anagogical" and "tropological" interpretations were fanciful, the abandonment of the four levels in the Protestant Reformation, with the claim that the text was self-explanatory, eventually resulted in literalism.[2] The claim can be made that our time is *more* literalistic than any other time in history. Not only were double, triple, and more meanings once seen in Scripture (and Scripture considered richer as a consequence), but our notion of history as the recording of "facts" is alien to the biblical consciousness. The ancients were less literalistic than we are, aware that truth has many levels and that when one writes the story of an influential person's life, one's perspective will color that story. Our is a literalistic mentality; theirs was a symbolical mentality. There can be no return to a symbolical mentality in its earlier forms; we no longer believe in four levels of scriptural exegesis or in a three-tiered universe.

Nor can many of us return to a symbolical mentality in its sacramental form; for instance, belief that natural and human objects and events are "figures" of the divine. For a traditional sacramental sensibility, the bread and wine of the Eucharist are symbols of divine nurture; they do not merely "point to" spiritual food, but really and truly *are* spiritual food. The things of this world participate in and signify what transcends our world. The sacramental sensibility depends upon a belief that everything is connected, that the beings of this world are analogously related to God (Being-Itself), and hence can be sacramentally related to God. The analogy of being by which all that is *is* because of its radical dependence on God ties everything together in a silent ontological web which reverberates with similarity within dissimilarity out to its farthest reaches. Even a corpse, says Augustine, is like God to the extent that it still has some degree of order left in its decaying flesh and emerging skeleton. In such a universe, everything holds together, everything fits, everything is related.

For a genuine symbolical sensibility such as Dante embraced in his *Divine Comedy*, the symbol—the finite object which signifies the infinite by participating in it—is neither literalized nor spiritualized. It does not become an idol or a mere sign. In our time, however, when there is skepticism concerning the unity of all that is, symbols tend either to be literalized (as in fundamentalism or the doctrine of transubstantiation) or spiritualized (as in Feuerbach or Protestant liberalism).

The medieval sacramental sensibility is not ours, either in theory or practice. Our time is characterized by disunity, by skepticism that anything is related to anything else, and by secularity. If there is to be any fresh understanding of the truth of images as a counter to literalistic truth, it will have to be one that takes seriously the characteristics of the contemporary sensibility.[3]

Before we leave this preliminary overview of literalism and the truth of religious language, it is necessary to add a word from social anthropology about *why* people cling to religious systems with such fervor, especially if they appear threatened by a secularized, relativistic, and pluralistic culture. As Clifford Geertz points out, human beings are "unfinished" at birth and must construct and order their world in ways that no other animals must do. Monkeys and bees are born into a monkey or bee "world" respectively—which is simply there for them. Having to construct our world, we are necessarily (if only subconsciously) protective of it and extremely anxious if it is threatened. We depend, says Geertz, so deeply on our constructions for our most basic sense of sanity that any threat to them is a threat to our very being.[4] Thus, one can conclude that people will be less open, less imaginative, less flexible during times of threat. They will be more literalistic, absolutist, dogmatic when the construction which orders their world is relativized, either through pluralistic perspectives from within the tradition or competing systems from without. Given the pressures against the traditional Christian imagistic system from, for instance, both the liberation theologies and from other world religions, this retreat into literalistic, absolutist hibernation is no surprise.

But literalism will not do. Much of this essay will be devoted to trying to show why it will not do and what the alternative is. Two thoughtful theologians point us in the right direction on the matter of religious language, the first with a straightforward admonition, the second with an analogy of religious language with poetic. British theologian Ian T. Ramsey has written:

> Let us always be cautious of talking about God in straightforward language. Let us never talk as if we had privileged access to the diaries of God's private life . . . so that we may say quite cheerfully why God did what, when and where.[5]

This admonition is never necessary for deeply religious people or persons aware of their own relative and limited perspectives. Old Testament scholar Phyllis Trible has written:

> To appropriate the metaphor of a Zen sutra, poetry is "like a finger pointing to the moon." It is a way to see the light that shines in darkness, a way to participate in transcendent truth and to embrace reality. To equate the finger with the moon or to acknowledge the finger and not perceive the moon is to miss the point.[6]

Or, to rephrase Trible's words for our subject, either to equate human words with the divine reality or to see no relationship between them is inappropriate. Rather, the proper way is "like a finger pointing to the moon." Is *this* the way "to participate in transcendent truth and to embrace reality"? I would agree with Trible that it is; I would call it the "metaphorical" way and will be elaborating on it as the form of religious language.

The Irrelevance of Religious Language

Turning now to the second problem facing religious language in our time—irrelevancy—we note that it also is a widespread phenomenon. In a secularized culture where the practice of regular public and private prayer is not widespread, this is bound to be the case. For many, the images in the Bible have sentimental significance from childhood days and happier times; for some, the biblical language creates a world of its own in sharp distinction from the evil modern world. But for many people, religious language, biblical language, has become, like a creed repeated too many times, boring and repetitious. We are essentially indifferent to it. And this is true despite the fact that biblical imagery is often vivid, powerful, shocking, and revolutionary. But all of the reasons given thus far for the "meaninglessness" of religious language have probably always been current. What distinguishes our time is various groups of people who are saying that traditional religious language is meaningless to them because it excludes them in *special* ways. In a more general sense, religious language in the Judeo-Christian tradition excludes us all, for it is largely biblical language; hence, its assumptions concerning social, political, and cultural matters are not ours. Entering the biblical world for many people is like going into a time warp in which one is transported to a world two thousand years in the past. We are aware of significant connections since both worlds are inhabited by human beings, but the images, problems, issues, and assumptions are different. In one way or another, we are all excluded from the biblical world and the tradition that has been formed from it: few if any of us identify easily or enthusiastically with images of demons, vineyards, Messiah and Son of man, kings, Pharisees, and so on. But the issues are much sharper and more painful for some groups: it is not simply that they do not identify; rather, they feel *specifically* excluded. The indifference and irrelevance that many people feel with regard to religious language is clarified by the critique of the more revolutionary groups, for their particular difficulties with religious language highlight issues that point directly to some of its basic characteristics. The feminist critique of religious language is especially relevant in this regard, for more than any of the other liberation theologies, feminist theology has focused on language, its power and its abuses. Three points in this critique stand out as significant.

First, feminists generally agree that whoever names the world owns the world. The Genesis story, according to the traditional, patriarchal interpretation, sees Adam naming the world without consulting Eve. For many feminists, this is a model of Western culture, including Christianity, which has been and still is a "man's world."[7] The feminist critique of religious language is an extremely sophisticated one, for it is based on a recognition of the fundamental importance of language to human existence. With Ludwig Wittgenstein, feminists would say, "The limits of one's language are the limits of one's world," and with Martin Heidegger, "Language is the house of being." We do not so much use language as we are used by it. Since we are all born into a world which is already linguistic, in which the naming has already taken place, we only own our world to the extent that the naming that has occurred is our naming. Feminist theologians are claiming that the world of Western religion is not their world; it was named by men and excludes women. The world of Western religion can become a world for women only if it is open to their naming. New naming, changes in language, are, however, no minor matters, for if one believes that language and "world" are coterminous, then changes in the one will involve changes in the other, and such changes are often revolutionary. The current resistance to inclusive or unbiased language, for instance, both at the social and religious level, indicates that people know instinctively that a revolution in language means a revolution in one's world.

Second, feminists are saying that the particular problem they have with Western religious language is its patriarchal character. It is not just that "God the father" is a frequent appellation for the divine, but that the entire structure of divine-human and human-human relationships is understood in a patriarchal framework.[8] "God the father," as we shall see, has become a model which serves as a grid or screen through which to see not only the nature of God but also our relations to the divine and with one another. "Patriarchy" then is not just that most of the images of the deity in Western religion are masculine—king, father, husband, lord, master— but it is the Western way of life: it describes patterns of governance at national, ecclesiastical, business, and family levels. We shall investigate this model in some detail at a later time, for it is one of the most prominent in the Judeo-Christian tradition. But the point I am stressing now is the total, overarching character of patriarchalism which contributes to the sense of exclusion on the part of women and hence prompts their criticism of the irrelevance of much of Western religious language to them. They say the model of "God the father" has become an idol. When a model becomes an idol, the hypothetical character of the model is forgotten and what ought to be seen as *one* way to understand our relationship with God has become identified as *the* way. In fact, as happens when a model becomes an idol, the distance between image and reality collapses: "father" becomes God's "name" and patriarchy becomes the proper description of governing relationships at many levels. The transformation of the paternal model into the patriarchal is an important case in point concerning what can happen to models when *one* dominates.

Feminist theologians are insisting that many models of God are necessary, among them feminine models, in order both to avoid idolatry and to include the experience of all peoples in our language about God.

Third, feminist theologians are saying that religious language is not only religious but also human, not only about God but also about us. The tradition says that we were created in the image of God, but the obverse is also the case, for we imagine God in *our* image. And the human images we choose for the divine influence the way we feel about ourselves, for these images are "divinized" and hence raised in status. For instance, earthly kingship gains in importance when the image of king is applied to God.[9] On the contrary, images that are excluded are not legitimated and honored; for instance, as feminists have pointed out, the paucity of feminine imagery for God in the Judeo-Christian tradition means a lower self-image for women in that tradition. The relationship between feminine imagery for the divine and the status of women in a society has been well documented in the history of religions.[10] One of the functions, therefore, of religious language is "naming ourselves" as we "name" God. Those who are conscious of being excluded from a religious tradition are most likely to recognize this important and often forgotten function of religious language.

In a number of ways, then, feminist theologians (and a similar case could be made by black and third world theologians) have shown why religious language is not meaningful in our time. Language which is not our language, models which have become idols, images which exclude our experience are three common failings of religious language, but they are especially evident to groups of people who feel excluded by the classical tradition of a religious faith.

Can Religious Language Be Revitalized?

If idolatry and irrelevance are the critical issues for religious language in our time, what remedies are possible for its revitalization? The crisis is too deep for patchwork solutions, for the problem lies in our most basic sense of "how things hold together." That is, many of us no longer believe in a symbolic, sacramental universe in which the part stands for the whole, the things of this world "figure" another world, and all that is is connected by a web of being. No longer believing in connections of this sort and hence afraid that our images refer to nothing, we literalize them, worshiping the icon in our desperation. Furthermore, we find them irrelevant for they connect us to nothing transcending ourselves: they are "just symbols." The question that looms before us is, I believe, a critical one for religious faith and expression: is it possible to have significant religious language, language that is true and meaningful, without classic sacramentalism? If we can no longer believe in a "figural" world—our world as a whole and in all its parts as a symbol of another world, a microcosm of it—can we still believe that our words about the divine are significant?

Let us consider this question more carefully. What are the characteristics of the classic sacramental perspective? The basis of the sacramental universe within Christianity (and there are similar perspectives in other religions) is the incarnation: the sense of divine immanence in the Hebrew tradition is brought to its apotheosis in the Johannine assertion that "the Word became flesh and dwelt among us." The full presence of God in an otherwise ordinary person, Jesus of Nazareth—as the Chalcedonian statement puts it, "fully God and fully man"—was the basis for a thoroughgoing sacramentalism. If God can be fully present in a particular human being, then all creation has the potential for serving as a symbol of divine immanence.[11] The natural and human orders of creation are not flat but two-dimensional: each thing is itself, but as itself, it is also something else—"news of God" as Gerard Manley Hopkins says. The world is alive with the presence of God; it "figures," shows forth, the divine in all its myriad particularity. Sacramentalism of this sort tends to be static and focused on the natural, not the historical, order. Incarnationalism, as the word indicates, is centered on the body, the flesh, not on human being as restless, moving, growing. The most extreme example of sacramentalism, the eucharistic doctrine of transubstantiation, illustrates clearly both the static and fleshly characteristics of the perspective. The bread and wine *become* the body and blood of Christ: two items of the naturalistic order are changed into what they symbolize. Actually, in this extreme case symbolization gives over to realism; the symbol is consumed by what it represents. But elsewhere in the symbolic perspective, the two dimensions exist in a hierarchical order of macrocosm-microcosm, spirit-body, Christ-church, man-woman, and so on. All is ordered, statically and hierarchically, with the body always "below," but permeated by spirit and capable of expressing and imaging spirit.[12]

In such a universe, of course, the meaning and truth of religious language are no problem. If the entire earthly order is a "figure" of the divine order, if each and every scrap of creation, both natural and human, participates in and signifies the divine order according to its own particularities, its own way of being in the world, then all that is "refers" to

Being-Itself and has "meaning," both in itself and as a symbol. Everything is connected hierarchically; hence, everything here below is meaningful both in itself and as a symbol of the divine.

Symbolic sacramentalism received systematic interpretation and ordering in the medieval doctrine of *analogia entis*, the analogy of being. This doctrine says, in essence, that every existing thing participates in Being-Itself, but analogously. That is, being is differentiated absolutely, so that while everything is connected as beings immediately and radically dependent on God, each thing has, is, its own act of being and hence is radically particular. The analogy of being does not paint the world all the same color; on the contrary, it stresses the glory of difference. Beneath the distinctions, however, everything is connected and this is the reason why everything in such a universe can be a symbol of everything else and, most especially, of God, who created everything out of the divine plenitude as a mirror and a reflection of the divine self. The analogical way, the symbolic way, rests on a profound *similarity* beneath the surface dissimilarities; what we see and speak of must be the differences, but we rest in the faith that all is empowered by the breath of God, Being-Itself.[13] The vision of God, the goal of all creation, is the belief that one day all of creation shall be one. The many shall return to the One, for the many are in secret one already.[14]

Now, try as we might, many if not most of us cannot work ourselves back into this mentality. If the destiny of religious language rests on a return to the traditional sacramental universe, if the significance of imagistic language depends on a belief that symbols participate in a transcendent reality, the future for religious language is grim. I do not believe either is the case—that we must or can return to such a sacramental universe or that the significance of images rests on symbolic participationism. In fact, we have not had a classic sacramental mentality for a long time (even though it hangs on in many quarters and, improperly understood, is the source of much literalistic realism in religious language). In effect, however, we have not had such a sensibility since at least the Protestant Reformation. One way to describe what occurred in the Reformation is a profound questioning of the symbolic mentality, a loosening of the connections between symbol and its reference. The eucharistic debate between Luther and the proponents of transubstantiation on the one hand, and between Luther and Zwingli on the other hand, reveals as much. Luther took a mediating position between the bread and wine as one with the body and the blood and these elements as a mere sign recalling them.[15]

To Luther, the bread and the wine were still symbols of Christ's body and blood, still participated in that reality, but in a way that I would call "metaphorical," for the assertions "This is my body" and "This is my blood" were not viewed as identity statements, but as including a silent but present negative. One critical difference between symbolic and metaphorical statements is that the latter always contain the whisper, "it is *and it is not.*"

I suggest, therefore, that one of the distinctive characteristics of Protestant thought is its insistence on the "and it is not." It is the iconoclastic tendency in Protestantism, what Paul Tillich calls the "Protestant Principle," the fear of idolatry, the concern lest the finite ever be imagined to be capable of the infinite. We see it in Martin Luther's "masks" of God, that God is revealed and veiled in all symbols; in John Calvin's notion of divine "accommodation" by which God stoops to our level by speaking in signs and images; and in an extreme form in Karl Barth's concept of *analogia fidei*, which insists that our language refers to God only as God from time to time causes our words to conform to the divine being.

The Protestant tradition is, I would suggest, "metaphorical"; the Catholic, "symbolical" (or "analogical" for contemporary Catholicism). I do not mean to suggest a hard and fast distinction here, but only a characteristic sensibility. The Protestant sensibility tends to see dissimilarity, distinction, tension and hence to be skeptical and secular, stressing the transcendence of God and the finitude of creation. The Catholic sensibility tends to see similarity, connection, harmony and, hence, to be believing and religious, stressing the continuity between God and creation. These caricatures are not meant to be directly related to the Protestant and Catholic ecclesiastical institutions or even to the theologies supported by these bodies. Not only are many Protestants "catholic" and many Catholics "protestant," but it is obvious that either tendency without the other would be insupportable. They are complementary. However, a sacramentalism of the medieval sort—the classic Catholic mentality—is not viable today, nor is it supported by most Catholics who seek a revitalization of this tradition. The most sophisticated revitalizations of the symbolic, sacramental tradition interpret it analogically, that is, in a way that stresses many of the characteristics of the metaphorical sensibility: its emphasis on the negativities, on the distance between image and what it represents, on its refusal of easy harmonies. Obversely, a Protestant sensibility which failed to see any connections or unity between God and the world would be totally negative and agnostic. A metaphorical perspective *does* see connections but they are of a tensive, discontinuous, and surprising nature.

One of the interesting and important characteristics of contemporary ecumenical theology is that it is neither traditionally Catholic nor Protestant, emphasizing neither easy continuities nor radical discontinuities, but some form of both. However, as David Tracy points out in his recent book, *The Analogical Imagination,* there are characteristic differences in the Christian community between those for whom experience in the world engenders primarily a sense of wonder and trust and those for whom it engenders primarily a need for healing and transformation.[16] The first moves from an awareness of harmony, taking the negativities into account, while the second moves from an awareness of the negativities, reaching toward a future harmony. They are two "ways," one not necessarily better than the other; it is the contention of this essay, however, that the Protestant sensibility is more characteristic of our time and is the place from which many of us must start. What we seek, then, is a form of theology, a form for our talk about God both at the primary religious level of images and the secondary theological level of concepts, which takes the Protestant sensibility seriously.

Metaphorical Theology

If modernity were the only criterion, our task would be relatively easy. But such is never the case in theology. Christian theology is always an interpretation of the "Gospel" in a particular time and place. So the other task of equal importance is to show that a *metaphorical theology* is indigenous to Christianity, not just in the sense that it is permitted, but is called for. And this I believe is the case. The heart of the Gospel in the New Testament is widely accepted to be the "kingdom of God"; what the kingdom is or means is never expressed but indirectly suggested by the parables of the kingdom.[17] The parables are by no means the only form in the New Testament which deals with the kingdom and we must be cautious lest we make an idol of them. However, as the dominant genre of Jesus' teaching on the kingdom, they suggest some central, albeit indirect, clues to its reality. As a form of religious language, the parables of the New Testament are very different from symbolic, sacramental language. They do not assume a believing or religious perspective on the part of the listeners to whom they are addressed; they do not assume continuity between our world and a transcendent one; they do not see similarity, connection, and harmony between our ways and the ways of God. On the contrary, they are a secular form of language, telling stories of ordinary people involved in mundane family, business, and social matters; they assume a nonbelieving or secular attitude on the part of their audience; they stress the discontinuity between our ways and the ways of the kingdom; they focus on the dissimilarity, incongruity, and tension between the assumptions and expectations of their characters and another set of assumptions and expectations identified with the kingdom. In other words, they are a form peculiarly suited to what I have called the Protestant sensibility.

They are so suited because they are metaphors, not symbols. They are metaphorical statements about religious matters, about what both transcends and affects us at the deepest level of our existence. What is it about a religious metaphorical statement which makes it more powerful than a symbolical statement? The answer to this question centers on the nature of metaphor and especially of metaphorical statements. To many people "metaphor" is merely a poetic ornament for illustrating an idea or adding rhetorical color to abstract or flat language. It appears to have little to do with ordinary language until one realizes that most ordinary language is composed of "dead metaphors," some obvious, such as "the arm of the chair" and others less obvious, such as "tradition," meaning "to hand over or hand down." Most simply, a metaphor is seeing one thing *as* something else, pretending "this" is "that" because we do not know how to think or talk about "this," so we use "that" as a way of saying something about it. Thinking metaphorically means spotting a thread of similarity between two dissimilar objects, events, or whatever, one of which is better known than the other, and using the better-known one as a way of speaking about the lesser known.

Poets use metaphor all the time because they are constantly speaking about the great unknowns—mortality, love, fear, joy, guilt, hope, and so on. Religious language is deeply metaphorical for the same reason and it is therefore no surprise that Jesus' most characteristic form of teaching, the parables, should be extended metaphors. Less obvious, but of paramount importance, is the fact that metaphorical thinking constitutes the basis of human thought and language. From the time we are infants we construct our world through metaphor; that is, just as young children learn the meaning of the color red by finding the thread of similarity through many dissimilar objects (red ball, red apple, red cheeks), so we constantly ask when we do not know how to think about something, "What is it

like?" Far from being an esoteric or ornamental rhetorical device superimposed *on* ordinary language, metaphor *is* ordinary language. It is the
way we think. We often make distinctions between ordinary and poetic
language, assuming that the first is direct and the second indirect, but
actually both are indirect, for we always think by indirection. The difference between the two kinds of language is only that we have grown accustomed to the indirections of ordinary language; they have become conventional. Likewise, conceptual or abstract language is metaphorical in
the sense that the ability to generalize depends upon seeing similarity
within dissimilarity; a concept is an abstraction of the similar from a sea
of dissimilars. Thus, Darwin's theory of the survival of the fittest is a
high-level metaphorical exercise of recognizing a similar pattern amid an
otherwise incredibly diverse set of phenomena.

The primary answer to the question of why religious metaphorical statements are so powerful is that they are in continuity with the way we
think ordinarily. We are not usually conscious of the metaphorical character of our thought, of seeing "this" in terms of "that," of finding the
thread of similarity amid dissimilars, but it is the only way a child's world
can be constructed or our worlds expanded and transformed. Of course,
there are important differences between ordinary and religious metaphorical statements which we shall fully note, but the first thing is to insist on
their continuity. Symbolic statements, on the other hand, are not so much
a way of knowing and speaking as they are sedimentation and solidifica-
tion of metaphor. For in symbolical or sacramental thought, one does not
think of "this" *as* "that," but "this" as *a part of* "that." The tension of
metaphor is absorbed by the harmony of symbol.

Another way to discern the distinction between metaphorical and sacramental thinking is to say that in metaphorical statements we always make
judgments. That is, we make assertions; we say "I am thinking about
'this' in terms of 'that'." The only times we do not think this way is when
we have already accepted a particular way of thinking of something. When
we already know something, that is, when we have accepted a perspective
on something, then we see and think about it "directly," or so it seems.
Actually, it is not the case that anything can be known or thought of
directly or literally; rather, we have simply acquired a way of looking at it
which is acceptable to us. Even as simple a statement as "this is a chair"
means only that I have made a judgment that I will think about this
object *as* a chair because there is sufficient similarity between this object
and other objects which I have called "chairs" in the past that I believe my

assertion is justified. The example may appear ridiculous but it was chosen because it illustrates metaphorical thinking at its most common, continuous, and instantaneous level. It is the same *kind* of thinking as the assertion "Jesus is the savior," inasmuch as here again one is making a decision to think of one thing in terms of another; in both cases, a judgment is involved that similarity is present. The differences between the two statements are vast and important, such as the degree of existential involvement and the much greater ignorance of the subject matter, as well as the novelty of the assertion in the second statement. The point to stress, however, is that human thought is of a piece, it is indirect, and it involves judgments.[18]

We have remarked that metaphor finds the vein of similarity in the midst of dissimilars, while symbol rests on similarity already present and assumed. But the difference is even more marked: metaphor not only lives in the region of dissimilarity, but also in the region of the unconventional and surprising. Both humor and the grotesque are distinctly metaphorical.[19] Humor is the recognition of a *very* unlikely similarity among dissimilars and we laugh because we are surprised to discover that such unlikes are indeed alike in at least one respect. A great many jokes take the form, "How is a _____ like a _____?" Likewise, the grotesque forces us to look at radical incongruity, at what is outside, does not fit, is strange and disturbing. Both are extreme metaphorical forms which point up a crucial characteristic of metaphor: good metaphors shock, they bring unlikes together, they upset conventions, they involve tension, and they are implicitly revolutionary. The parables of Jesus are typically metaphorical in this regard, for they bring together dissimilars (lost coins, wayward children, buried treasure, and tardy laborers with the kingdom of God); they shock and disturb; they upset conventions and expectations and in so doing have revolutionary potential. In this regard, one could characterize symbolic, sacramental thinking as priestly and metaphorical thinking as prophetic. The first assumes an order and unity already present waiting to be realized; the second projects, tentatively, a possible transformed order and unity yet to be realized.[20]

Perhaps the most striking evidence of the revolutionary character of the New Testament parables is the redefinition they give to conventional understandings of the monarchical, hierarchical metaphors of "kingdom" and "rule." God's "kingdom," we discover from the parables, is not like any worldly reign; in fact, its essence is its opposition to the power of the mighty over the lowly, the rich over the poor, the righteous over the unrighteous. It is a *new* rule which is defined by the extraordinary reversal of expectations in the parables as well as in the life and death of Jesus.

The characteristics of metaphorical thinking we have suggested—ordinariness, incongruity, indirection, skepticism, judgment, unconventionality, surprise, and transformation or revolution—especially as they are realized in Jesus' parables, have persuaded many people to think of Jesus as a parable of God.[21] That is to say, the life and death of Jesus of Nazareth can be understood as itself a "parable" of God; in order to understand the ways of God with us—something unfamiliar and unknown to us, about which we do not know how to think or talk—we look at that life as a metaphor of God. What we see through that "grid" or "screen" is at one level an ordinary, secular story of a human being, but also a story shot through with surprise, unconventionality, and incongruities which not only upset our conventional expectations (for instance, of what a "savior" is and who gets "saved"), but also involve a judgment on our part—"Surely this man is the Christ." In contrast to incarnational christology, however, parabolic christology does not involve an assumption of continuity or identity between the human and the divine; it is not a "Jesusolatry," a form of idolatry. It is, I believe, a christology for the Protestant sensibility and the modern mentality.

All the foregoing comments on metaphor, parable, and Jesus as a parable require considerable elaboration. Perhaps, however, these brief introductory remarks are sufficient for us to attempt to advance a case for a metaphorical theology. If metaphor is the way by which we understand as well as enlarge our world and change it—that is, if the only way we have of dealing with the unfamiliar and new is in terms of the familiar and the old, thinking of "this" as "that" although we know the new thing is both like *and* unlike the old—if all this is the case, then it is no surprise that Jesus taught in parables or that many see him as a parable of God. For he introduced a new, strange way of being in the world, a way that could be grasped only through the indirection of stories of familiar life which both "were and were not" the kingdom. And he himself was in the world in a new, strange way which was in many respects an ordinary life but one which also, as with the parables, called the mores and conventions of ordinary life into radical question.

A metaphorical theology, then, starts with the parables of Jesus and with Jesus as a parable of God. This starting place does not involve a belief in the Bible as authoritative in an absolute or closed sense; it does not involve acceptance of a canon or the Bible as "the Word of God." In fact, such a perspective reverses the direction of authority suitable both to Scripture and to the Protestant sensibility. For what we have in the New Testament are confessions of faith by people who, on the basis of their experience of the way their lives were changed by Jesus' Gospel and by Jesus, *gave* authority to him and to the writings about him. The New Testament writings are foundational; they are classics; they are a beginning. But if we take seriously the parables of Jesus and Jesus as a parable of God as our starting point and model, then we cannot say that the Bible is absolute or authoritative in any sense except the way that a "classic" text is authoritative: it continues to speak to us. What must always be kept in mind is that the parables as metaphors and the life of Jesus as a metaphor of God provide characteristics for theology: a theology guided by them is open-ended, tentative, indirect, tensive, iconoclastic, transformative. Some of these characteristics appear "negative," in the sense that they qualify any attempts at idolatry, whether this be the idolatry of the Bible, of tradition, of orthodoxy, or of the Church. In such a theology *no* finite thought, product, or creature can be identified with God and this includes Jesus of Nazareth, who as parable of God both "is and is not" God. Against all forms of literalistic realism and idolatry, a metaphorical theology insists that it is not only in keeping with the Protestant sensibility to be open, tentative, and iconoclastic but that these are the characteristics of Jesus' parables and of Jesus' own way of being in the world.

On the other hand, metaphorical theology is not just a modern version of the *via negativa* or an exercise in iconoclasm. It not only says "is not" but "is," not only no but yes. If the parables of Jesus and Jesus himself as a parable of God are genuine metaphors, then they give license for language about life with God; they point to a real, an assumed similarity between the metaphors and that to which they refer. The many parables of the kingdom tell us something about the rule of God, of what it means to live in the world according to God's way. Jesus as a parable of God tells us actually and concretely (though, of course, indirectly) about God's relationship to us. In other words, a metaphorical theology is "positive" as well as "negative," giving license for speech about God as well as indicating the limits of such speech. Such a theology, as is true of all theologies, must be concerned not only with *how* we speak of God but *what* we say of God. On the question of how we speak of God, a metaphorical theology is firmly opposed to literalism and idolatry of all kinds; on the question of what we say about God, metaphorical theology again turns to the parables and to Jesus as a parable for beginning, foundational clues.

The parables of the New Testament are united by a number of characteristics, of which one of the most outstanding is their concern with *relationships* of various kinds. What is important in the parables is not *who* the characters are (a static notion) but *what they do* (a dynamic one). The plot is always the heart of a parable, what a character or several characters decide in matters having to do with their *relationships with each other*. Whether one thinks of the parable of the Prodigal Son, the Good Samaritan, the Unjust Steward, or the Great Supper, it is relationships and decisions about them that are critical.[22] Just as the central Old Testament religious language is relational—focused on the covenant between God and Israel; so the central New Testament language is relational—focused on persons and their way of being in the world in community. Likewise, if we look at Jesus as a parable of God, we have no alternative but to recognize personal, relational language as the most appropriate language about God. Whatever more one may wish to say about him, he was a person relating to other persons in loving service and transforming power.

I have emphasized the word "person" for two reasons. First, as we were made *in the image of God* (Gen. 3:27), so we now, with the model of Jesus, have further support for imagining God in *our* image, the image of persons. This means that personal, relational images are central in a metaphorical theology—images of God as father, mother, lover, friend, savior, ruler, governor, servant, companion, comrade, liberator, and so on. The Judeo-Christian tradition has always been personalistic and relational in its religious languages. This need not be seen as crude anthropomorphism, but as foundational language, the dominant model, of God-talk. Such language, however, is not the only appropriate religious language: no *one* model can ever be adequate. We find—both in Scripture and in our tradition—naturalistic, impersonal images balancing the relational, personal ones: God as rock, fortress, running stream, power, sun, thunder, First Cause, and so on. The Judeo-Christian tradition has had a decidedly personalistic rather than naturalistic tendency, with appalling consequences for the exploitation of the natural environment. This tradition is personalistic, however, not in an individualistic but in a relational sense, and it is therefore appropriate and required that a revolutionary hermeneutic of this tradition broaden relationship to its widest dimensions, including the entire natural world. In any case, a metaphorical theology will insist that *many* metaphors and models are necessary, that a piling up of images is essential, both to avoid idolatry and to attempt to express the richness and variety of the divine-human relationship.

The second reason for stressing the word "person" is to underscore, in as strong and definitive a way as possible, that it is not patriarchal language which is licensed by Jesus as parable of God. The Christian tradition, and the Jewish as well, have been and still are deeply patriarchal. We will be giving substantial time to this issue, for the profound penetration of the patriarchal model not only in theology but also in the structures of Western culture makes it a critical one for any metaphorical theology to consider. What is stressed in the parables and in Jesus' own life focuses on persons and their relationships; therefore, the dominance of the patriarchal model in the Christian tradition must be seen as a perversion in its hegemony of the field of religious models and its exclusion of other personal, relational models. The dominance of the patriarchal model is idolatrous in its assumption of privileged appropriateness. To put the issue in its simplest form, God's name is not "father" although many Christians use "God" and "father" interchangeably as if "father" were a literal description of God.

A metaphorical theology, then, will emphasize personal, relational categories in its language about God, but not necessarily as the tradition has interpreted these categories. On the contrary, if one looks to the parables and Jesus as a parable to gain some preliminary understanding of what "person" means and what "relationship" means, both applied to us and to God, one finds not a baptizing of conventional hierarchies of relationships, whether these be of class, race, sex, or whatever, but a radical transformation of our expectations. For instance, if we are to say "God is father" it is both true *and* untrue, and even where true, it is different from conventional views of patriarchal fatherhood. If we are to call ourselves "children" in relationship to God, this is a limited and in some respects false image. There are personal, relational models which have been suppressed in the Christian tradition because of their social and political consequences; they are, however, as appropriate as the fatherhood model and are necessary both to qualify it and to include the images of personal, relational life of large numbers of people whose experiences have been excluded from traditional Christian language. To mention but two examples in passing, "mother" and "liberator" are metaphors of profound personal relationships with vast potential as models for God. They arise out of the depths of human relational existence and are licensed by the parabolic dimension of the New Testament, not in a literal way (the words do not appear), but in the sense that the characteristics we associate with "mother" and "liberator" fit with (and, of course, also do not fit with) the surprising rule of God as we have it in the parables and the parable of Jesus.

But a metaphorical theology cannot stop with metaphors, with the parables and the life and death of Jesus as extended metaphors of God's rule. Metaphor, parables, and Jesus as parable *fund* theology, but are not theology. If we wish to be precise, we must make a distinction between primary and secondary religious language, between metaphorical and conceptual language. But it is impossible to keep the distinction clear because most primary religious language is implicitly conceptual and most secondary theological language is latently imagistic. The parables of Jesus cry out for interpretation—not for *one* interpretation, but nonetheless for answers to the question, "What does this parable mean?" The richness of imagistic language means that it will always spawn many interpretations. Likewise, the biblical story of Jesus' life and death, an extended metaphor itself and packed with many supporting metaphors (Jesus as Messiah, as Son of man, as Suffering Servant, and so on), is not just a story but is already highly interpreted. What the story *means* is the perspective from which it is told and not something tacked on to pure, unadulterated images. Or if we think of Paul's letters, we see a mixture of images and concepts, the images moving in the direction of concepts in the sense that, for instance, when Paul tells us we are buried with Christ so that we might rise with him, he also tells us what this means (baptism, or the newness of the Christian life). Or if one considers the Nicene Creed, one sees a mixture of imagistic and conceptual language: the phrase "God of God, Light of Light, Very God of Very God, Begotten not made, Being of one substance with the Father" and so on was deemed necessary to interpret the imagistic language "one Lord Jesus Christ" and "Son of God." Whether the interpretations are good ones, are appropriate, or are still meaningful to us is beside the point. What is critical at the moment is that *some* interpretation is necessary; imagistic language does not just tolerate interpretation but *demands* it.

Thus, metaphorical theology does not stop with metaphors but must deal with the entire gamut of religious/theological language. Robert Funk has noted that it is a tortuous route between Jesus' parables and systematic theology.[23] Indeed it is, but that route must be traversed, for to stop at the level of images, of metaphor, of story is inevitably to give over either to baptizing certain images (usually biblical ones) as alone appropriate or to finding religious images sterile and meaningless. In other words, in terms of the twin issues of idolatry and irrelevance in religious language, *moving beyond* metaphors is necessary both to avoid literalizing them and to attempt significant interpretations of them for our time. It is impossible just to tell "the simple story of Jesus" and it was not told that way in the first place, for the many "stories" of Jesus in the New Testament are each told within several layers of interpretation.

In the continuum of religious language from primary, imagistic to secondary, conceptual, a form emerges which is a mixed type: *the model*. The simplest way to define a model is as a dominant metaphor, a metaphor with staying power. Metaphors are usually the work of an individual, a flash of insight which is often passing. But some metaphors gain wide appeal and become major ways of structuring and ordering experience. Thus, T. S. Eliot's Wasteland or W. H. Auden's Age of Anxiety became perspectives from which modern culture was perceived. There are many kinds of models—scale models, picture models, analogue and theoretical models, as well as root-metaphors which are similar to models but of wider range. For our preliminary purposes, however, the main point is that models are a further step along the route from metaphorical to conceptual language. They are similar to metaphors in that they are images which retain the tension of the "is and is not" and, like religious and poetic metaphors, they have emotional appeal insofar as they suggest ways of understanding our being in the world. The example we have used before, "God the father," comes readily to mind: it is a metaphor which has become a model. As a model it not only retains characteristics of metaphor but also reaches toward qualities of conceptual thought. It suggests a comprehensive, ordering structure with impressive interpretive potential. As a rich model with many associated commonplaces as well as a host of supporting metaphors, an entire theology can be worked out from this model. Thus, if God is understood on the model of "father," human beings are understood as "children," sin is rebellion against the "father," redemption is sacrifice by the "elder son" on behalf of the "brothers and sisters" for the guilt against the "father" and so on.[24]

Models, as is true of metaphors but in an organic, consistent, and comprehensive manner, give us a way of thinking about the unknown in terms of the known. As Max Black says, a model gives us a "grid," "screen," or "filter" which helps us to organize our thoughts about a less familiar subject by means of seeing it in terms of a more familiar one. He gives the example of seeing a military battle in terms of a chess game. The chess model will help to understand tactics and the movement of armies; as he shrewdly notes, however, it also "screens out" certain other aspects of battle—for instance, we will not think of blood and death if we use only the chess analogy.[25] Models are necessary, then, for they give us something to think about when we do not know what to think, a way of talking when we do not know how to talk. But they are also dangerous, for they exclude other ways of thinking and talking, and in so doing they can easily become literalized, that is, identified as *the* one and only way of understanding a subject. This danger is more prevalent with models than with metaphors because models have a wider range and are more permanent; they tend to object to competition in ways that metaphors do not. In many Old Testament psalms the psalmist will pile up metaphors for God in a riotous *melée*, mixing "rock," "lover," "fortress," "midwife," "fresh water," "judge," "helper," "thunder" and so on in a desperate attempt to express the richness of God's being. But models do not welcome such profusion; even in the case of models of the same *type* (for instance, "God the mother" along with "God the father") there is often great resistance. This is due, in part, to the literalization of models and it is probably the single greatest risk in their use.

It should be evident by now, however, that in all matters except the most conventional (where widely accepted perspectives or models are already operating), thinking by metaphor and hence by models is not optional but necessary. And this is true in the sciences as well as in the humanities. It is sometimes supposed that science deals with its subject matter directly, empirically; science is "factual" whereas poetry and religion are "spiritual, emotional, or imaginative." Unlike them, science does not need the indirection of metaphor but can move inductively from empirical observations to theory and from theory to verification in the "real" world. This positivistic view of science is fortunately no longer the only force in science; rather, what one finds is that much of the most interesting and suggestive work on models is being done by scientists, especially physicists. Relatively little has been written by theologians on models in religion; however, the literature on models in science is enormous, going back a good twenty-five years. As physics comes increasingly to deal with invisibles such as subatomic particles, behaviors of entities that must be imagined rather than observed, it finds itself in a position similar to poetry and religion in that it must attempt to understand the unknown in terms of known models. Also, as more and more conclusions in physics (as well as in many of the other sciences) are expressed in mathematical formulas, models become the only way of connecting scientific knowledge both with ordinary language and with other domains of science. Finally, and most importantly, scientists need models for discovering the new; to think of the new in terms of the old, so long as one does not collapse the two, can often, through the dialectic of similarity and dissimilarity, provide a breakthrough.

There are other uses of models in science as well. But the critical point for our preliminary purposes is to note the widespread acceptance of models in science as well as in many other disciplines. One finds thinking by models in biology, computer science, education theory, political science, ethics, psychology, sociology, and so on. The self-conscious use of models, in regard to both their benefits and their risks, is a common phenomenon in most fields of study. What this means, among other things, is that poetry and religion, the two fields which have always known they must think via metaphor (and as a consequence have been denied by many as dealing in knowledge—truth and meaning), now find that their way of metaphor and indirection is widely accepted as necessary in all creative, constructive thought. A scientist doing a routine experiment does not need models, but a scientist devising an experiment to test a hypothesis may very well need to try out various models in order to locate what is unfamiliar about the present case. And so it is in all creative ventures. What we do not know, we must simulate through models of what we do know.

Because of the centrality of models in science and the amount of analysis available on scientific models, we will be looking carefully at some of this material for possible insights into the ways models function in theology. We will discover, for instance, that as interpretive, explanatory devices religious models share structural characteristics with scientific models; but because models in religion emerge from existential experience, they have affectional dimensions as do poetic metaphors. But a metaphorical theology cannot stop at the level of models. To be sure, considerable interpretive activity takes place at such a stage: as dominant metaphors, models manifest priorities within a religious tradition; as organizing networks of images, they are well on the way to systematic thought; as comprehensive ways of envisioning reality, they implicitly raise questions of truth and reference; as metaphors that control the ways people envision both human and divine reality, they cannot avoid the issue of criteria in the choice of certain models and the exclusion of others. A further step of interpretation, however, is called for: conceptual interpretation and criticism.

Concepts and theories arise from metaphors and models; they are an attempt to generalize at the level of abstraction concerning competing and, at times, contradictory metaphors and models. By "concept" we mean an abstract notion; by "theory" we mean a speculative, systematic statement of relationships underlying certain phenomena. A concept is an idea or thought; a theory organizes ideas into an explanatory structure. Concepts, unlike metaphors, do not create new meaning, but rely on conventional, accepted meanings. Theories, unlike models, do not systematize one area in terms of another, but organize concepts into a whole. These definitions are only minimally helpful, however, for they are too neat and compartmentalized for a metaphorical theology. If our thesis holds that *all* thought is indirect, then all concepts and theories are metaphorical in the sense that they too are constructions; they are indirect attempts to interpret reality, which never can be dealt with directly. Concepts and theories, however, are at the far end of the continuum and rarely expose their metaphorical roots. These distinctions mainly show the different functions of metaphor, model, and concept or theory in the *one* task of interpreting our being in the world.

Conceptual language tends toward univocity, toward clear and concise meanings for ambiguous, multileveled, imagistic language. In this process something is lost and something is gained: richness and multivalency are sacrificed for precision and consistency. Conceptual thought attempts to find similarities among the models while models insist on dissimilarities among themselves. The relationship, however, is symbiotic. Images "feed" concepts; concepts "discipline" images. Images without concepts are blind; concepts without images are sterile. In a metaphorical theology, there is no suggestion of a hierarchy among metaphors, models, and concepts: concepts are not higher, better, or more necessary than images, or vice versa. Images are never free of the need for interpretation by concepts, their critique of competing images, or their demythologizing of literalized models. Concepts are never free of the need for funding by images, the affectional and existential richness of images, and the qualification against conceptual pretensions supplied by the plurality of images. In no sense can systematic thought be said to *explain* metaphors and models so that they become mere illustrations for concepts; rather, the task of conceptual thought is to generalize (often in philosophical language, *the* generalizing language), to criticize images, to raise questions of their meaning and truth in explicit ways.

An example of the movement from parable toward conceptual thought can be illustrated briefly by the career of "the kingdom of God." I would call "the kingdom of God" the root-metaphor of Christianity which is supported and fed by many extended metaphors, the various parables. No *one* parable is adequate as a way of seeing the kingdom, and all the parables together undoubtedly are not either, but they are all that is provided. Many extended metaphors are necessary to give meaning to the model of the kingdom; taken together they display certain common features which are not illustrations of the kingdom so much as exemplifications of it. The process of understanding and interpreting these common features is not deductive or inductive but dialectical: "the rule of God" at this stage *is* all of the parabolic exemplifications. In the hands of Paul and his notion of "justification by faith," however, we move to a higher level of interpretation by a concept generalizing on that rule. Paul Ricoeur points out, and I believe rightly, that Paul's notion is in continuity with the foundational language of "the kingdom of God" and the underlying parables, but it is less particular, more generalized; less concrete, more abstract; less imagistic, more univocal. Ricoeur calls Paul's concept a "translation language," a semi-conceptual mode of discourse which remains under the control of the hermeneutical potential of metaphor *because* it preserves the tension of the foundational language.[26]

For another example of the relationship among metaphors, models, and concepts, one must remember that metaphors and models of God will range widely and have various degrees of dominance within a tradition: person, king, rock, mother, savior, father, fortress, lover, liberator, helper, and many more. We must ask questions of these models. Which ones are dominant? Why should certain ones be dominant? Are they consistent? Are the central models comprehensive? To whom are they significant? To whom are they meaningless or objectionable? Are they fruitful in the sense that they help us to understand our lives better, and are they commensurate with other matters we hold to be important? Do they fit with lived experience or do they have to be rationalized in order to be held? All of these questions and more fall under the heading of the critique of metaphors and models that is the task of conceptual thought.

Systematic thought also tries to organize all the dominant models in a tradition into an overarching system with a key model of its own. For instance, for Paul it was justification by grace through faith; for Augustine, the radical dependence of all that is on God; for Aquinas, the analogy of being whereby each creature participates in and glorifies God through realizing its proper finite end; for Schleiermacher, the feeling of absolute dependence; for Barth, the election of all people to salvation in the election of Jesus Christ before the foundation of the world. Each of these is a radical model, which could be called a "root-metaphor": "a root-metaphor is the most basic assumption about the nature of the world or experience that we can make when we try to give a description of it."[27] Each root-metaphor is a way of seeing "all that is" through a particular key concept. It is also thinking by models and, as is evident, even these root-metaphors are still metaphors: at the highest level of abstraction and generalization one does not escape metaphor (the exceptions are symbolic logic and higher mathematics which do not pretend to refer to reality as lived).

Therefore, we will focus on *models* because, as mediators between metaphors and concepts, they partake of the characteristics of each and are an especially fruitful type of expression to investigate for a metaphorical theology. The aim of a metaphorical theology, as we recall, is to envision ways of talking about the relationship between the divine and the human which are nonidolatrous but relevant: ways which can be said to be true without being literal; ways which are meaningful to all peoples, the traditionally excluded as well as the included. Such a theology, I believe, is appropriate to the Protestant sensibility and I have suggested clues to its character from the parables of Jesus and Jesus as parable. In this framework, moreover, models are critical because models are dominant *metaphors*: they retain the tension of metaphor—its "is and is not" quality which refuses all literalization. Models are also *dominant* metaphors: they are dominant within a tradition both because they have earned that right as "classics" which speak to people across many ages and because they have usurped that right to the false exclusion of other metaphors. Both their right and their usurpation of right must be taken into account.

The tasks of a metaphorical theology will become clear: to understand the centrality of models in religion and the particular models in the Christian tradition; to criticize literalized, exclusive models; to chart the relationships among metaphors, models, and concepts; and to investigate possibilities for transformative, revolutionary models.[28] The goal of this analysis can then be thought of as an attempt to question the *didactic* tradition of orthodoxy over the more flexible, open, *kerygmatic* point of view epitomized in the parables and Jesus as parable. What must be done in a metaphorical theology is to open up the relationships among metaphor, model, and concept for the purpose both of justifying dominant, founding metaphors as true but not literal *and* of discovering other appropriate dominant metaphors which for cultural, political, and social reasons have been suppressed.

The final task of a metaphorical theology will be a reforming, transforming one. As metaphorical, such theology can never be simply a baptizing of the tradition, for that would mean giving up the *tension* which is at the heart of metaphor. The classic models of the Christian tradition have been and still are hierarchical, authoritarian ones which have been absolutized. As feminist theologians have become increasingly aware, the orthodox tradition did a thorough job of plumbing the depths of one such model, the patriarchal, as a way of being articulate about God. Feminists have become conscious of the profound structural implications of this model as a form of ecclesiastical, social, political, economic, and personal oppression. The problem does not lie with the model itself of "God the father," for it is a profound metaphor and as true as any religious model available, but it has established a hegemony over the Western religious consciousness which it is the task of metaphorical theology to break. The "outsiders" to the mainline Christian tradition— women, blacks, third world people—are questioning the hierarchical, authoritarian, patriarchal models of Western theology. If Christianity is a universal religion (and not a tribal one for white, middle-class males), such voices are legitimate and necessary. As an example of one such voice, we will look at new religious images and models being suggested by women and we will do so in the spirit of openness to the future and to the unity that lies in the future, a spirit appropriate to a metaphorical theology. As Ursula LeGuin, a fantasy and science-fiction writer, says, truth lies in the imagination.[29] This may be only half a truth, but it is the half we most often forget.

2 Metaphor, Parable, and Scripture

The claim has been made that a metaphorical theology is appropriate and necessary for two reasons: metaphor is the way we think, and it is the way the parables—a central form of expression in the New Testament—work. These are related assertions, for the power of the parables stems, in part, from that basic movement by indirection from the known to the unknown—the heart of metaphor. Our first task, then, must be to establish both the centrality of metaphor for human understanding and to show the metaphorical character of parables. We need to deal as well with the question of the status both of Jesus' parables and Jesus as a parable, if we are to claim theological centrality for them and here, of course, we will be involved in the issue of the authority of Scripture. Hermeneutical questions dominate metaphorical theology, and the ones we will raise in dealing with scriptural texts, while critical, are not more important than those dealing with the tradition or with our contemporary social and political situation.

Having looked at metaphor, and parables as metaphors, we will turn next to a further stage of religious and theological language: the model. Before attempting a treatment of models in theology, in chapter 3 we will focus on models in science and in other fields. We will note similarities and differences between scientific and theological models, in order to see why models are central—what their uses are as well as their dangers. In chapter 4 we will move to an analysis of models in theology, the relationship of models to metaphors on the one hand, and to concepts on the other. We will look at some specific models in Christian theology and we will raise the questions of the meaning and reference of models as well as criteria for appropriate, adequate models. Finally, in chapter 5 we will focus on the model "God the father" as a way of bringing together the issues of idolatry and irrelevance, for more than any other dominant model in Christianity it has been absolutized by some and, recently, found meaningless, if not destructive, by others. It can serve, then, as a test case for a metaphorical theology in its task of envisioning nonidolatrous but relevant models of the relationship which lies at its center.

The issues on which we focus—the problems of the idolatry and irrelevance of religious images in our time—are critical ones. I do not suppose that my modest suggestions can do anything more than, at most, raise the question of whether the *way* in which these issues have been dealt with—a way I would describe as guided by the didactic, orthodox tradition—is not counterproductive. What I wish to suggest is that another way, a way I would describe as the *kerygmatic, parabolic tradition*, a way which depends on metaphor, is not only found in Christian sources but is at the heart of human understanding. We will not relinquish our idolatry in religious language unless we are freed from the myth that in order for images to be true they must be literal. Nor will we find religious language relevant unless we are freed from the myth that in order for images to be meaningful they must be traditional. Metaphorical theology, as is true of the parables, demands that our understanding and speech in religious matters be open-ended, tensive, secular, indirect, iconoclastic, and revolutionary. It demands that the central model in Christianity for human and divine life—the model of personal, relational existence as found in the story of Jesus—be allowed to guide us both in form and in content.

Metaphor

> Metaphor is as ultimate as speech itself, and speech as ultimate as thought.
> . . . Metaphor appears as the instinctive and necessary act of the mind exploring reality and ordering experience.[1]

If this comment by literary critic John Middleton Murry were an isolated one, it could be dismissed as the prejudice of a humanist who would like to see the process of thought in his field of poetry be the model for all human thought. But this is not the case. The voices insisting on the primacy of metaphor are legion, coming from philosophy, the sciences, religion, the arts, and the social sciences.[2] It is as if, after centuries of dormancy, the world has finally woken up to the significance of Aristotle's adage that the greatest thing by far is to be a master of metaphor. But the level at which metaphor is appreciated in all fields of human inquiry today is a more basic one than suggested by Aristotle. For it is not geniuses who are being congratulated for their ability to use metaphor; rather, it is being asserted that metaphor is indigenous to all human learning from the simplest to the most complex.

In the animal world, and in our own beginnings, all that is known is bodily sensations. But unlike the other animals for whom the meanings of things are largely instinctive and adhere to the things signified, the essence of our uniqueness is that we use our bodily sensations as signs to stand for something else. Signs become symbols: the thing stands for and represents something else. Thus, "water" is not merely something that feels good on a dry throat, a bodily sensation, but also a symbol of refreshment and renewal (as well, paradoxically, of drowning and death). The animal world is *there*; our worlds are constructed. And they are constructed in a phenomenally economical way, by an infinite number of borrowings, cross-sortings, and associations. We start with very little— our bodily sensations as all that we are aware of directly—and we build from them. An analogy of how the process works is seen very clearly in the alphabet of the Indo-European languages: from its twenty-six letters, millions of words are created—a vast inverted pyramid of words with an infinite number of subtle shades of similarity and dissimilarity with one another. An unabridged dictionary is an outward and visible sign of the inward workings of the human mind in its incredible metaphorical capacity. The most outstanding feature of the human mind is its *mobility*, its constant, instantaneous power of association, its ability to be forever connecting this with that. It is as if everything in the world were similar to everything else, in at least one respect, and the task were to locate the similarities, especially the significant ones. When we learn a new thing, we invariably say, "I see it now," meaning that I connect the new thing in some way with what I already know. We cannot learn or understand except through connection, through association.

What is largely an unconscious process in a child's metaphorical construction of its world through acquiring an expanded vocabulary, becomes more conscious and manifest as we turn to examples in philosophy and science—two fields which, unlike the arts, have not usually been seen as dependent on metaphor. David Burrell points out that Plato's dialectic, in its constant movement from question to provisional answer to further question, is a form of the metaphorical process evident in ordinary language. In both instances, movement towards the truth is achieved by stretching language, by analogies with the familiar through borrowings, by judgments of aptness and appropriateness.[3] In logic of this sort, "truth" is never reached; rather, approximations are achieved to which persons commit themselves, but the process continues. A metaphorical pattern for rational human understanding is essentially a dramatic pattern for human knowing and becoming, a pattern which focuses on mobility, open-endedness, and tentativeness in its commitments.

Similarly strong cases for the centrality of metaphor could be made were we to look at the writings of philosophers such as Whitehead, Wittgenstein, Heidegger, or Ricoeur. Any philosophy which understands language as the essence of human being, which sees the distinction of the human animal to be its image-making capacity, is bound to perceive philosophy's attempts to know and express reality on a continuum with the indirection of language, in other words, as relying on metaphor. If language always stands between us and reality, if it is the medium through which we are aware of both our relationship to "what is" and our distance from it, then metaphor is both our burden and our glory, from the first words of children to the most complex forays on reality by philosophers.

But if we take philosophy in the more general sense, not as philosophy of language or philosophy which gives priority to language, but simply as conceptual or abstract thought, an understanding of philosophy that would include Descartes, Kant, and Spinoza, can we still say that metaphor is central? Kenneth Burke points out that "abstraction" means "drawing from," the drawing out of similar strains and motifs from dissimilar situations.[4] The principal tasks of conceptual thought—analysis, classification, and synthesis—all depend on this process of "drawing out" similarities within dissimilars. As Burke notes, "the business of interpretation is accomplished by the two processes of oversimplification and analogical extension."[5] When we interpret, that is, when we analyze, classify, and synthesize a series of events, structures, objects, or whatever, we suppress the ways in which they are dissimilar because we have discovered significant similarities among them. It goes without saying that what we find to be significant is so from our own limited perspective: metaphorical thinking, which is to say, all thinking, is intrinsically perspectival. We say "this" is like "that," but we realize that it is also *not* like "that" and that other ways of linking up the similarities and dissimilarities are possible.

When we turn to the sciences, whether mathematics or the natural or social sciences, we also find metaphor to be central. Perhaps it is most surprising to those who suppose that metaphor belongs only in the arts and religion to discover it at the most basic level in mathematics: the numerical analogue. Seeing the similar number among otherwise disparate entities is a metaphorical act, as in six apples, six moons, six ideas, six generous acts.[6] In the social sciences the ubiquity of metaphor is obvious: the human being has been seen as a child of God, as half-angel and half-beast, as a machine; the state has been viewed as an organism and a mechanism; the brain has been understood through the metaphor of the computer and vice versa. When one turns to physics, the evidence for the importance of metaphor in the form of models is extensive. The critical nature of models in atomic physics, the inability of this area of study to do without models, is vividly captured by physicist Mary Hesse remarking on the use of models when entities such as protons and neutrons are observable only in virtue of their remote effects:

> It is as if the properties of cricket balls were known to us, not by seeing and handling them, but only by hearing a sharp impact as a batsman hits out and observing shattered windows. To speak of *atomic particles* at all is to employ a model based on dynamics and electrostatics.[7]

In a situation such as this in which the entity in question cannot be observed, it must be imagined in terms of something else with which we are more familiar. In this case, metaphorical thinking in terms of the use of models is not illustrative, ornamental, or merely heuristic, but essential if one is to talk about the entities at all. Jacob Bronowski speaks for many philosophers of science when he insists that ideas in science, as in any other field, are derived from images:

> We cannot form any theory to explain, say, the workings of nature without forming in our mind some pattern of movement, some arrangement and rearrangement of the units, which derives from our experience. (That is why, for example, the reasoning of physics is always arguing about waves and particles, which derive directly from our physical experience.) In this sense, the whole of science is shot through and through with metaphors, which transfer and link one part of our experience to another, and find likenesses between the parts. All our ideas derive from and embody such metaphorical likenesses.[8]

These several witnesses to the importance of metaphor in philosophy and the sciences are mentioned here only to make the point that metaphor is not the possession of poetry or the burden of religion as has often been supposed, but is evident in all fields and at the most basic level of their understanding and conceptuality. As we shall see, it is, in fact, the constructive thinkers in various fields who regard metaphor most highly. They recognize with Coleridge that the creative act, whether it be the solution to a mathematical puzzle, the writing of a poem, or a new and fruitful way to view the dynamics of world economics, is a selection, combination, and synthesis of the already familiar into new wholes. We never create—as the tradition says God did—out of nothing, but use what we have, seeing it in a new way. The new way is not simply a reshuffling of the old, for metaphorical thinking recognizes the *unlike* as well as the *like*, but it uses the similar to move beyond it into the unknown. The process of creation can be compared to a Rorschach test where one sees a pattern similar to something which is vaguely familiar and the mind jumps to fill in the unknown gaps in order to see it whole.[9] The whole that one sees is not identical with anything with which we are familiar, but the similarity has enabled us to see a new thing. Arthur Koestler's monumental study, *The Act of Creation*, gives hundreds of examples of breakthroughs in various fields, especially in science, through the "bisociative" ability of the human mind which, if freed from conventional matrices, "sees" new similarities formerly blocked.[10] The most famous example is undoubtedly Archimedes in his bathtub, but Koestler mentions many others: Lord Kelvin came to the idea of the mirror galvanometer after noticing a reflection of light on his monocle; Newton saw that the moon behaved like an apple; Pasteur recognized the analogy between a spoiled culture and a cowpox vaccine.[11] As Koestler notes, seeing the similarity that has not been seen before in two previously unrelated matrices of thought is the essence of discovery—and this is metaphor in its most obvious and brilliant form.

These remarks on metaphor, its ubiquity and importance, are not meant to suggest that "everything is metaphor." I am not suggesting that "metaphor" is the ultimate metaphor for interpreting human beings or even for describing the nature of language. While in many ways we are the "metaphorical creature" and language is profoundly metaphorical, if we are not to absolutize metaphor we must view it as *one* way—albeit a highly suggestive and fruitful way—by which to understand particular aspects of human being, especially those pertaining to expression and interpretation, creation and discovery, change and transformation. I do not believe, however, that it is an adequate perspective from which to view our sensuous, affectional, and active lives at their base level. Of course, this level of human existence, when expressed and interpreted, comes under the metaphorical, but it also lies beneath it, is its funding, and is more basic than it. In a sense, we feel more than we can express, we know more than we can interpret. Metaphor deals with expression and interpretation, not with the depths of human existence that lie even beyond words. This is a difficult distinction to maintain, because in a sense everything human beings feel and know is already interpreted and hence metaphorical; but just as it makes little sense to talk of metaphorical language unless there is a nonmetaphorical language (dead metaphors, dictionary meanings), so it makes little sense to talk of "seeing this as that" unless there is a nonmetaphorical base. This base, difficult as it is to stipulate, deals, it seems to me, with our sensuous, affectional, and active lives at the most primordial level. There are some things that lie too deep for words, among them, for instance, the touch of another human being, what occurs in human silence, the terror that can grip us in the night, or an act of human compassion. These are not metaphors, but the stuff from which metaphor is made.[12]

Having looked at the centrality of metaphor, we need to define it as precisely as we can. The history of efforts to understand the nature of metaphor begins with Aristotle whose view constitutes one of the two major perspectives on it. In spite of his appreciation for its importance, his relegation of it to the mark of genius indicates he saw it principally as a rhetorical device rather than as central to language as such. His view can be called "substitutable" while the other major view sees metaphor as "unsubstitutable." That is, Aristotle's understanding of metaphor, and the opinion that prevailed until the nineteenth century (except for Vico in the Renaissance who suspected that metaphor was considerably more important than his predecessors or anyone else until Coleridge), was that what metaphor said could be said some other way. But, increasingly, over the last two centuries, that opinion has been reversed and metaphor has been seen not as a trope but as the way language and, more basically, thought works.

The principal contemporary theorists on metaphor as unsubstitutable are I. A. Richards and Max Black. Richards says, "we all live, and speak, only through an eye for resemblances" and Black agrees.[13] The ways in which their understandings of metaphor differ are subtle and not crucial for our argument. What follows is an amalgam of their views as well as of other theorists, notably Douglas Berggren, Walter Ong, Nelson Goodman, and Paul Ricoeur. Richard's definition is a good beginning: "In the simplest formulation, when we use a metaphor we have two thoughts of different things active together and supported by a single word, or phrase, whose meaning is a resultant of their interaction."[14] The most important element in this definition is its insistence on *two active thoughts which remain in permanent tension or interaction with each other.* Thus, in the example from Black mentioned earlier, "war is a chess game," the vitality of the metaphor depends upon keeping both thoughts and what Black calls their "systems of associated commonplaces" active in the mind. The meaning of the phrase, "war is a chess game," is not the same as "war is *like* a chess game" which implies a simple comparison, describing war as similar to chess. As Black says, "looking at a scene through blue spectacles is different from *comparing* that scene with something else."[15] The difference is that the *tension* is lost, what Ricoeur calls the "is and is not" quality of metaphor. By retaining the interaction of *two* thoughts active in the mind, one recalls, as one does not with a simile, that the two are dissimilar as well as similar. One difficulty with simile in contrast to metaphor is that simile softens the shock of the linkage through its "like," reducing an awareness of the dissimilarity, and hence allowing us to slip into literalistic thinking. A metaphor that works is sufficiently unconventional and shocking so that we instinctively say no as well as yes to it, thus avoiding absolutism. The difficulty with dead metaphors, of course, is that the shock and thus the tension is lost and literalism follows. Religious metaphors, because of their preservation in a tradition and repetition in ritual, are especially prone to becoming idols.

The tensive or interactive view of metaphor also reveals the fact that *both* fields or subjects are influenced or changed by being brought into relationship with the other. The names of these fields vary among theorists: Richards calls them "vehicle" and "tenor"; Black, "subsidiary" and "principal" subject; but, whatever the name, in our example of "war is a chess game," both war (as tenor or principal subject) and chess (as vehicle or subsidiary subject) undergo change by being thought of in relationship to the other. Thus, although chess is the filter or screen through which war is seen and hence influences our view of war, chess is also seen differently—in the present case as "warlike." This is a very important point for religious models because the human images that are chosen as metaphors for God gain in stature and take on divine qualities by being placed in an interactive relationship with the divine.

A third point which is only implicit in Richard's definition but one which he as well as Black, Ong, and Ricoeur all stress is that metaphor belongs to the semantics, not the syntax, of language. That is, it is concerned with meaning: it is in the form of assertions, of judgments. Metaphor of this sort, and at the level at which we are dealing with it, is not words but sentences with a subject and a predicate. The rhetorical, ornamental view of metaphor which sees it as a literary trope tends to concentrate on metaphorical words or phrases—for instance, Shakespeare's metaphor of "salad days" for Cleopatra's youth—rather than on two matrices of thought which are brought into conjunction with each other through a judgment of significant similarity.

Two points are crucial here: the indirection and tentativeness of all judgments and the structural, organizational power of metaphor. As Walter Ong points out, judgment is always binary; we can grasp nothing in itself but only as related to and set apart from something else.[16] Metaphor, because of its explicitly binary nature, is a reminder that we never apprehend simply and in a unitary fashion as idealism would have it. The "bifocal" or "twinned" vision of metaphor—what we have called the tension of metaphor which actively entertains the similarity and dissimilarity of both subjects—is a reminder, says Ong, of the duality which is always at the heart of human truth and judgment. Moreover, in the semantical view of metaphor, the judgment of similarity (and difference) has structural and organizing possibilities because we are dealing here with two *matrices* of thought, two systems of associated commonplaces. The most fruitful metaphors are the ones with sufficiently complex grids to allow for extension of thought, structural expansion, suggestions beyond immediate linkages. Thus, in this sense, "liberator" is a good metaphor for God because it entails a complex structure for thought which can be elaborated. Similarly, chess is a complex game which teases the mind into new connections with war the longer one reflects on it. It is because some metaphors have structural possibilities that, as we shall see, models can develop from them, for models are dominant metaphors with comprehensive, organizational potential.

There is, however, a deeper level to the semantics of metaphor: it is not just that a judgment is being made that one subject is both like and unlike another, but the tension of duality in such a judgment is, as Ricoeur insists, between a literal or conventional interpretation which self-destructs and an extended, new interpretation which is recognized as plausible or possible.[17] Thus, war is not literally seen as a game of chess (as Ricoeur points out, such an assertion is literally absurd), but because *both* subjects and their systems of associated commonplaces are actively entertained together, one can see a kind of sense, a nonliteral sense, to the assertion. The response to a metaphor is similar to the response to a riddle: one "gets" it or one does not, and what one "gets" is the new, extended meaning which is a result of the *interaction* of the subjects. Nelson Goodman expresses it colorfully when he says that "metaphor, it seems, is a matter of teaching an old word new tricks—of applying an old label in a new way."[18] Or as he says elsewhere, "a metaphor might be regarded . . . as a happy and revitalizing, even if bigamous, second marriage."[19] In more prosaic terms, metaphorical meaning depends upon a literal, conventional base as our point of contact, but through being applied to a new field, new meaning is created. As Ricoeur puts it, reality is redescribed through metaphor. This is a weighty assertion, resting on the capacity of metaphor both to rely on a literal meaning and to subvert and extend it through transformation. As we shall see, the parables of Jesus and Jesus as a parable are metaphorical in this sense. While we shall often be dealing with questions of the reference and truth of metaphor, a few initial remarks may be helpful. When Ricoeur says that metaphor redescribes reality, at one level he is only saying that in metaphor old views of reality are traded for new ones. As Goodman says in his characteristically colorful way, "a metaphor is simply a juvenile fact, and a fact a senile metaphor."[20] While metaphor does not refer to the conventional or literal view of the aspect of reality in question, neither does it refer to "another world" or to no reality outside itself. As an assertion, it has not only meaning but reference, not only internal sense but outward directionality. And the reality to which it refers is the ordinary world to which every interpretation refers.[21] The theory of gravitation refers to that world in one way; a poem in another; a philosophy of organism and process in a third way; the parables of Jesus in yet another way. Each models reality in a different way; none has direct or literal access to it. Metaphor is basically a new or unconventional interpretation of reality, whether that interpretation refers to a limited aspect of reality or to the totality of it. John Donne's line of poetry, "I am a little world made cunningly," is a redescription of reality as is Heraclitus's root-metaphor of change as the nature of reality.

The centrality of metaphor in all constructive fields—our world as modeled and we as the modelers—means that the question of the truth of metaphor cannot be dealt with in a direct, literalistic, positivistic way. What we consider realistic or literal is, as Goodman points out, what we are used to; traditional labels are old metaphors.[22] Even in science, which has a more settled context or set of conventions for its "facts" than do other fields, unrelated empirical truths are not significant. What matters in science as in other fields is whether individual "facts" fit into some whole, raise or answer significant questions, are related to other facts. The criteria of truth for a hypothesis in science are not unlike criteria applied to metaphors in poetry and religion: "Truth of a hypothesis . . . is a matter of fit—fit with a body of theory, and fit of hypothesis and theory to the data at hand and the facts to be encountered."[23] One speaks of a metaphor as apt or appropriate because it fits into the assumptions of a poem or into a system of doctrines or to life as lived. The hypothesis or metaphor may well transform or even revolutionize the conventional theory or set of expectations, but in either case it is not considered true because it corresponds with some uninterpreted reality but because it gives us a more apt, fitting way of interpreting reality than did the traditional view.

Finally, some comments on the abuse and dangers of metaphor are now appropriate. The greatest danger is assimilation—the shocking, powerful metaphor becomes trite and accepted. A parable by Franz Kafka makes the point with eerie power:

> Leopards break into the temple and drink up the sacrificial wine; this is repeated over and over again; eventually it becomes predictable, and is incorporated into the ceremony.[24]

Habit will always, it seems, triumph over novelty, no matter how shocking the novelty. Jesus said, "This is my body," and instead of surprise, joy, or disbelief, we do not even hear the metaphor. Colin Turbayne has listed three stages of metaphor.[25] Initially, when newly coined, it seems inappropriate or unconventional; the response is often rejection. At a second stage, when it is a living metaphor, it has dual meaning—the literal and metaphorical—and is insightful. Finally, the metaphor becomes commonplace, either dead and/or literalized. At this stage, says Turbayne, we are no longer like the Wizard of Oz who knew green glasses made Oz green, but, like all the other inhabitants of Oz, we believe that Oz *is* green.

What has occurred, of course, is that similarity has become identity; the *tension* that is so critical in metaphor has been lost. This is an ever present danger in religious metaphors, though also in scientific ones, for in both cases models of reality, especially ones with long-term and widespread backing, are identified with reality. "It is," says Douglas Berggren, "the familiar, or inherited or submerged metaphor which is the most dangerous."[26] Religion is obviously a prime candidate for housing familiar and submerged metaphors, since religious images—through tradition and ritual —seldom change and become accepted as ordinary language. But scientific models are equally susceptible, in part because science is not usually perceived as even trafficking in models.

Moreover, a metaphor used frequently, a metaphor that is believed in as the "thing itself," affects attitudes at profound levels. All metaphors, at least in poetry and religion (but also in advertising), have a strong attitudinal component, for we respond at an affectional level to metaphors which have significant associations for us. Thus, at an amusing level we can see Turbayne's point when he says, "a Dry-Martini health drink loses its flavor";[27] at a more serious level, when we see God as "suffering companion," we have a different attitude toward the deity than when we see God as "hunter." But metaphors that are literalized affect our attitudes at subconscious levels. If one believes that the death of Jesus *is* (literally) a substitutionary sacrifice to free all others from sin and guilt, that belief will have a more pervasive influence on one's attitudes than if one sees it as one interpretation among other possible ones. To sum up, one must be careful of metaphors; they are not to be taken lightly.

In conclusion, we recall that human thought and language grow and change by seeing one thing in terms of another: they are intrinsically metaphorical. Explicit or alive metaphors make us aware of this mobile, tensive characteristic of our way of being in the world. The distinctive features of alive metaphors can be summed up in the following way: a metaphor is an assertion or judgment of similarity and difference between two thoughts in permanent tension with one another, which redescribes reality in an open-ended way but has structural as well as affective power.

Parable

George Caird, a biblical scholar, says that "all, or almost all, of the language used by the Bible to refer to God is metaphor. . . ."[29] This is an opinion widely shared among contemporary biblical scholars and means that as we turn from a general treatment of metaphor to the principal text of the Judeo-Christian tradition what we find is corroboration of the importance of metaphor for religious language. Caird notes that in the Bible God speaks to us in similitudes: "I spoke to the prophets, it was I who gave vision after vision; I spoke through the prophets in parables" (Hos. 12:10). Moreover, we have no language but analogy for speaking about God, inadequate as such language is: "To whom will you liken me? Who is my equal? With whom can you compare me? Where is my like?" (Isa. 46:5).[30] As we turn, then, to a treatment of Jesus' parables as metaphors and Jesus as a parable, we note that their metaphorical nature is not an anomaly in the Bible but of a piece with its characteristic language.

Two notes of Old Testament imagery for God are especially pertinent for our study: its rich variety and its personal, relational character. The strong iconoclasm of the Old Testament, its fear of making graven images of God, resulted in a superabundance of images, none of which was to be regarded as literal or even adequate. As one exegete says, "A Hebrew sucked the juice out of each metaphor as he used it, and threw the skin away at once."[31] The Hebrew poet piled up and threw away metaphors of God, in the hope of both overwhelming the imagination with the divine richness and undercutting any idolatrous inclination to absolutize images. This characteristic of Old Testament language about God is a useful reminder that many as well as novel images are appropriate and necessary to both avoid idolatry and remain relevant to a people's experience of God. But within the plethora of Hebrew images, there is one category that stands out—personal, relational images. While nonhuman images are frequent and especially powerful for intimating feelings of the sublime and mysterious as well as for balancing images which domesticate, God as thunder, lion, torrent, bear, and ocean is, nonetheless, a less-frequent way of speaking of the divine than God in personal images. All human actions and attitudes are ascribed to God in the Old Testament and the five most common metaphors are king/subject, judge/litigant, husband/wife, father/child, master/servant.[32] The hierarchical, patriarchal nature of these metaphors will be dealt with later; the positive point I wish to make now is that they are personal and relational metaphors.

It is no surprise, then, when we turn to the New Testament to find that Jesus' chief metaphor for God is a personal one—that of "father"—and that his parables are concerned with relations among persons. Nor is it a surprise to find the parables themselves to be metaphors, with some of the "throwaway" qualities of iconoclastic Hebrew imagery. No *one* parable tells us of "the kingdom of God" and even all together they do not add up to a definition of the kingdom, to a doctrine or concept of the kingdom.[33] The two notes of iconoclasm with variety of images and emphasis on personal, relational metaphors continue in the New Testament.

There are new directions, however, for religious language suggested by the parables and Jesus as a parable.[34] First, the New Testament in general and the parables in particular do not talk *about* God as much as the Old Testament does. The focus of the language here is not on the divine nature and characteristics; rather the language is considerably more *indirect*. This feature is especially evident in the synoptic gospels; in John we see direct language about God, but in John and in other parts of the New Testament we have already moved into more secondary, conceptual language from the primary, imagistic base of the synoptics.[35] The synoptic gospels do not introduce startling new language about God so much as a new *way* to talk about the divine-human relationship and this suggests a second new direction for religious language. It is a language of *extravagance*. As we shall see, one of the outstanding features of the parables is the element of the extraordinary, of radicalism, of surprise and reversal. They are metaphors with considerable shock value, for their intention is to upset conventional interpretations of reality. Yet, and here we come to a third new direction, the parables introduce this note of extravagance in a curiously *mundane, secular* way: through seemingly ordinary stories about ordinary people engaged in ordinary decisions.

These characteristics of indirection, extravagance, and mundanity are epitomized in *the* parable of the New Testament, the story of Jesus. This "metaphor" above all others in the New Testament is in many ways the most obvious one and at the same time the most difficult to grasp. It is obvious that the New Testament is written from the perspective of faith in Jesus as the critical interpretive framework for understanding the divine-human relationship. It is difficult to grasp because this "parable" is a human life, the most complex and multidimensional of all metaphors, with unlimited possibilities for interpretation.

These characteristics of indirection, extravagance, and ordinariness are ones we have met before in our discussion of metaphor and it is because of these similarities and others that parables have been called extended metaphors. The importance for our project of understanding parables as metaphors is substantial, for we are suggesting the possibility of a metaphorical theology, a theology which is on a continuum with our basic way of knowing and interpreting our world. We hope to establish that religious knowing and interpreting are not something superimposed on and alien to the human way of being in the world—the old reason-versus-faith dichotomy—but that both "reason" and "faith," or as I would prefer to say, ordinary interpretation and religious interpretation, are metaphorical in origin and in process. That is, both are tentative, indirect judgments with the difference mainly in the degree of novelty, extravagance, or tension they display. If it can be established that the critical form of Jesus' teaching, the parables, is metaphorical, and further, that the life and death of Jesus himself is a parable of God, then a case can be made that modes of interpretation founded on these sources should also have metaphorical characteristics.

Two qualifications are necessary at this point. First, I am not arguing that the parables or Jesus as a parable are the only form in the New Testament, but only that this form is a central one and provides a plausible interpretive framework for the work and person of Jesus. Second, I am not attempting to eliminate differences between images and concepts in theology, but only to show that they are on a continuum and exist in a symbiotic relationship. I wish to show that the parabolic, kerygmatic beginnings and the conceptual, didactic tradition are or should be on a continuum. It is for this reason that we will focus on models, because they are a mixed genre, partaking of both image and concept.

The parables of Jesus as extended metaphors already display features of models. That is, in the parables the kingdom is not said to be this or that, for the thread of similarity between a parable and the kingdom is not a particular event or object; rather, the kingdom is likened to a whole structure of events. The kingdom of God is always *intimated indirectly* through telling a story: a man who found a special pearl and sold all he owned to buy it; a woman who turned her house upside down to locate a lost coin; sowers who scatter seed, some on good and some on poor ground; a son who leaves home and returns repentant; a man who invites his reluctant friends to a banquet and ends up opening his table to everyone. What is crucial in these stories is the *plot*; they are exemplars, not discrete poetic metaphors. As Ricoeur has said perceptively, the interactive partners in permanent tension in a parable are two ways of being in the world, one of which is the conventional way and the other, the way of the kingdom.[36] A parable is a judgment or assertion of similarity and difference between two thoughts in permanent tension with one another: one is the ordinary way of being in the world and the other, the extraordinary way.

The plot of a parable forms one partner of the interactive metaphor while the conventional context against which it is set is the other partner. Reality is redescribed through the tension generated by these two perspectives. Thus, in the parable of the Great Supper (Luke 14:16–24), the guests who by convention should be invited to such a feast—the "worthy" —are usurped in the plot of the parable by the unconventional guests— the "unworthy." We *know* the worthy guests because of conventional standards of worth, but it is only through the plot of the parable that we glean a dim sense of how the unworthy guests might be considered worthy according to a new standard. That sense depends upon the tension between the two standards, a tension that redescribes reality as conventionally understood. The *action* in a parable is indicative of the kerygmatic quality of parables, for they are paradigms of persons encountering the kingdom, not abstractly, but concretely and existentially. A parable says: if you want a suggestion of what the kingdom is, listen to this story of a man who invited worthy guests to dinner, and when the guests declined claiming business and family obligations, the man invited social outcasts to his feast. That whole story is the extended metaphor and what it models is the kingdom: the structure of human relationships which it suggests; its inversion of expectations; its intimation of a set of priorities; its existential, ordinary, and secular quality—all of this is the grid or screen which allows us to see what life in the rule of God is like. It is obvious in this example that one cannot get the point of the story except by keeping the tension between the two descriptions of reality (of how life is to be lived in the world), for the "point" of a parable is not a moral, concept, or resolution, but the play of the interactive partners which, as C. H. Dodd says, "teases" the imagination into participatory thinking.[37] What it causes us to think about is life under the reign of God, and the parables, while giving no definitions of that life, provide exemplars or models of it.

As many critics have remarked, the outstanding feature of the parables and the feature which is at the heart of the tension in the parables is their *extravagance*.[38] While the stories are, at one level, thoroughly ordinary and secular, events occur and decisions are made which are absurd, radical, alien, extreme. In the naturalistic or nonhuman parables, the ones dealing with the mustard seed, the lost coin, the buried treasure, the pearl of great price, and so on, the extreme quality appears in the passion for the rule of God, its overriding importance in relation to everything else. Most of the parables, however, are personal and relational, concerned with ordinary and extraordinary, or conventional and radical, ways of dealing with other people: the Unjust Judge (Luke 18:1–8), the Prodigal Son (Luke 15:11–32), the Wicked Husbandman (Matt. 22:33–41), the Great Feast (Luke 14:16–24), the Good Samaritan (Luke 10:29–37), the Laborers in the Vineyard (Matt. 20:1–16). All of these parables are stories about absurd, alien, or radical ways of relating to others, given conventional standards. Robert Funk has summed up the tension between these two ways in the phrases, the "logic" of merit and the "logic" of grace.[39] These and many other concepts attempting to summarize what the parables mean are appropriate and inevitable; at this stage of our considerations, however, what is critical is the mobile, tensive, dramatic, extravagant quality of the parables, which functions in the play of two different basic orientations to reality.

Ricoeur sums up this quality of the parables by suggesting that parables work on a pattern of orientation, disorientation, and reorientation: a parable begins in the ordinary world with its conventional standards and expectations, but in the course of the story a radically different perspective is introduced that disorients the listener, and finally, through the interaction of the two competing viewpoints, tension is created that results in a redescription of life in the world.[40] The uneasiness generated by the disorientation of a parable, introduced by the alien perspective, is nicely suggested by John Dominic Crossan: "I don't know what you mean by that story, but I'm certain I don't like it."[41] A parable is, in this analysis, an assault on the accepted, conventional way of viewing reality. It is an assault on the social, economic, and mythic structures people build for their own comfort and security. A parable is a story meant to invert and subvert these structures and to suggest that the way of the kingdom is not the way of the world. Or, as Crossan says, a parable asks the question: "Why things might not be just as well some other way rather than the way we expected and presumed?"[42] If we review in our minds the central relational parables of Jesus, we see again and again expectations being reversed: an elder son who does not get what he "deserves"; late workers who are paid the same as early ones; a feast that is given for the poor and "unworthy" when the prominent guests decline; a Samaritan who comes to the aid of a Jew while "religious" people walk by on the other side.

Throughout the parables, then, two standards—or we could say, two models—are in permanent tension with each other, and the effect of their interaction, for anyone who allows himself or herself to be personally involved, is profound disorientation. Thus, not "liking" the parables is the appropriate initial reaction to them. Crossan says the parables place the listener "on the edge of the raft" and what this means is the end of conventional security: "You have built a lovely home, myth assures us: but, whispers parable, you are right above an earthquake fault."[43] Ricoeur insists on the same point when he says that the reorientation in a parable is of an open-ended and relative sort, which does not allow us to remake our world according to a new set of rules and standards.[44] If this is the case with parables, then "Christian" politics, art, morals, economics, philosophy, and so forth, are all questionable ventures, unless undertaken with appreciation for the relativity and partiality of all such "systems." What the parables stand for is opposition to *all* forms of idolatry and absolutism, *even* the new orientation to reality brought about through the parables' redescription of reality. The permanent function of parables is to enhance consciousness of the radical relativity of human models of reality, even when these models are "divinely inspired," that is, based on the new way of the kingdom.

If we follow this analysis of the parables, we come to two conclusions regarding the basis for a metaphorical theology. First, some clear indications for method are suggested and these can be summed up in much the same way as we described the metaphorical perspective: *a theology influenced by the parables would be open-ended, tensive, secular, indirect, iconoclastic, and revolutionary*. As we shall see, these methodological characteristics will undergo changes as we move from parables to models to concepts, but they definitely provide some criteria both for the construction and criticism of theology. Secondly, some suggestions emerge from the parables for the critical content of theology: *the focus is on relational life*. As in the Old Testament where the central metaphors for God are personal, so in the New Testament relational models predominate.

These characteristics for both the method and content of theology continue when we look at other forms in the New Testament—notably, the sayings, healings, and miracles of Jesus. As William A. Beardslee points out, paradox, exaggeration, and hyperbole in the proverbial sayings jolt the listener out of conventional expectations and make it impossible to create a continuous project out of one's life.[45] While sayings such as "Whoever seeks to gain his life will lose it, but whoever loses his life will preserve it" (Luke 17:33) and "Love your enemies, do good to those who hate you" (Luke 6:27) are not metaphors, they have the same structure as the parables of two interacting perspectives—one conventional and the other radical—in permanent tension with each other. The proverbial sayings, while more conceptual than imagistic, bring about similar results of disorientation through the intensification provided by hyperbole and paradox. We can extend this pattern still further if we look at the healings and miracles of Jesus. In the healing stories, conventional expectations are overturned through radical deeds by Jesus which bring about strange and unexpected events: the sick are restored to life. Likewise, in the miracles, the course of ordinary life and what can be expected in this continuum is broken and the unexpected and extravagant occurs. The healings and miracles need not be understood as bizarre phenomena, which are contrasted with the teachings of Jesus (i.e., the parables) considered as sensible, moral tales; but all can be seen on a continuum, as words and deeds which have similar characteristics. Such a view makes the teaching more extraordinary and the healings and miracles less so.

All these remarks come into clearer focus when we consider *Jesus as a parable of God*. John Dominic Crossan says, "Jesus proclaimed God in parables, but the primitive church proclaimed Jesus as the Parable of God."[46] Leander Keck says, "Jesus concentrated on parabolic speech because he himself was a parabolic event of the kingdom of God."[47] Initially, it seems strange to speak of Jesus as a parable, for the traditional way to interpret the person and work of Jesus does not include such language. The orthodox christology of Chalcedon not only moves from "above" to "below," from God to Jesus, but from person to work, while the interpretation of Jesus as a parable of God questions both of these assumptions. It is in the Antiochene rather than the Alexandrine tradition, starting from below, from the story of Jesus in the synoptic gospels. Many theologians today feel that an incarnational theology, a theology from above such as the Johannine "Word became flesh" perspective, is not possible in a time when the credibility of God is undermined.[48] And yet, as Keck points out, while one cannot today move from God to Jesus, neither can one have Jesus without God: "No one can deal with Jesus of Nazareth without confronting the question of God, because his concentration on God and his kingdom is what was constitutive of Jesus."[49]

How is it possible to confront the question of God in a way that takes seriously both the central concerns of the New Testament and the modern sensibility? One possible way is to interpret Jesus as a parable of God for, as we have seen, the parables focus on the kingdom; they are a secular, indirect, open-ended form of religious language which does not assume prior belief in God; and they are a form of Jesus' work manifesting characteristics which are also evident in other forms of his work such as the healings and miracles. Thus, Jesus as a parable of God means starting from "below," starting with the work and moving indirectly to the person. There is little doubt but that this was the way that the early Church arrived at its confession of Jesus as the Christ: from experiences of healing, forgiveness, and renewal in relation to this man came the attempt to say who he was. The work of Jesus forces the question of his person. Of course, the point of view from which the New Testament is written is one which has already made considerable progress in identifying Jesus as in a special if not unique relationship with God. The many titles ascribed to him—Messiah, Son of God, Son of man, and so on—are metaphors from the Hebraic tradition which provide familiar screens through which to interpret the strange and marvelous work of this man. But the work came first and the direction was from below to above.

The metaphor of "parable" for the work and person of Jesus is ideally suited to express these emphases. It is necessary to be precise when making this assertion and not lapse into rhetoric. It is sometimes said that all we need is "the story of Jesus"; the issues involved in christology and soteriology are, however, much too complex and weighty to permit such sentimentality and evasion of thought. We must look as carefully as possible at what it means to call Jesus a "parable" of God.

The first thing to say about Jesus as a parable of God is that through the whole network of his life, deeds, and death we are asked "to look Godward through that pattern," as Leander Keck says, for "in ongoing reflection on what is implicit in the coordinates of Jesus' pattern, one's understanding of God can be realigned by what one is permitted to see, and compelled to see, by looking at God through Jesus."[50] The implications of taking Jesus as a parable of God are initially twofold. First, given our interpretation of parable as extended metaphor and metaphor as unsubstitutable, Jesus' work is *essential* for our understanding of God. A parabolic christology is not a weak or lightweight christology which sees Jesus merely as a heuristic fiction, helpful but dispensable. A metaphor is not an ornament or illustration, but says what cannot be said any other way; likewise, Jesus as parable of God provides us with a grid or screen for understanding God's way with us which cannot be discarded after we have translated it into concepts. Doctrine, necessary and appropriate as it is, does not replace the metaphors that fund it. Second, Jesus as parable *realigns* our understanding of God; he does not initiate it. Whether religious or nonreligious, everyone who encounters Jesus as a parable of God does so with preconceptions of God. As a true and novel metaphor, Jesus as parable reorders and upsets our familiar, conventional understandings of God by means of the unfamiliar, unconventional pattern he introduces. The interactive partners in permanent tension in the parable that is Jesus' life are the prior understandings we have of proper life under God in the world and the way of the kingdom, which was the focus of his entire existence. Just as the parables center on the kingdom, so does the life and death of Jesus.

Thus, the centrality of both Jesus and the kingdom is presented in a parabolic christology. This focus gives credibility to the judgment that to see Jesus as a parable of God is a legitimate interpretation, for any view that either made Jesus marginal or something other than the kingdom central to the New Testament would be highly questionable. But, more specifically, what does it mean to call Jesus a parable of God? Leander Keck and John Donahue, two biblical scholars who have analyzed Jesus' career in these terms, insist that there is an inner connection between the parabolic mode of speech and the mode and motive of his work. We need to look more closely at this connection. As we have seen, in Jesus' parables two ways of being in the world are set in permanent tension with each other through the plot of a story. Through extravagance in these brief dramas, conventional mores are questioned and the listener is asked to make a decision. Can the story of Jesus be seen in this light? Is it possible to say that the heart of the drama of Jesus' life and death is the tension that it manifests between accepted ways of relating to God and to others *and* a new way that he does not so much tell us about but *is* in all his words and deeds? Are his life and especially his death extravagant and radical, a shock and a scandal which, when encountered seriously, call into question the comfortable homes that our myths have built for us? Is Jesus himself the whisper that our presumed security rests on an earthquake fault and that only a radically different kind of security, one based on utter trust in God, will provide us with houses, albeit never "solid" ones, in which to live?

If we were to interpret the work and person of Jesus in this light, several points would be stressed. First, it would be christology from "below." That is, one central mark of a parable is that it works through the ordinary and secular, by indirection, to bring about insight. Questions of the work would definitely precede those about the person and the questions raised would allow for many different interpretations and answers. While there have been many theories of the atonement, there has been only one orthodox position on the person of Jesus. But if Jesus' whole life is seen as a parable, the same flexibility and conceptual richness permitted in the work would be encouraged for understanding "who" he was and is. The mundane, secular starting point means that judgments about who Jesus is and what he did necessarily permit skepticism, doubt, or uncertainty. A metaphorical statement is, as we recall, always a judgment of similarity (and difference) between two thoughts: Jesus "is and is not" God. Metaphorical statements are never identity statements; hence, idolatry, "Jesusolatry," is avoided, and while we look through the story of Jesus to gain an understanding of what it means to live under God's rule, we cannot make the illegitimate move of identifying Jesus with God.

This has immense importance for Christian assessment of other religions which, on the orthodox view of Jesus' identity with God, are excluded from significant revelation. If Jesus is understood as *a* parable of God, one which Christians claim is a true one, then other religions can make the claim that they also contain metaphorical expressions of divine reality. In spite of the difficulties in adjudicating alternative and conflicting claims, to deny such possibilities is to limit God to a "tribal" status and ultimately to make an idol of Christianity. Likewise, to see Jesus as a parable and thus to deny his identity with God is important for peoples whose experience has been excluded due to the particularity of Jesus' person and history, for instance, for women who feel excluded by Jesus' maleness. A parabolic christology relativizes Jesus' particularity while universalizing the God of whom Jesus is a metaphor. Hence, openness to other manifestations and expressions of divine reality is not only encouraged but mandated.

Second, we have stressed the personal, relational focus of the New Testament parables, and when we turn to Jesus as a parable, we see that Jesus' way of being in the world was one which embodies this focus. The first thing to notice, for instance, about Jesus' characteristic address to God as "father" is not the foundation it provided for a patriarchal model to God, but its relational, personal character. It was for Jesus a term of great intimacy and affection which described his own sense of utter trust in God. Likewise, the thrust of his teachings as well as his healings was toward persons, their way of relating to others, their wholeness and health, both physical and spiritual. Most importantly, that mode was exemplified or modeled in his own person, in his dealings with the poor, with women, with outcasts, and with foreigners. Thus, a theology dependent on Jesus as parable will focus on the quality of relationships among differing kinds of persons; in such theology ethics can never be an appendage to systematic theology, but at its heart. For this reason, the liberation theologies which insist on the priority of "orthopraxy" over "orthodoxy" have a strong case.

Third, Jesus' mode of relating to other people and to God could be characterized as radical, shocking, unconventional. The tension in the "plot" of his life is one of constant interaction between the ways of the world and the ways of the kingdom. One sees the tension he created with established ways wherever one turns in the Bible: in relation to the kingdom of God, he questioned the importance of the natural family, religious structures, marriage, wealth, and nationalism. As Keck says, "he not only tells shocking stories but leads a shocking life towards a shocking end."[51] John Donahue notes that in the Gospel of Mark, for instance, the most frequent responses to Jesus are surprise, awe, wonder, and fear at the disturbing, unsettling quality of the man and his deeds.[52] Jesus' life, as an embodiment of the kingdom, is one partner in the drama; the other protagonist is the economic, political, religious, national, and social mores of his time. This is not to say that Jesus' was, in a direct sense, a revolutionary concerned with social change; however, as Keck points out, since "the kingdom of God is not the fulfillment of the present but a rectifying alternative to it . . . the God of the kingdom is not the ideological bulwark of the status quo, but a threat to it."[53] Both the scandal and trust of Jesus' life come into sharp focus in his death, for the cross is both the supreme offense to the ways of the world and the greatest test of trust against conventional evidence. The cross, however, is more than the scandal and trust of Jesus' life; it is also a parable of God's *way* of dealing with evil, a way different from that of conventional ways. Not only is the way of the kingdom opposed to the evil ways of the world, but as theologian Maurice Wiles points out, in the parable of the cross we see embodied a different conception of the pursuit of the good, a conception in which good is found not by separation from evil but by suffering identification with it.

> So the parable of the cross points the human imagination to a vision of God as participant in the continuing conflict with evil, identifying himself at whatever cost with both the perpetrators and the victims of that evil. It is through the cross that he is most clearly seen as "the God for whom nothing is expendable except himself."[54]

If Jesus is a parable of God, it is at the cross that the parable will be heard by those who have ears to hear, for here God's suffering love embraces both the sinner and those sinned against.

Several notes have emerged from our consideration of Jesus as a parable of God. Like a parable, the life and death of Jesus is a mundane, ordinary story raising in an indirect way through his work the question of his person. As with the parables, the focus of Jesus' life is on persons and the mode of their relations with one another and with God, epitomized by Jesus' relation with God as "father" and with others as brothers and sisters. Finally, the extravagance, unconventionality, and radicalism of the parables is reflected in Jesus' conflict with established mores and most acutely in his death on a cross which inverts expectations of the destiny of a "savior." The disciples, those who hear the parable that is Jesus, find that their own lives must reflect the same parabolic qualities. As Donahue says of Mark's Jesus: "Response to this parable puts the ordinary askew. It involves a challenge to the total fiber of life."[55] Like Jesus, "who" we are depends to a great extent on what we do; the intimate relationship between being and doing in the Judeo-Christian tradition militates against both empty spirituality and overintellectualism. Likewise, the Christian life is preeminently one of relationship, in trust toward God and love towards others, as was true of Jesus' life. Moreover, like Jesus we are called to life in but not of the world, to lives that always stand in criticism of the status quo and that press toward fulfillment in the kingdom. Finally, as Jesus is a parable of God, so are his disciples parables of Jesus: we "are and are not" his followers. Like all metaphorical judgments, this assertion of faith, of reflecting his image and of similarity with him, is a relative, open-ended, tensive statement which makes no pretense at identification or possession. Just as parable puts distance between Jesus and God, so it puts distance between Jesus and his followers: we reflect his ways but in our own ways, and there are other ways besides his. Christians judge his way to be a good, perhaps the best, way, but it is not exclusive.

Scripture

The closing words of the above paragraph are relative ones. They suggest that a metaphorical theology, one based on parables and Jesus as parable, will differ from traditional views of the authority of Scripture. One of the distinctive marks of metaphorical thinking is its refusal of identity: if all of our knowing is seeing one thing in terms of something else, those terms can never be collapsed. Whatever we know, we know only by indirection; hence, distance is forever between us and what we know. If we know God by the indirection of the Bible, then the Bible "is and is not" the word of God. The Bible is a metaphor of the word or ways of God, but as metaphor it is a relative, open-ended, secular, tensive judgment. It is, as we shall attempt to show, the premier metaphor, the classic model, of God's ways for Christians, but as a metaphor it cannot be absolute, "divinely inspired," or final. The status of Scripture is a crucial issue for a metaphorical theology which is attempting to speak to the issues of idolatry and irrelevance, for conservatives absolutize Scripture, refusing to admit its metaphorical quality while liberation theologies, especially radical feminist theology, relativize Scripture to the point of undercutting the relevance of its basic images. The status of Scripture is also critical for a theology based on parables and Jesus as parable, since the level and kind of authority of the text in which these forms appear must be established.

Three critical issues face us. First, we will consider briefly the nature of interpretation in the broad sense as our way of being in the world as well as in the specific sense of the interpretation of texts. Second, we will consider Scripture as the classic text of the Christian tradition and the authority it has in such a view. Third, we will examine two perspectives on texts and tradition, one with conservative tendencies and the other potentially revolutionary, in order to see which view fits best with a metaphorical theology.

"To interpret or not to interpret" is not a human choice: we are hermeneutical creatures. To say that we are hermeneutical, that to interpret is the distinctive human way of being in the world, is identical to saying that we are linguistic, for, as we have seen, language is at base metaphor, either dead or alive metaphor. We are not usually aware of interpreting because in our daily dealings with the world we accept and use the conventional linguistic glasses provided by dictionary definitions and the perspectives of our culture, class, and society. We become conscious of our hermeneutical nature when new metaphors are presented to us or forced upon us: to see oneself as an organism, a free individual, a child of God, or a member of the master race are all metaphors of the self, though some of these interpretations appear more metaphorical than others. The depths of our interpretive nature defy our best archeological digging as this fine statement by Nelson Goodman indicates:

> The catch . . . , as Ernest Gombrich insists, is that there is no innocent eye. The eye comes always ancient to its work. . . . Not only how but what it sees is regulated by need and prejudice. It selects, rejects, organizes, discriminates, associates, classifies, analyzes, constructs. It does not so much mirror as take and make; and what it takes and makes it sees not bare, as items without attributes, but as things, as food, as people, as enemies, as stars, as weapons. Nothing is seen nakedly or naked.[56]

"Nothing is seen nakedly or naked": if this is true, as it appears to be at the basic level of perception—of what the eye takes in—then how much more true it has to be at the level of the metaphors by which we construct our social, cultural, political, and religious worlds. If we cannot "see a fork" except by means of a model or gestalt of "fork" (which, of course, can range from a pointed wooden stick to gold, three-pronged table service), then how could we see the blooming, buzzing confusion of the more complex and sophisticated dimensions of our world except through organizing patterns and structures? These patterns and structures are large-scale metaphors, or more accurately, models, systems of interconnecting metaphors which order experience for us. Whether consciously or unconsciously, all people live by metaphors: a militant ecologist lives consciously by an organic model of the world, but a farmer does also, although perhaps in a less explicit fashion. To become aware of the metaphors that govern basic perspectives is, among other things, a political act, for the possibility of change both at the personal and public levels depends upon consciousness of hidden metaphors. As Kenneth Burke notes, the choice of metaphors is *the* hermeneutical act, for a metaphor by definition is "a device for seeing something *in terms of* something else."[57] Once we become aware that we *are* interpreters and interpretation means seeing one thing in terms of something else, in other words, using one thing as a perspective on something else, then we have forever lost what we thought we had—the innocent eye.

When we turn to texts, then—a text such as Scripture—we realize that here also there is no such thing as the innocent eye, neither the eye which selected, rejected, and organized the text nor our eye which, when reading or listening to it, also selects, rejects, and organizes. This makes the analysis of metaphors much more complicated than we have previously considered. A metaphor is not only the tensive interaction of the partners in the metaphor itself, but also the tension created by the perspectives of both speaker and hearer. A text is not a bit of language we take in like food, but, as contemporary hermeneutical critics have insisted, it is *discourse*—someone speaking out of one complex context to someone else who also inhabits a complex context. The focus of the attention of both speaker and hearer is the text, to be sure, but in order to understand that text appropriately and with any degree of accuracy, the basic metaphors or "prejudices," as the philosopher of language Hans-Georg Gadamer says, must be taken into account. To say that both speaker and hearer have "prejudices" or basic organizing metaphors is not a negative statement; it means only that no eye is naked, that texts are interpretations by speakers and that hearers come to texts with interpretive frameworks of their own by which they prejudge what a text means. Hence, the total interpretive situation of a text is a complex triad of speaker, text, and hearer in which many possibilities are present for misunderstandings, differences of opinion, varying interpretations, and revisions of previous interpretations.

Some helpful guidelines for appropriate and reasonably accurate interpretations of texts have been suggested by Gadamer which are worth considering.[58] He suggests that the best way to approach a text is, initially, in an open and accepting way with the expectation that the text has something important to say. Because basic texts in a tradition, including Scripture, are universal in intent and capable of speaking across generations, one assumes that one *can* hear what the text wants to say in spite of its initial strangeness due to cultural differences. Gadamer, unlike Dilthey and Schleiermacher, does not believe that interpretation arises only because of misunderstanding and alienation, but also and primarily because of a desire to hear what the text has to say. As one begins to grapple with a text, readers find their initial "prejudices" being questioned by the text, just as their interests and concerns open up the text to them. Gadamer compares the process to a game in which the reader is absorbed by the movement and becomes a part of the process or engages in Socratic dialogue with the text, questioning it and being questioned by it as the process continues. What emerges from serious interaction with a text is what he calls a merging of "horizons" of the reader and the text; that is, the perspectives of each fuse and a new interpretation comes about, for, as he insists, "we understand in a different way, if we understand at all."[59] In other words, the interpretation that results from this process is not the text alone, nor the intention of the speaker, nor any interpretation prior to the present hearer, but a new thing which has been influenced by all of the foregoing but is not reducible to any of them. The implications for the question of the authority of Scripture are clear. It means there is no "canonical" or absolute text or interpretation: a text is never "there," pristine and absolute, but exists only in relationship to its hearers *and* no interpretation can be final, for a text only has meaning in relationship to hearers, all of whom come with different interpretive contexts.

Gadamer is not suggesting that *any* interpretation of a text is as good as any other. Not only does he state that texts must be taken with utter seriousness in the "game" or "dialogue" by which they are understood, but he also insists that the best interpreters are those who have been exposed to many classical interpretations of the text in question. Thereby they are prepared to ask the right questions and intuit the most appropriate answers. Just as a classic performance of a musical score or a play becomes a standard for later performances, so also wise interpretations of the basic texts of a tradition by great exegetes become guides for future interpreters. Gadamer is by no means suggesting that all interpretations are of equal merit or that later interpretations are better than earlier. In fact, as we will see later, his point of view is potentially conservative. What he does very well is tell us how to appreciate and accept the texts of a tradition; what he does not do is suggest how that tradition can be changed.

We have reviewed Gadamer's hermeneutics in detail because he, better than any other contemporary philosopher of interpretation, sees the connection between interpretation and metaphor; that is, that interpretation is movement from a familiar base—one's own "prejudices"—to a new, changed perspective through interaction with another and unfamiliar base which is the text. Through the tension created by the interaction of the familiar and the unfamiliar, something new emerges which is the fusion of the two horizons. Gadamer's own words are worth quoting on this point:

> What I am describing is the mode of the whole human experience of the world. I call this experience hermeneutical, for the process we are describing is repeated continually throughout our familiar experience. There is always a world already interpreted, already organized in its basic relations, into which experience steps as something new, upsetting what has led our expectations and undergoing reorganization itself in the upheaval. Misunderstanding and strangeness are not the first factors, so that avoiding misunderstanding cannot be regarded as the specific task of hermeneutics. Just the reverse is the case. Only the support of the familiar and common understanding makes possible the venture into the alien, the lifting up of something out of the alien and thus the broadening and enrichment of our own experience of the world.[60]

This description of the experience of interpretation as "the mode of the whole human experience of the world" is nearly a correlate of what we have described as metaphorical thinking. In both instances, the familiar meets the unfamiliar and, in the process of trying to understand the unfamiliar, tries out various perspectives on it—sees it *as* something else—which it "is and is not." In both cases, we make judgments which have to undergo revision as we come to clearer recognition of the process by which the new, unfamiliar thing is both like and unlike what we already know. Gadamer's metaphors of "game" and "dialogue" are helpful for suggesting the nature of this process, as they stress the mobile, open character of human thought when it is growing, when we are learning a new thing. Finally, Gadamer's perspective aligns with metaphorical thinking in that in both cases thought has no closure and is radically relative: no judgment is final, no interpretation absolute, no perspective exclusive.

We conclude, then, that interpretation, both as our basic way of being in the world and as applied to texts, is very close to what we have described earlier as metaphorical thinking. They are two names for the same process, for as Burke says, "to consider A from the point of B is, of course, to use B as a *perspective* upon A."[61] What metaphor does is to consider A from the point of view of B and what interpretation does is to see something from a particular perspective: they are the same process. What this means, of course, is that metaphorical thinking, as we have described it, is not something alien, esoteric, or "poetic," but simply a precise way of describing what we do when we interpret: we see "this" as "that," we find the thread of similarity with the familiar in the unfamiliar situation and move beyond where we were before as we work through the process of "is and is not" toward new understanding.

It is now necessary to consider more carefully what *kind* of text Scripture is as we move to specify its authority for Christians. When we consider the sort of text Scripture is we see, as hermeneutical critics such as Gadamer and Ricoeur point out, that it epitomizes what a great text should be. A great text is a poetic text in the broad sense of a particular fiction or reconstruction of reality as universally applicable across generations. It can be contemporaneous or "timeless" in that it speaks a universal language through its own particularity, not because it says one thing, but because it can say many things. It is rich, open, diverse, for as a poetic text it is constituted by metaphors open to many interpretations. As such, it is also a classic text which lives beyond its own time as it meets and accommodates itself to the experiences and interpretations of diverse peoples. We shall argue that the authority of Scripture is the authority of a classic poetic text and that such a notion of authority is substantial and enduring, both because *its authority is intrinsic* (the world it presents, that is, the reality it redescribes, speaks with power to many people across the ages) and because *its interpretation is flexible* (the world it presents is open to different understandings).

To call Scripture a poetic text does not of course mean that it is poetry in the narrow sense or that it is a fairy tale and hence "false" in contrast to an empirical or scientific text which is "true." As we have seen, such a division is simplistic, for all language is construction. There is a difference, however, between poetic and nonpoetic texts: the poetic text is one constituted by novel, tensive metaphors; it does not rely on accepted linguistic conventions, but presents new, alternative descriptions of reality.[62] A poetic text, such as Shakespeare's *Hamlet* or Eliot's *The Wasteland*, presents an alternative world which the reader enters through a suspension of the ordinary world. There are, of course, connections with ordinary reality in poetic fictions, but in order to appreciate the power of its alternative world, one must suppress ordinary reality for the time being, allowing the new world of the text to control one's perceptions.

In a very similar way, Scripture as a whole and in its many parts redescribes reality by presenting the reader with an alternative world. It is a "world" in the sense of a way-of-being, an ontological stance, a mode of existence, and it is presented in a highly particular fashion through concrete images and stories. Like other poetic texts, the Bible principally *shows* a world through concrete narratives and dramas rather than *telling* about the world, though one must be careful to recognize the close connection in Scripture of the poetic and the didactic. Similarly, as other poetic texts demand both a moment of intense concentration on the world presented as well as a moment of assimilation to one's already constituted world, so with the Bible attention must be focused on the text in order for the novelty of the world it offers to be assimilated appropriately and powerfully. Finally, as with other poetic texts, many interpretations of Scripture are possible, for the mark of a poetic text is its novel metaphorical character.[63] *The Brothers Karamazov* is a great poetic text while "pop" novels are not, both because of the fresh particular metaphors in *The Brothers*—the tensiveness of its language—and because of the complex, novel metaphor, or world as a whole, which it itself is. The richness of the metaphorical quality of a great work means that it will not only bear many interpretations but also demands them. It is not a travesty, then, to interpret the Bible in many different ways, but precisely what should occur given the nature of the text.

But Scripture for Christians is not only a great poetic text; it is its classic poetic text. What is meant by calling it the classic Christian text? Frank Kermode distinguishes between an "imperial" and a "modern" classic. An imperial classic is a founding text of a civilization resting ultimately "on the notion of a moment privileged, timeless yet capable of contemporaneity with all others," while the modern view abandons the idea of an absolute classic, for as Kermode says, "the only works we value to call classic are those which . . . are complex and indeterminate enough to allow us our necessary pluralities."[64] An imperial classic is closed, absolute, allowing for translations but only minor interpretive changes, while the modern classic is open, relative, pluralistic in interpretation. The first view assumes that the classic will accommodate itself to all generations while the second feels that interpretive work is critical to show the relevancy of the text.

The difficulties with these views of the classic are evident: the first refuses to deal significantly with the issue of appropriation, while the second refuses to take the text itself with sufficient seriousness. But it seems evident from our treatment of the Bible as the *poetic* classic of Christianity that these difficulties can be avoided, for the essence of a great poetic text is that through its particular images it *does* speak universally, but in a way that is open to diverse rather than fixed interpretations. A classic is not the sort of text that says just one thing nor is it the sort of text that can be made to say anything. The dual emphases which we have stressed—the moment of intransitive attention to the text suspending our own worlds and the moment of appropriation integrating the world of the text into our worlds—mean that the process of understanding a classic appropriately is a complex dialogue which has both limits and flexibility. David Tracy, who also understands Scripture as a classic text, sums up this dialogue when he says, "The classics, with their two notes of permanence and excess of meaning, always demand interpretation, never mere repetition nor simplistic rejection."[65]

James Barr suggests an understanding of the authority of Scripture similar to the one we are presenting when he says that the Bible functions as the classic model for the Christian understanding of God.

> The fundamental model was first worked out and decisively appropriated in the Old Testament. That model was reaffirmed, restated, and reintegrated in Jesus. Christian faith is faith which relates itself to this classic model. The God in whom Christians believe is the God who was known in the Bible; the Jesus in whom they believe is the Jesus of the New Testament.[66]

As "classic model," the Bible is here understood as an interpretive grid or screen by means of which many dimensions of Christian experience of God are given shape. The Bible as classic model means not that the Bible is absolute, perfect, or final (no model is), but as Barr says, "The status of the Bible is one of sufficiency rather than perfection."[67]

We deal with such classic foundational models in many other areas; for instance, the United States Constitution or the Parthenon at Athens. Each has attained a stature in its field as a classic, in these cases, as a model of a certain kind of government and a style of architecture to which future generations return again and again. If one wants to know what guides the spirit of American democracy, one looks to the Constitution (in addition to other and more current sources); if one wishes to understand the epitome of Greek architecture, one studies the Parthenon (in addition to other sources). Neither is absolute: American democracy is not identical with the Constitution and Greek architecture is not exhausted by the Parthenon. Each functions as a classic model; to put it negatively, one could *not* appreciate American democracy or Greek architecture adequately unless one attended carefully to these models. They are implied in the structure of each, for they are foundational. Similarly, to try to comprehend Christianity without the Bible would be a travesty, for the Bible provides the classic model affirming the centrality of Jesus of Nazareth and witnessing to the God present in Jesus as the God already known in Israel. To understand Scripture as the primary model or classic of Christian faith means that in it we have the initial or foundational witness to or interpretation of the activity of Jesus as the saving activity of God. The Bible does not exhaust Christian faith, for many other classics provide guidance also: the creeds; the works of theologians; the great liturgies, hymns, sermons, prayers, and confessions or autobiographies of the Church. But these secondary classics test themselves against *the* classic, the model called the Bible.

There are significant advantages to seeing the Bible as the poetic classic or classic model of Christianity, especially for our issues of idolatry and irrelevance. As model, the distance between the Bible and the reality it is attempting to express is always maintained. A model or metaphor is, as we have stressed, never identifiable with its object; the Bible as model can never *be* the word of God, can never capture the ways of God. As model, the Bible can never be an idol. As poetic classic, the Bible continues, as does any great poetic work, to speak universally; its particular metaphors and the world it describes metaphorically have proven themselves across the ages to many diverse peoples when the Bible has been interpreted as other poetic texts are interpreted—existentially, flexibly, openly. David Tracy's description of the power of the classics is very much to the point here: in the classics "we recognise nothing less than the disclosure of a reality we cannot but name truth. . . . Here we find something valuable, something 'important'; some disclosure of reality in a moment that must be called one of 'recognition' which surprises, provokes, challenges, shocks and eventually transforms us."[68] It is not a mistake, then, to deal with the Bible as "great literature"; such a description should be seen as intrinsic to its religious power and relevance, not as a maneuver to retain interest in it among skeptics and unbelievers. As poetic classic, the Bible cannot be irrelevant, or more accurately, the Bible has proven itself *to be* relevant time and time again.[69] The Bible as *model* underscores the relative, groping character of this very human work; the Bible as *poetic classic* underscores the enduring centrality which this book has for all who call themselves Christians.

One profound limitation of the Bible as classic text is that it suggests conservatism and the power of tradition. The very word "classic" has connotations of "perennial," "basic," "standard setting," "beyond criticism." I believe that our qualifying words "poetic" and "model" not only speak to the issue of the inherent conservatism of the classic, but, as I hope to show, suggest both its reforming and revolutionary power. The tradition of hermeneutics, however, which we have found helpful in this chapter, the tradition of Heidegger influencing both Gadamer and Ricoeur, has conservative leanings. When language is equated with being and when the texts which allow being to emerge are poetic ones, the basic task of hermeneutics is to listen to the call of being through language and to accept what it says, not to criticize or change the language. In a Heideggerian perspective, we are not in control of language, but are called into being by language. This is not the place for an extensive critique of this point of view, but it is necessary to point out its conservatism, for its first concern is not how one can criticize a language tradition but how one appropriates it.

Both Gadamer and Ricoeur are critics of this type, although Ricoeur less so than Gadamer, for Ricoeur does not equate language with being; rather, he sees metaphor as the *redescription* of reality—language can renovate and revise our vision of being. Nonetheless, Ricoeur's devotion to a "hermeneutics of recollection or restoration" versus a "hermeneutics of suspicion" means that, like Gadamer, he is principally interested in what language says to us, not in its possible false consciousness or the oppressive cultural structures it may mask as absolutes.[70] What both Ricoeur and Gadamer do very well is show us how we can become integrated into a tradition, appropriate it as our own, overcome our initial alienation to it, allow its poetic universality to speak to us and our concerns. However, especially in the case of Gadamer who appears to appreciate with singular sensitivity the historical relativity both of speaker and hearer, it is surprising that he does not consider the possibility that the texts of a tradition may be victims of ideology, of "prejudices" not merely as preunderstandings but as distortions of such a sort that the universality of the texts is undercut. "Historicity" appears to mean not cultural, sociological, or economic determination to Gadamer, for he does not see that some texts, whether consciously or not, can and have been written out of a form of historicity (racism, nationalism, sexism, imperialism) that distorts their universality in basic ways.[71] What Gadamer is aware of, and Ricoeur as well to a lesser extent, is the power of tradition as well as its positive characteristics—its graciousness, wisdom, rightness. As Gadamer says, "There is no way to free oneself of tradition . . . we stand always within tradition, and this is no objectifying process, i.e., we do not conceive of what tradition says as something other, something alien."[72]

The difficulty with this view, of course, is that many *do* experience tradition as alien and here we must part company with Gadamer. Marxist hermeneuts such as Jürgen Habermas have clearly contended that the hegemony of linguisticality makes criticism of a tradition impossible: the subject is submerged and passive within tradition.[73] Habermas insists that we must have resources for questioning traditions; reflection is necessary to break up "the dogmatism of life-practices"; language can serve to legitimate ideology and must be criticized for distortions brought about by economic and social privilege in a culture. Language *deceives* and one central task, says Habermas, is to refuse acceptance of its deceptions.

The relevance of this debate between Gadamer and Habermas to a tradition such as Christianity is evident: it is not an esoteric discussion of linguistics but concerns the central issue of how authoritative texts should be considered. Is one's basic attitude toward them one of acceptance or suspicion? Is one to be a receiver of a tradition or a reformer of it? Does one approach the Christian tradition as a listener or a critic? My own judgment is that a modified hermeneutics of restoration is the appropriate stance for Christians in regard to Scripture and the tradition built upon it. Ricoeur moves in this direction with his view of religious language as redescription of or reorientation to reality; in other words, his is not an unqualified acceptance of language's opening to being. Rather, what distinguishes his position from Gadamer's is, I believe, its metaphorical quality: whatever "is" is not to be accepted, for what religious language as metaphor does is to insist on the "is not" as well as on the "is." Ricoeur introduces a distinctively negative note, a note of disorientation, of nonidentity, of distanciation, of the future as different from and alienated from the present.

We are concerned, in part, not only to avoid idolatry—any identification of our words or traditions with being-itself—but also to show the relevance of the Christian tradition to those whose experience the tradition has rejected or distorted. Therefore, Ricoeur's correction of Gadamer is critical to us. For as we have tried to suggest, if the Bible is understood as a *poetic* classic or classic *model*, its metaphorical characteristics mean that tension, dialectic, openness, change, growth, and relativity must be intrinsic to a proper understanding of its authority. Thus, reform and revolution, perhaps one or both, are features integral to biblical authority. To question linguistic distortions within Scripture and the tradition would not be alien or wrong, but precisely what is called for, given the particular kind of text the Bible is and its authority. To see false consciousness, to unearth deceptions and prejudices due to cultural biases, to substitute revised metaphors and models for distorted ones—all of this would be not only permissible but what a theology based on Scripture as poetic classic must do. Metaphorical theology, most basically, insists on the dialectic of the positive and the negative, on the "is and is not," and that tension permeates every aspect of it, from its founding text to the most recent theological essay.

The conclusion to which our reflections on metaphor, parable, and Scripture have brought us could be summed up in the aphorism: *to be a believer is to be on a continuum with being human.* To be a human being is to interpret, to think of "this" as "that," to make judgments concerning similarity and difference, to think metaphorically. To be a believer is to follow the way of the parables and Jesus as parable, to live with the tension between the kingdom and the world, never identifying the one with the other while aware of the transformation of the world by the kingdom. Whether as human being or believer, we never overcome the distance between ourselves and our world; the main difference between a "secular" and a "religious" perspective is the degree of tension between ourselves and reality. Religious people are less comfortable in the world, aware of the difference between things as they are and things as they ought to be; they are conscious of the metaphorical "is and is not." A deeply metaphorical perspective such as that based on parable demands a way of being in the world characterized by a high degree of tension, relativity, iconoclasm, and change.

As we turn now to models—which are substantive, organizing metaphors and the next step in our journey towards conceptual, systematic thought—we will be concerned to see in what ways the parabolic base has been retained in theology and in what ways it has been changed or lost. Unfortunately, too little attention has been paid to models in theology and as a consequence the continuum between parables and concepts has not been sustained. For models, partaking of both metaphorical and conceptual characteristics, are a critical although often hidden and unappreciated middle term which may well instruct us on whether, as Ricoeur says, the foundational language of parable has been retained in the translation languages of theology.[74] It is because of this lack of research into the nature of models in theology that we turn next to consider models in science and other fields where they have been studied more extensively. Our purpose in this detour is of course not to give an exhaustive survey of the functions of models in these fields nor to enter any internal debates concerning the importance of models in other disciplines, but only to gain insight into the functions and importance of models in theology. Because models have been "silent" in theology they can be temptations to idolatry; because they have been highly resistant to change, they can be temptations to irrelevancy. Since our purpose is to sketch the outlines of a metaphorical theology based on parable which will both avoid idolatry and be relevant to our times, it should be obvious why we must track the model to its hidden lair.

3   Models in Science

Midway between the unintelligible and the commonplace, it is metaphor
which most produces knowledge.[1]

Once again, it is a provocative statement by Aristotle which guides us
as we now turn to the ways in which models function in various fields of
knowledge. Aristotle identifies metaphor, the essence of models, as the
primary cause or agent of knowledge. Contemporary thinkers in a wide
range of fields, including the natural sciences, anthropology, psychology,
sociology, political science, computer science, and the various arts appear
to agree with Aristotle, for one of the distinctive marks of mid-twentieth-
century thought is a weakening of the positivistic stranglehold of the last
two centuries and an awakening to awareness of the power of metaphor.
Interest in metaphors and models ranges from the most comprehensive
"root-metaphor" or "archetypes" by which people define their culture and
their view of reality to highly specialized, complex scientific models that
allow scientists to be articulate about increasingly abstract and otherwise
unavailable entities. We begin with the most general uses of models in a
variety of fields and move to their most specific functions in atomic
physics. We hope that such a survey will not only underscore the importance of metaphorical thinking in fields not usually considered as open
to or needing it, but also provide some specific insights to help us better
understand models in theology.

Models in the Social Sciences
and Technology

All that has been said about metaphor so far pertains to model, for a
model is, in essence, a sustained and systematic metaphor. To characterize
war as a chess game is not to employ a passing metaphor, but a model,
for it is the structure or set of complex relationships among the chess
pieces that tantalizes the mind and lures us to meditate on the model.
Perhaps our first and most basic experience with models is the young

child's hero worship of an older sibling, a sports or movie celebrity, as a model to emulate. Faced as we are, early and late, with the vast desert of unfamiliarity which is the self, we "pass over"—contemporary theologian John Dunne says—to the life stories of others in order to illumine the great mystery of the self.[2] A great deal of self-knowledge is gained in this indirect fashion; much of the fascination in reading novels and autobiographies or biographies lies in the models they provide for the most central of all human tasks, the discovery of self-identity. Such "role models," unlike discrete metaphors, are systematizing, organizing grids or screens, offering complex and detailed possibilities for analogical transfer to another life. A child who patterns her life after a film actress or sports star is engaging in the same *kind* of process as the Christian who follows the ancient practice of "the imitation of Christ." In both instances, a model of something presumably better known and more familiar is being used to provide structure and insight into something lesser known and unfamiliar. Abraham Heschel says that the human being "always looks for a model or an example to follow. What determines one's being human is the image one adopts."[3] While no *one* model can possibly be adequate to the uniqueness and mystery of individual selves, much of our journey toward defining the self consists of a long series of partial, inadequate, and rejected models which we try on for size. In sum, thinking in terms of models is one of our earliest and most continuous epistemological experiences.

What happens on the individual, personal level occurs also at the level of whole societies and civilizations. As one social commentator remarks, "to future generations, an age may be known by the metaphors it chose to express its ideals."[4] Just as individuals model themselves after others, so entire cultures seek and achieve defining metaphors that provide ways of organizing and speaking intelligibly about a vast array of details which, without the models and metaphors, would be chaos. Thus, a whole network of associations accompany such dominant metaphors as "the Dark Ages," "the Renaissance," "the age of anxiety," "the silent generation," "the age of Aquarius." These models not only provide ways of talking about culture but also influence attitudes toward culture, for the commonplaces associated with these metaphors have powerful positive and negative overtones. Moreover, the models are obviously partial and inadequate; if taken literally, they are absurd, and if not balanced by other metaphors, they are simplistic.

The power of such models, however, cannot be denied. One has only to think of a recent model for the city—"the concrete jungle"—to appreciate how it both expressed attitudes of fear and desire for escape on the part of many who fled to the suburbs, but also created that fear and desire for escape because reflection on the associations of "concrete jungle" brought about a self-fulfilling prophecy. Sociologists are increasingly conscious of the profound level at which metaphors determine beliefs and actions both of individuals and societies. As one commentator writes: "If we think of events of our lives as controlled by witches or even controlled by some force known only to witches, we shall behave in one way; if we think that the course of our experience is a matter of statistical probabilities, we shall behave in quite another way."[5] Another cultural analyst has noted that a dominant model for society—society as an organism—has recently undergone change in the United States.[6] During the McCarthy era in the 1950s the organism seemed to be internally healthy but was infected by "germs" from without in the form of the evil of communism. Now, however, he suggests that the evil threatening the societal organism is perceived as coming from within; it is a cancer for which there is no cure, and as a consequence, deep pessimism has set in. It is evident in such a shift of models from "evil without" to "evil within" that profound changes will follow not only in morale but also in decision making at military, political, and social policy levels.

Another example of the control of models on social matrices is graphically illustrated in a study conducted by two anthropologists on the importance of males in Bororo society who lived in terms of the model presented by the macaw bird. Two crucial characteristics of effective models which we will meet throughout our study are clearly operating in the following description: *specificity* and *distance*. A good model is concrete and detailed *and* must be sufficiently different from its principal subject to spark insight ("men are macaws" fulfills this criterion while "tigers are lions" does not).

> By examining the world of macaws as it exists with reference to the Bororo, Christopher Crocker [one of the anthropologists] was able to isolate a cluster of specific features that show the metaphor as a precise statement about the place of men in Bororo society. The macaw, we learn, is a woman's pet. It is kept in her hut and fed by her. It is also associated with spirit. Other animals might be domestic or associated with spirit, but only the macaw is both. Men in a very real sense live in a woman's world: descent is matrilineal and marriage is uxorilocal; they are, broadly speaking, kept by women. They are also, in contrast to women, associated with spirit, especially in the context of the men's hut that is situated in the center of the village.[7]

The model is effective for the following reasons: there are significant similarities between men and macaws in Bororo society so that isomorphism or similarity of structure is evident; the model is *specific* as well as common to Bororo society so that an entire network of associations can be discovered with its principal subject; "men" and "macaws" are sufficiently unlike so that the model always retains its *distance* from its principal subject and can continue to supply novel points of contact by means of the "neutral analogy" (the aspects of a model which are not yet designated as either relevant or irrelevant). Finally, it is evident how determinative of behavior this model must be for Bororo males (and females), and how a change in model—for instance, to "men are tigers"—could well foster as well as reflect a social revolution.

The models controlling societal behavior are more often than not partially and sometimes totally concealed, for they exist, as anthropologist Victor Turner insists, "between the full brightness of conscious attention and the darker strata of the unconscious, a set of ideas, images, concepts . . . these are the models of what people believe they do, ought to do, or would like to do."[8] The entire enterprise of advertising rests on exploiting this subliminal level where hidden metaphors of self-fulfillment are titillated: the makers of an advertisement juxtaposing cigarettes, cowboys, lovers, snowcapped mountains, and firelight know well the power of this collage to create a subliminal, embryonic model of pleasure.

Most of us live most of the time within the power of models of which we are unaware. The models are part of a "paradigm," an entire set of assumptions about what we believe we do, ought to do, or would like to do. Such paradigms are simply the basic conventions, largely unquestioned, which the establishment of a society in its religious, political, economic, and educational institutions defends and into which it initiates the young. But occasionally, as Turner says, "liminal" thinkers emerge, those who are conscious of an anomaly, something in their experience that cannot be fitted into the conventions, and if the anomaly is sufficiently powerful, they break the paradigm by proposing a new model. These people are "the unacknowledged legislators" of humanity and are found in all fields: they are the creative philosophers, poets, scientists, theologians, or psychologists. One has only to think of such names as Plato, Jesus, Galileo, Freud, Darwin, or Einstein to grasp immediately the function and importance of liminal thinkers, those who are always crossing new thresholds. Within the new paradigms they create future generations live: we accept "Socratic dialogue," "the kingdom of God," "the heliocentric system," "the super ego," "evolution," and "relativity," not as the shocking models that originally revolutionized basic perceptions of reality but as ordinary ways of being in the world.[9]

Models are not only important for anthropology and sociology but also for political science. As Martin Landau, a political theorist, notes, political science has always employed metaphors; hence, the conflict over the use of models is irrelevant, for "the choice is not between models and no models, but between a critical consciousness of their use and uncritical acceptance."[10] The use of models in political theory is as old as Plato's *Republic* and Hobbes's *Leviathan*. Augustine made a significant contribution with his models of the City of God and the City of Man. Two enduring political models have been the machine and the organism, with the former dominant during the seventeenth and eighteenth centuries, while the latter emerged in the late nineteenth century with the rise of evolutionary thought and has achieved prominence in the twentieth with the influence of ecological awareness. The last four centuries have been largely scientific ones and it is therefore no surprise that the mechanistic model was the critical one lying behind the composition of the United States Constitution in the eighteenth century. The American government was constructed not of and by human beings, but as a mechanism with separation and balance of powers. Alexander Hamilton's statement clearly shows that the state is a perfectly adjusted machine which works well when the pushes and pulls of its parts are in harmony: "Make the system complete in its structure; give a perfect proportion and balance to its parts, and the power you give it will never affect your security."[11] The consequences of different models are obvious if, for instance, we consider expectations of appropriate behavior in machine versus organic models. In the organic model, where citizens are seen as parts of a body, it is "natural" to demand sacrifice of one part for the good of another, but such altruism makes no sense in a machine model where power controlled by checks and balances rather than mutual support is the effective criterion.

These models in the human sciences are, for the most part, archetypes or root-metaphors. That is, they are large-scale, total models for human reality—the self, society, the state, and so on. The models selected at this level are of the broadest type: person, machine, organism, health, and disease—models with rich structural networks suggestive of multiple relations as well as emotional associations evoking commitment. At this level a model must be both *specific*, in order to refine concepts and make distinctions, and *comprehensive* in scope, in order to include wide ranges of experience. Finally, great care must be exercised lest the models by which we structure ourselves and our world tyrannize us, for such models easily become literalized. We live *within* these models and may forget the tension that is crucial to the proper use of models: people are *not* their heroes, a society is *not* an organism, the state is *not* a machine. As R. P. Braithwaite cautions us, "the price of the employment of models is eternal vigilance."[12]

On a more popular level, we also observe the predominance of models in the behavioral sciences and computer technology. In the world of business and politics, models are used to predict investment behavior, voting patterns, political coalitions, committee and group behavior.[13] The Gallup Poll, for instance, attempts to predict national elections through the use of a model of the electorate; here the model really represents a smaller version of the larger complex, a type of "scale model." Just as spacecraft models are employed for predicting the behavior of full-sized ships, so relevant details and factors in a voting sample are organized on a small scale in an attempt to project the results on to the entire electorate. True scale models such as the model airplane are among the oldest and most obvious examples of models; they work in miniature, attempting to retain all the details of the original. We delight in doll houses, miniature working cars, and similar models. Scale models of this sort, however, are the least useful kind of model, for we learn nothing new from them. Models used by the behavioral sciences to predict behaviors of various sorts are considerably more sophisticated in that they focus on key variables by simplifying detail. The difficulty with predicting behavior, however, is that too many details are present; a political poll attempts to lift out significant variables, overlooking minor ones, in order to attain a pattern. For instance, in simulation games—which are simplified models of more complex situations—the goal is to see, through the controlled use of a few key facts and variables, how particular groups of people will interact.

Models in the behavioral sciences are entirely heuristic; that is, they are pragmatic and expendable. As we shall see, models in science and in theology are not dispensable but essential, and while no one model may be permanent, some models are always necessary. Nonetheless, the use of models in the behavioral sciences clearly highlights the necessary dialectic between detail and simplification: while models must be sufficiently detailed to provide rich linkages between the two subjects, they also need to simplify the details of the principal subject. A model of an overly detailed aerial photograph cannot be a copy of it, for no insight is possible into the principal features of the photograph unless certain aspects of it are highlighted. A map of a city is useful only if it is a model and not a copy noting every building and street light. Simplification always involves distortion, and, as we shall see, this is one of the main reasons why many models are necessary for any complex phenomenon.

A final, contemporary use of models is found in the computer science field. If an age is known by the metaphors it chooses to express its ideals, then ours is undoubtedly the computer age. We not only dignify the computer by modeling it (in some of its logical relations) after the human brain, our mark of distinction; we also perceive the workings of our minds on the model of the computer by an inversion of models. As Weller Embler insists, we worship the electronic brain, and "presently we shall wish that our nerve cells were as clever as electron tubes, quite forgetting that it was our nerve cells that had the wit to create electron tubes."[14] Even though the remark, if made now rather than twenty-five years ago, would substitute transistors for electron tubes, the point is still the same: machines are like us, not we like them, and it is our inversion—of modeling ourselves after machines—that has resulted in positivism. The admonition is well taken, for it presses home two dangers of models: both the selection that we permit to guide us and the distance or tension that must always prevail in the use of models. Moreover, the computer example illustrates beautifully the great temptation as well as problem when models are inverted. As we shall see, theological models are especially prone to inversion, for the human features chosen to provide models of God are raised to divine status and become "godlike."

Our survey of the use of models in various fields has yielded some insights concerning their nature and function which need to be summarized. Of primary importance, models provide a way of talking about an unfamiliar area: they give intelligibility to the unintelligible. And models, unlike discrete or passing metaphors, yield this intelligibility in a structural or comprehensive manner. They provide a network of language to be expanded so that we can say many things about an unfamiliar area of investigation. At least three subsidiary points have emerged regarding these structural, comprehensive models. First, the most effective models are *specific*, common ones: good models like "body," "machine," "person" are concrete and well known. Second, the best models are sufficiently *different* from their principal subjects so that insight is generated through encountering similarity in spite of difference. Third, helpful models manifest a *dialectic* of simplicity and detail: models must simplify and order the seemingly chaotic detail of the principal subject, but they must also provide sufficient complexity to offer suggestive connections.

By saying this much on the basis of a preliminary study of models, we are also able to identify a number of crucial issues regarding the use of models. Since a model offers a path to intelligibility, presumably on the basis of some similarity between the model and the modeled, it is evident that no *one* model can ever be adequate. As we recall, at the heart of all metaphorical thinking lies the "is and is not"; hence, many models must be entertained. The implications of this admonition for theological models are significant, as we shall see. We have also noted the profound influence that models have on attitudes, for most of the powerful models carry strong emotional associations of a positive or negative character. Since major models are often concealed or hidden, we are seldom aware of their effect on us: we live *within* our models as fish live in the sea. Moreover, models not only influence our feelings toward the principal subject but also make us feel differently about the model itself—through inversion. In short, we begin to feel similarly toward computers and minds when each models the other, just as we feel similarly about God and human beings when each serves as the model for the other.

The principal danger in the use of models is, as we have stressed, the loss of tension between model and modeled. When that distance is collapsed, we become imprisoned by dogmatic, absolutistic, literalistic patterns of thought. A tradition or society then embraces but one model which it perceives not as *a model* but as "the way things are." The characteristics of metaphorical thought are lost—its flexibility, relativity, and tension. In circumstances such as these, "liminal" thinkers are likely to arise, because they are conscious that human experience is too diverse, complex, and mysterious to be packaged in just one box. Certain aspects of their experience are anomalous to the conventional paradigm and a change of models is necessitated. Whether that change will produce a reformation or a revolution (i.e., a paradigm shift) depends on the profundity of the basic models of the tradition as well as on the tradition's flexibility in admitting limitations in these models. Needless to say, these reflections on the dangers and revision of models have enormous implications for Christian theology, for it is a tradition which has been prone to forgetting both the relativity of its central models and to elevating them to the exclusion of other models. The key to the proper use of models is, once again, to remember always the metaphorical tension—the "is and is not"—in all our thinking and interpreting.

These insights on the functions and limitations of models are corroborated and given precision in the natural sciences, for here we find the most extensive and careful treatment of models. Thus we turn to models in natural science, especially in physics, and since this is a complex issue, we will approach it in a way intended to provide an adequate context for understanding the contemporary importance of models in this field.

First, since support for the importance of models is invariably accompanied by an appreciation of the imagination, we shall briefly review current views of science which connect it with ways of thinking operative in the humanities. Second, we shall consider Thomas Kuhn's notion of "paradigm" as the context within which science normally operates. Third, we will then examine different types of models in science and the two major points of view regarding their functions and importance. Finally, we shall evaluate the central issues and insights pertinent to the use of models in science for the purpose of identifying contributions to their function in theology.

Natural Science, the Humanities, and the Imagination

One of the most important revolutions in the philosophy of science during the last thirty years is the turn away from a narrow positivistic view of science as empirical, inductive, certain, and totally verifiable to an understanding of it—at least in its most creative and profound aspects—as more like than unlike other human ways of knowing.[15] What one discovers again and again, both from creative scientists and from the theoreticians of science, is an appreciation of the imagination in science. For instance, Max Planck, the discoverer of quantum theory, insists that the pioneer scientist must have "a vivid imagination, for new ideas are not generated by deduction, but by *artistically* creative imagination."[16] Arthur Koestler, in his study on the nature of creativity (*The Act of Creation*), focuses on examples not from the arts but from the sciences, and he identifies the critical factor in creative breakthrough as the analogical ability of the human brain to associate in novel ways. Since relations in nature are presumably infinite, it is the person possessing the power to connect unconventionally, imaginatively, who can offer new ways of relating natural phenomena, ways which often prove to be more comprehensive and fruitful than current alternatives. Since the identification of new patterns or structures in nature is at the heart of the scientific enterprise, *imagination*—understood as analogical association of novel and significant similarity in spite of difference—*is essential to scientific thinking.*

Such a view of thought corresponds closely to what we have called the metaphorical: it is the basic human ability to construct the world through novel and ever changing patterns of similarity and difference. It is no surprise, then, to find models emerging in scientific theory and practice as a crucial component. As we have seen, models are the hypotheses of structure or set of relations we project from an area we know reasonably well in order to give intelligibility to a similar structure we sense in a less-familiar area. From this point of view, a model is the concrete manifestation of the imagination's intuition of significant similarity between two previously unrelated areas. Max Black insists that the exercise of the imagination provides the common ground between the humanities and the sciences and that when models in science come to be universally accepted in scientific culture, the gap between them will be partly filled, "for science, like the humanities, like literature, is an affair of the imagination."[17]

The impetus toward appreciating the role of the imagination and models in science comes, as should be evident, not from a general desire for rapprochement between science and the humanities, but from science itself. It has occurred because of a change over the last century both in the theory and practice of science. The popular view of science as objective, mechanistic, substance oriented, materialistic, and deterministic is an outmoded seventeenth-century view which few scientists now embrace.[18] The popular view is based on the Newtonian system in which everything real was constituted by mass particles or atoms acting on each other by impact and gravitational attraction: it is an entirely materialistic and matter-oriented universe. It not only supported the Cartesian dualism of mind and body in an attempt to save the human mind from materialism, but also separated faith and reason in order to save religion from reductionism. In the eighteenth century the separation widened and God was banished from the world (resulting in yet another dualism of spirit and matter), with the deity's only function being one of a mechanic who set the world in motion: the providential, active, immanent God made no sense in mechanistic materialism. If matter alone is real, then "fact" is limited to the empirical and material, and "truth" is no longer a flexible term embracing religious and natural knowledge, but is limited to what can be known through the senses.

It is especially noteworthy for our purposes that during the years 1640–80 conscious attempts were made to eliminate metaphorical language. Not only was the Bible interpreted literally (in ways it never had been interpreted before), but also the language of philosophy and theology was pruned of ambiguity, imagery, repetitions, and contrasts.[19] The outrageous metaphors of the seventeenth-century metaphysical poets—John Donne the outstanding example—portend a lack of ease with metaphorical language as natural and accepted parlance. Metaphor was lost in the eighteenth century and with its demise we find imagination consigned to poetry while reason is restricted to logic and the sciences. It is not difficult to see how Newtonian science and its concomitants form a clear line of tradition to present-day positivism. It is in essence a *nonmetaphorical* way of perceiving the world and everything in it. Biblical literalism and idolatry were its byproducts—an attempt to save "the word of God" from being consigned to poetry on the one hand or reduced by reason on the other. As a consequence of these strategies, the Bible has been turned into an idol—perfect and absolute, closed to human interpretation.

We cannot here elaborate the recovery of a more integrated understanding of human thought. We must note, however, the renewed interest in the role of the imagination in the nineteenth-century Romantics, both in literature and theology. But the move had to come from within science itself, and this did not occur until the evolutionary view of the universe forced the recognition that change and development, not mechanism and determinism, was the more fruitful and plausible way to view reality.

What the doctrine of evolution opened up, theories of relativity and quantum physics corroborated. And now, instead of "particles of matter existing in an absolute framework of space and time,"[20] relativity informs us that there are no absolute measurements possible and quantum physics informs us that the ultimate particles are not "substances" as Newton supposed, but receding pulses of energy so elusive that all we can say about them is that sometimes they behave like "waves" and sometimes like "particles."[21] An accurate description, then, of elementary particles of matter is impossible, not only because "they do not exist as 'immutable facts' . . . but only 'as a possibility for being or a tendency for being,'"[22] but also because all attempts to measure their motions are relative, since there is no simultaneous time at different points in space.[23] The possibility of describing and measuring the "traces" or "resonances" of the elusive ultimate particles is further complicated by "the uncertainty principle"; that is, given the fact that any measurement disturbs and influences these entities, there are limits imposed on the accuracy of measurement. In other words, the experimenter influences the results. What emerges is a picture, not of objective, material substances being described and measured by a neutral observer, but rather of a network of movements and relationships in which the scientist is a participant.

The implications of this view of science—admittedly at its most elusive frontier, atomic physics—are significant. Among them are the end of determinism and substance as well as absolute objectivity and certainty; instead, we find stress on relativity, the importance of *relations and process* rather than substance, and an appreciation of the scientist as participant rather than as observer. The universe is not a collection of bits of matter moving in boxlike space with absolute velocity, especially when the human observer enters the picture. That is, all our knowledge is *our* knowledge and subject to the limitations of the human mind and body. At base, the new science tells us that the measurements of mass and dimensions of a body change as it moves relative to us and that matter is constructed out of what is mysterious, inconceivable, and forever in motion.[24] Where in this picture is there support for the old dualism between an objective, neutral "reason" as the faculty suited to investigate phenomena from a scientific perspective versus a subjective, involved "imagination" as the faculty for interpreting the world from a humanistic perspective? Many philosophers of science are now insisting that in science as in religion, the basic epistemological situation of *all* investigators and interpreters is of being *in* a world that we create in our attempt to discover those patterns of which it is most patient.[25] We begin in a primitive condition of rapport with the world and all our various forays to interpret that world, whether scientific, artistic, religious, philosophical, or whatever, refer finally to that one .world, either to its nature or its desired transformation.

This suggests that scientific, like humanistic, thinkers propose their interpretations as metaphors and models. In other words, what would a *literal* language of reality be, and is scientific language "literal" in the sense of a picture or a copy of reality? Philosopher of science Ian Barbour insists that it is not; that scientific description of the world is *one* symbolic system which is partial and selective (as are all other symbolic systems): "In physics problems, an elephant on a slippery river bank becomes a mass with a coefficient of friction, and a Beethoven symphony becomes a set of molecular vibrations."[26] If there is no "literal" language for reality but only various symbolic systems patterning it in different ways, then it is evident that science is a metaphorical enterprise along with all other systems of interpretation. This means, of course, that the *tension*, the recognition of the metaphorical "is not," must prevail in scientific views of "truth" as well as in humanistic ones. Scientists today are well aware that "facts" are theory-dependent, that there are no literal facts, that all exist within interpretive frameworks, and that these frameworks or paradigms can and have changed over the centuries. Thus, as Koestler notes, "What we call 'scientific evidence' can never confirm that a theory is *true*; it can only confirm that it is *more true* than another."[27]

The broadest interpretive context, or set of assumptions, guiding the work of science is called a "paradigm." Just as the assumptions or beliefs called "Christianity" could be called the paradigm within which Christian theologians conduct their work, so scientists live within paradigms as their chief interpretive frameworks. We now turn to a consideration of scientific paradigms in the hope of clarifying the ways in which science is metaphorical and uses models.

Paradigms

It comes as a surprise, if not a shock, to many people to learn that normal scientific activity is carried on within a set of assumptions which are relative and changing, but that is, of course, precisely the modern view of science. Koestler, comparing this phenomenon to schools and movements in the arts—the way, for instance, "a Rembrandt nude differs from a nude by Manet"—writes: "Thus, contrary to appearances and beliefs, science, like poetry or architecture or painting, has its genres, 'movements,' schools, theories which it pursues with increasing perfection until the level of saturation is reached where all is done and said—and then embarks on a new approach, based on a different type of curiosity, a different scale of values."[28] There are significant differences between movements in science and in the arts, but it is important to realize that in science as in other ways of knowing there is no "innocent eye": even science is never conducted "naked" vis-a-vis nature.

The movements or interpretive frameworks in which normal science does its work have been called "paradigms" by Thomas S. Kuhn, who, over the last fifteen years, has created a stir within the scientific community with his insistence that scientists conduct their work within a basic set of assumptions, shared beliefs, key models, and accepted exemplars.[29] We cannot here enter the debate on the subtleties of Kuhn's position or the detailed criticisms of it, for our interest lies elsewhere, in understanding paradigms as a basic metaphorical strategy and in weighing their value for theological reflection.

While Kuhn's major work, *The Structure of Scientific Revolutions*, has been criticized as both vague and radical, he has refined and clarified his position over the years so that it is now more precise and less unconventional. The most recent, revised definition he gives for paradigm is "a disciplinary matrix" that includes three elements: "symbolic generalizations," the formal or logical expressions, such as mathematical formulas, used by scientists without question; "models," which give preferred analogues, whether held heuristically or ontologically; and "exemplars," which are concrete problem solutions accepted as paradigmatic.[30] This view is more modest and less sweeping than Kuhn's earlier understanding of paradigms, which one critic characterized as including metaphysical, sociological, and artifactal dimensions; that is, a paradigm involves a set of beliefs about the nature of reality, institutional or community habits, and widely accepted classic works or models.[31]

Whatever the precise definition, at its most general and certainly most influential, a paradigm has been seen as "a set of commitments that scientists possess when they are pursuing normal science."[32] Ian Barbour's description of how a set of commitments works—for instance, those comprising Copernican astronomy, Newtonian physics, or the theory of relativity—is worth quoting:

> Most scientific endeavor is carried on within the framework of such a 're-ceived tradition' which defines the kinds of explanation to be sought. The tradition influences the concepts through which the scientist sees the world, the expectations by which his work is governed, and the language he uses.[33]

Controversy has raged over whether these commitments are metaphysical or merely heuristic; that is, whether normal, working science demands existential commitment to a world view or only "as-if" beliefs about the world. Controversy has also raged over the issue of the subjectivity of the scientist who works within a paradigm; that is, does the set of guiding assumptions make all criteria for verifying hypotheses so theory laden that significant objectivity is lost? Some scientists do believe that both theories and models refer to reality while others do not; also, while the extent of subjectivity was overemphasized in Kuhn's original work, as he himself admits, there is widespread agreement that because of paradigms no scientific theory can be conclusively verified or falsified.

The discussion of paradigms in science has drawn the methodology of the sciences and the humanities closer together. While it is undoubtedly an exaggeration to say, as Kuhn once did, that a paradigm change involves a conversion, a new way of seeing, it is evident that the person trained in a scientific tradition "sees" what the untrained cannot. For instance, in a bubble-chamber photograph, a beginning student sees only confused, broken lines while the nuclear physicist sees a record of subnuclear events.[34] A scientist from an earlier century with a different set of basic commitments and shared assumptions would presumably see still something else. Similarly, a painter of the Impressionist school and one from the Surrealist movement will "see" a landscape differently; adherents of Buddhism and of Judaism will likewise interpret death or the purpose of life differently according to the shared assumptions of the communities to which they belong. Hence, paradigms appear to be universal phenomena which provide total contexts for interpretation. As such, they are highly resistant to change. This is not to suggest that the paradigms of science are totally unverifiable or held against contravening evidence, for neither is the case. The fact that in the scientific community there is only *one* paradigm at a time—for instance, creationism and evolution are not simultaneously supported—means that agreement on the better, more fruitful paradigm is much wider in science than in the arts or religion. Also, observation exerts considerable control over theories; while a theory cannot be *conclusively* verified or falsified, continued negative results will eventually undermine it, whereas, for instance, religious belief in the providence of God does not appear to be destroyed by any amount of negative evidence. In sum, to understand science as operating within paradigms not only suggests significant connections with movements, schools, and doctrines in the arts and religion, but also displays yet another way to express metaphorical thinking as basic to human understanding of the world.

A final and highly significant point in regard to scientific paradigms concerns the way they change. As Kuhn and others point out, normal science consists principally of solving small puzzles within the accepted and unquestioned first principles of the paradigm. In their daily experiments laboratory scientists do not question the theory of relativity; rather, they solve puzzles within that accepted set of assumptions. As Kuhn notes, however, what does not fit into the framework often is not "seen"; problems that cannot be solved within it are usually overlooked.[35] There is a sense, then, in which a scientific paradigm—and we shall see the same phenomenon in religious paradigms—may serve as a set of blinders, eliminating peripheral vision or disturbing anomalies. If the issues or factors that do not fit the paradigm or are neglected by it become sufficiently anomalous, if the pressure they exert builds to the point that the paradigm appears to have major inadequacies, then a revolution occurs. In such a crisis, an alternative set of assumptions may become preferable or may appear more fruitful, better able to deal adequately with a wider range of phenomena, more suggestive for further discovery. Such changes are not accomplished unless an alternative is available; for science, like other fields, never operates without an interpretive framework. When such a major shift occurs, as in the change from Newtonian to quantum physics, the old data is seen in a new way; familiar terms acquire altered meanings; the view of the field—its methods, goals, system of relations—undergoes a sea change.

The degree of change in theological revolutions, by contrast, is less marked, for the old tends to survive along with the new in ways more profound than in scientific revolutions, but the stress on anomaly, on a paradigm which can no longer cope, functions similarly in both science and religion. The religious revolution identified with the name Jesus of Nazareth and minor revolutions by Paul of Tarsus, Francis of Assisi, Martin Luther, John Wesley, Friedrich Schleiermacher, Karl Barth, and present-day liberation theologians occurred because the traditional paradigm could no longer cope with significant dimensions of experience. On the one hand, a basic paradigm—the "Christian tradition" with its shared set of assumptions—has endured throughout the crises which have reformed it, and that paradigm is the one identified, as I would express it, with the parables of Jesus and Jesus as parable of God. On the other hand, each of these revolutions marks a reform of the tradition in ways similar to a paradigm change. In any case, it is certain in religion, as it is not in science, that the traditional shared assumptions in the form of major models survive and survive with power if that tradition is to preserve its intrinsic, distinctive character, even though the changes brought about through significant anomalies are profound ones. Religious paradigms more readily absorb change than scientific ones. While it is obvious that there is never total agreement within a religious paradigm on the essential assumptions and beliefs of that paradigm, a religious paradigm is not infinitely flexible; otherwise, there would not be distinct religions in the world. This is an important point, for it impinges directly on the issue of the continuing relevance of the Christian tradition to groups such as feminist Christians, who find their experience a critical anomaly to which Christianity traditionally has not attended. The question they ask is whether Christianity has the resources as well as the openness to address the anomaly they pose, or whether they must, in order to be true to their experience, base themselves in another paradigm.

Types of Models and Two Views
of Models in Science

In Kuhn's most recent description of what constitutes a scientific paradigm, he lifts up as one of its crucial characteristics preferred analogues or models which scientists accept, either heuristically or ontologically. So far we have considered models in various fields, including the natural sciences, only in the broadest sense. A paradigm is a set of basic assumptions or commitments in a field of study or a tradition which defines the issues considered, the methods used, the answers allowed. A root-metaphor or archetype is, like "organism" or "machine," a well-known commonplace in which we transfer the vocabulary appropriate to it to a less-familiar field of investigation. But Kuhn is suggesting a much more specific type of interpretive framework than either paradigm or archetype, and it is to this kind of model we now turn.

The major type of model used in contemporary science is the "theoretical model," which, as Max Black points out, consists "in *talking* in a certain way."[36] Such models differ substantially from what they model and hence are not in any significant way similar to "scale models." They also differ from what Black calls "analogue models" where, unlike the scale model, there is a change of medium as, for instance, in hydraulic models of economic systems or in the use of electrical circuits in computers.[37] The critical feature here is exact structural correspondence between model and modeled—every relation in the one must be found in the other. In contrast to both these types, theoretical models are not constructed; rather, they are grids or screens providing a vocabulary which, while based in one field, is found appropriate to another. Thus, theoretical models are, in essence, metaphors, but their distinguishing feature is the stress on similarity of *structure* between model and modeled. Science is concerned with the way things work, with behavior and with relations. Hence, it is the network of relations and modes of functioning from an area whose workings are understood, projected as a pattern of possible explanation to an area where the relations and functions are not yet understood, which is at the heart of the scientific use of models.

Ian Barbour's definition of a theoretical model sums up these points: "A *model* in science is a systematic analogy postulated between a phenomenon whose laws are already known and one under investigation."[38] Three points on the nature of models are implied in this definition: first, there must be an analogy or similarity between the model and the modeled; second, the similarity must be of a structural sort pertaining to the basic workings or laws of the two fields; third, the analogy must be systematic, that is, suggestive of many connections, all of which are, presumably, not immediately evident. These points are related to the nature, function, and status of models in science. Most scientists hold that in order to use a model, one must have some sense of its appropriateness, that is, some evidence of similarity of structure (isomorphism) between the two fields. Most scientists also hold that the principal uses of models are twofold: explanation of laws and structures of the new field provided by the "positive analogy," and discovery of new laws and structures by the "neutral analogy." Scientists differ on whether models are heuristic (helpful, but of passing importance with no commitment concerning their relation to reality), or essential (a permanent feature of science with a commitment to their partial but genuine ontological status). They also disagree on the nature of scientific explanation: whether it is satisfied by mathematical formulas or whether models are necessary for explaining new and unfamiliar material by connecting it with already known laws and structures. Scientists tend to agree that similarity of structure constitutes the critical relationship between model and modeled, and that the neutral analogy generates new discoveries.

Hence, while there is widespread agreement on the *usefulness* of models in science where isomorphism obtains, especially in generating new discoveries, there is disagreement over the *continuing importance* of models, both in terms of their explanatory role and their ontological status. We might call the two views the "low" view and the "high" view: the first finds models useful but not permanent and holds them in an "as-if" manner with no ontological commitment; while the second finds models of central and lasting importance and holds them, to varying degrees, as referring to reality, "as the way things are." These views are intended to suggest characteristic directions toward lesser and greater significance assigned to models rather than to divide philosophers of science into one camp or the other. Many of the differences between them pertain not only to models, but derive from more general views of the relations of scientific constructs (whether models or theories) to the world.[39]

This overview now needs to be elaborated and we begin with a few examples of theoretical models in science. As we have suggested in a general way, science is concerned with how things work, with the behavior of physical phenomena. One of the most common and helpful strategies to accomplish this end is to compare the behavior of a new phenomenon with one whose structure is already known. The physicist E. Mach illustrates this point in the following statement:

> What a simplification it involves if we can say, the fact A now comports itself, not in one, but in many or all of its features like an old and well-known fact B. The moon comports itself as a heavy body does with respect to the earth; light like a wave-motion or an electric vibration; a magnet as if it were laden with gravitating fluids, and so on. We call such a description *an indirect* description.[40]

The value of such models is that they provide simplified structures which make the behavior of new phenomena intelligible. The laws governing behavior are transferred by analogy between the two sets of phenomena, the point which is also stressed in another well-known model: "The billiard ball model of gases is that set of assumptions according to which the molecules comprising a gas exert no forces on each other except at impact, travel in straight lines except at instant of collision, are small in size compared to the average intermolecular distance, etc."[41] E. H. Hutten describes the basic function of scientific models as suggesting "rules of usage," semantic rules for an unfamiliar area; that is, models not only loosen the tongue, but because of isomorphism, give directions: "For example, the oscillator model when applied in the theory of specific heat allows us to say this. The atom is a small mechanical particle; it is bound to the crystal lattice with the force proportional to the displacement; it has only kinetic and potential energy; and so we know what the atom can do under the circumstances."[42] He generalizes the functions of models in a very clear and helpful way when he writes: "The model prescribes a context, or gives a universe of discourse; it so sets a limit to what can be said; the content of the theory, and the logical range of the sentences in it, is therefore determined; and the meaning of the sentences is specified."[43] It should therefore be evident that scientific models, unlike models in sociology, anthropology, or theology, usually depend upon another complex and, from a layperson's perspective, recondite scientific field; a set of commonplaces associated with a well-known term such as organism or machine is not sufficient. The function of the models is to illuminate the structure or behavior of a lesser-known phenomenon; hence, detail, in *scientific* terms, of the behavior of other, better-known phenomena is what is needed. Thus, the web of explanation expands, for accepted theories are used as models for phenomena that do not yet have theoretical explanations, but whose structure appears to be sufficiently similar to warrant the projection of the better- to the lesser-known area.

An especially interesting case of models in science, from the theological perspective, is the complementary use of *both* wave and particle models for atomic entities. Why not one or the other or a third which will reconcile them? None of these alternatives is acceptable to scientists because electrons sometimes behave like waves and sometimes like particles; neither model is adequate, yet neither can be eliminated, and no reconciling third is available. Moreover, when electrons behave like particles their wave behavior is less evident and vice versa. In other words, the models while complementary are also in some respects contradictory. Niels Bohr suggests that the complementarity principle reveals human conceptual limits and if we try to force nature into one mold (such as wave) we preclude the full use of other molds (such as particle). What this means in the case of atomic physics is summarized by Ian Barbour:

> Thus we must choose between complete causal *or* spatio-temporal descriptions, between adequate wave *or* particle models, between accurate knowledge of position *or* momentum. The more one set of concepts is used, the less can the complementary set be applied simultaneously. We have successive and incomplete complementary pictures that cannot be applied simultaneously.[44]

While Bohr says the idea for the complementary models came to him from the Bible and in metaphoric form, i.e., that one could not know someone simultaneously in the light of love and in the light of justice,[45] theologians should not overreact to this gesture from science toward religion. What is important is not the source of Bohr's inspiration, but two other factors. First, of course he is incorrect in supposing that biblical love and justice are contradictory or mutually exclusive; but second, and more important, the use of complementary models in science is a critical reminder that models are never literal, that all models are partial, that more than one model is necessary. Atomic physics is not the only case of the use of complementary (and at times contradictory) models in science: in biology, mechanistic and organic models are used; in psychology, behavioristic and introspective models. While it is desirable not to encourage unnecessary dichotomies in any field (nor for theologians to feel malicious delight that physicists may have to settle for contradiction and paradox), the acceptance of complementarity with its accompanying implications of limitation, partiality, and multiple models is, once again, what I would call metaphorical thinking—an awareness that all modes of interpretation are inadequate approximations and will at best give us only limited insight.

Scientific models make this point effectively—not only complementary models, but any scientific model—for theoretical models typically simplify by omitting complicating factors and by using approximations. Sir James Jeans, writing on the use of two models for the same phenomenon in science, compares them to two maps of North America on different projections—neither will represent the whole truth but each will represent some aspect of it. So long as we only draw our maps on flat pieces of paper, such imperfections, he says, are inevitable. Jeans concludes: "The pictures we draw of nature show similar limitations; these are the price we pay for limiting our pictures of nature to the kinds that can be understood by our minds."[46] One might want to ask Sir James what other kinds of pictures would be possible, but apart from that small evidence of scientific hubris, the comparison of models with maps is a suggestive one. It calls to mind once again that a variety of models is necessary and that the most important issue in the use of models is the temptation to literalism and absolutism.

The critical question and the one that distinguishes the "low" from the "high" view is how essential are models in science? Are they heuristic, largely for discovery and illustration, or are they a permanent part of a theory, which not only allows for further discovery beyond the attainment of a minimal theory, but also permits explanation in terms other than mathematical formulas? The low view proposes a limited function for models: the main use for a model is the deduction of isomorphism between the better- and lesser-known structures and, once this has been accomplished, the model may be discarded. The sensibility of the low view is heuristic: one treats a model "as if" it pertained to the principal subject but one need not make a commitment that it really does. There is a tendency toward instrumentalism in this view: theories need models to put flesh on mathematical skeletons—illustrations which the *cognoscente*, the expert, can do without. An instrumentalist view of models is similar to C. S. Lewis's description of a "Master's" metaphor in which one knows what one wants to say and illustrates it for others, as contrasted with a

"Pupil's" metaphor in which the speaker is in the position of learner and has no means other than the metaphor to express the subject.[47] D. A. Schon makes the point graphically:

> . . . we sometimes use metaphors as devices for explaining theory when they were actually essential to the formation of the theory. In discussing a theory of genes, the lecturer may say, "Think of it, if you will, as a kind of code," when in fact he has no other way of thinking of it.[48]

It is necessary to be careful at this point so as not to suggest that "everything is metaphor" in science. We have refused this aphorism in a general epistemology, for there must always be an accepted, familiar set of conventions in order for new learning to take place.[49] Certainly in the case of science, which possesses a broader and more refined set of accepted conventions for its kind of knowledge than do most other fields, it would be insupportable to suggest that science is nothing but metaphor. Nonetheless, there is still the question of how important models are—whether, as Peter Achinstein says, a model is "an approximation useful for certain purposes,"[50] or as Niels Bohr says, "quantum theory . . . provides us with a striking illustration of the fact that we can understand a connection though we can only speak of it in images and parables."[51]

The key issue that appears to distinguish the low- and high-view people is the nature of scientific explanation; that is, the degree of relevance or connection with known data necessary for an adequate explanation of a novel phenomenon. This issue has relevance to theological models, for explanation in theology as well as in science is often abstract and intramural. The low-view people are influenced by a narrower understanding of scientific explanation, what is called the "hypothetico-deductive" theory, according to which "the scientific method consists in making observations, forming hypotheses to explain them, deducing consequences from these hypotheses, and performing experiments to confirm or disconfirm the hypotheses."[52] In other words, a phenomenon is explained when it is subsumed under a general law subject to some kind of verification. The process is deductive and nonanalogical; there is no attempt to link the new phenomenon to what is already known through the use of models; that is, a partial explanation of the new phenomenon. Rather, explanation is complete when a mathematical formula has been attained and laboratory experiments have verified that the new phenomenon falls under a known law. Only positivists consistently hold to this view of explanation; the low-view people obviously go well beyond it in their appreciation for the heuristic functions of models. Nonetheless, their view that models are expendable suggests that the "explanation" that counts is the mathematical one, while the explanation that would make connections through models to other ranges of scientific knowledge is marginal. In other words, the goal of scientific explanation is not to build up a world of interconnecting networks of theories and models to explain how phenomena work on a grand scale, but rather to subsume phenomena under particular laws which may or may not have any relation to one another.

And yet, if explanation is to take place in language that communicates beyond the most narrow confines of specialists, it must be in terms of models. Logic alone makes this point, as one philosopher of science illustrates when he says, "an explanation of X cannot be non-X, since one cannot deduce X from not X, nor can the explanation be X, since no explanation is offered by showing that a thing is itself. . . . X can be explained by Y if it is shown that X is both like and unlike Y."[53] Thus, explanation by models, by linking the new to the old, by connecting new phenomena to accepted theory by using the latter as a model for the former, is what we have called metaphorical thinking. The low-view people are essentially nonmetaphorical thinkers; though, appreciating as they do the role of the imagination in science and the importance of models heuristically, they are by no means literalists. Nonetheless, they do not see the importance as well as the necessity of association, connection, similarity and difference, as the essence of explanation, but are satisfied by the subsumption of phenomena under known laws. One of the chief values of models is that they communicate to outsiders in ways theories do not; because of their relative simplicity and familiarity they can introduce the nonexpert to insight otherwise unavailable. Most theologians insist they would be lost without the continuing use of their models, but so, say the high-view people, would scientists who care about explaining scientific theory to nonscientists.

Low-view adherents should be clearly distinguished from positivists who have little use for models, believing it is possible to proceed directly from observation to theory. Scientific positivists have their colleagues in theology, for the assumption that it is possible to go directly from observation to theory without the critical use of models has its counterpart in those who assume it is possible to move from "the story of Jesus" to doctrine without the critical aid of metaphors and models. Few creative scientists today are positivists; the debate now is between low- and high-view supporters. Both groups acknowledge the importance of the imagination in scientific work, support the critical role of models, and are aware of the limitations of models. The significant differences between them pertain to the role of models in scientific explanation and the ontological status of models.

In summary, we have considered the nature and function of theoretical models in light of low and high views of models. While models are being used with increasing frequency in science, suspicion about them is still strong. One of the values for theologians studying the use of models in science is the constant warning by scientists on their use—cautions that religious traditions are prone to forget. However, the principal value for theology of studying scientific models is the stress on their importance, not their limitations. The high-view people underscore the permanent significance of models in science and it is to their contributions that we now turn.

Central Insights from Scientific Models Pertinent to Theology

High-view supporters, such as Mary Hesse, E. H. Hutten, Frederick Ferré, Ian Barbour, Rom Harré, and N. R. Hanson, display a somewhat different sensibility than low-view adherents. They do not merely accept the use of models as a heuristic device but see them as a permanent and proper mode of scientific operation. They stress the view that scientific discovery, like all constructive forays into the world, is a profoundly imaginative act and that it takes place within a paradigm, a set of assumptions which guides its questions and provides the context for its answers. In other words, high-view supporters are self-consciously metaphorical, aware of the relativity and open-endedness of scientific theories, conscious that these theories are founded on models and are permanently wedded to models, ready to give qualified but genuine commitment to models as reflecting reality. The thought of these people displays the fundamental characteristics of all metaphorical thinking—its tension, openness, indirection, iconoclasm, growth, and change. This should come as no surprise, given the nature of contemporary science. While seventeenth-century science did not display these characteristics, twentieth-century science not only does, but in many ways is also the progenitor of them.[54] If we recognize that these characteristics are inherent in the parables and in Jesus as parable, as I believe they are, we also realize that it is recent science that has reintroduced them to Western culture and made them not only respectable but also necessary for thoughtful people who would see life as a whole. For these characteristics of thought are not, I contend, the province of one field or restricted to a particular subject matter. We find them, to be sure, in such seemingly distant cousins as parables and contemporary science, but their "discovery" in such apparently unlikely and disparate places is a witness to their presence in *all* human interpretive activity. Thus, if we would see life as a whole—in its religious, scientific, personal, and public dimensions—these characteristics of metaphorical thought must operate everywhere.

Scientists who support a critical role for models can do much to show us the way. In part, of course, this is due to the popular assumption that if scientists say it is so, then it must be the case, for their basic methodology is "objective" in contrast to the "subjectivity" of religion and the arts. While contemporary science itself does not support this view, it nonetheless dies hard; in any event, what can and needs to be shown is the basic similarity of method for knowing and interpreting (with due acknowledgment of differences) in science and in other fields.

Many of the characteristics of metaphorical thinking are evident in the following statement on theoretical models by Ian Barbour:

> . . . theoretical models are novel mental constructions. They originate in a combination of analogy to the familiar and creative imagination in creating the new. They are open-ended, extensible, and suggestive of new hypotheses . . . such models are taken seriously but not literally. They are neither pictures of reality nor useful fictions; they are partial and inadequate ways of imagining what is not observable.[55]

What is distinctive about this statement is its hearty endorsement of imagination in science, which it judges adequate to deal with reality in a qualified way. That is, models, the products of imagination, are neither literal pictures of reality nor mere useful fictions, but partial, though inadequate, ways of dealing with what really is. Needless to say, scientific models are not the products of imagination in the sense of whimsical, idiosyncratic personal preferences: Barbour says models "originate in a combination of *analogy to the familiar* and creative imagination" (italics added). As previously stressed, isomorphism in some sense is at the heart of a scientific model, a point emphasized by high-view as well as low-view people; a model which could not be shown even by the most sophisticated and indirect modes of scientific verification to be isomorphic would be highly suspect. Nonetheless, what is critical and, for our purposes, noteworthy, is that Barbour's statement on theoretical models in science could be read, word for word, as a good definition of models in theology. With one exception, it can serve as an outline for insights from scientific models pertinent to the function of models in theology. That exception—the lack in this particular statement of any mention of relations or structure as the central content of a scientific model—is supplemented by Barbour's statement that "a model is a symbolic representation of selected aspects of *the behavior of a complex system* for particular purposes" (italics added).[56]

With this correction, let us focus on several points in particular. These points form a whole which can be expressed in the following way: a model in science aims at *discovering* that *structure or set of relations* in an unfamiliar area which is believed to be a genuine but partial *reflection of its reality*. Three main points emerge here. First, models are concerned with *discovery*, with opening up the unintelligible to intelligibility, with generating new hypotheses and suggestions, with enlarging what is known and accepted. Second, models are concerned with *behavior*, with how something works, with systematic structure; thus, the content of a model is the network of relations it displays. Third, models are at the same time *both true and untrue*; they invite existential commitment but in a qualified manner; while believed to be appropriate, they are also held to be partial and inadequate.

The stress on discovery in scientific models is universal among high-view supporters. This is the case largely because these people believe that science functions to enlarge our understanding of what makes things go, how they work, and how different systems and objects relate to each other. Unlike the low-view adherents who support a narrower view of explanation, the high-view insist that a scientific explanation of a phenomenon ought to be articulated in the most extensive terms possible, linking it by means of models to already established theories. The goal is intelligibility and this will occur only through constant pressure at the frontiers, forging chains of interconnecting networks of incipient theories and accepted models. Models are thus cognitively oriented for the purpose of understanding the world and not, as the low-view insists, mainly for suggestiveness or illustration. Scientific discovery is, says the high-view, projection, through the creation of plausible structures (models), of explanatory mechanisms for new phenomena. By such means, widely divergent domains of understanding are linked together in freshly intelligible ways.

In classical physics and quantum mechanics the linking of new theory to the old is called the "Correspondence Principle." As E. H. Hutten points out, in an eminently clear statement, one of the best ways to accomplish this, especially in view of the increasingly abstract nature of physics, is through models:

> The succession of theories is in the direction of ever-increasing abstraction. We are able to construct a more abstract theory by using a model. The model offers certain analogies, mainly in structure and function, to the situation for which it is a model. The model is a bit of established, known theory—and so we obtain an equation which is then interpreted in terms of the new theory. The new interpretation is linked to the interpretation in terms of the old theory by the Correspondence Principle. . . . Thus we reach ever higher levels of abstraction in our thinking by using the model as a ladder; and we achieve a better understanding of nature by discovering and describing processes that are ever more remote from the level of ordinary experience. This better understanding is represented by a higher level of integration of concepts given by the new theory. Pushing outwards the frontiers of knowledge also improves its integration, for we can see better how things hang together and how our concepts are related to each other.[57]

This is a highly suggestive statement on the interlocking processes of discovery and explanation, with models as critical to both dimensions.[58] Apparently, the process is one of a continuous dialectic between models and theories, in which the world is both discovered and explained through the projection of models, their testing in some fashion, the linking of them to established theory, and a reoccurrence of the pattern. Change, flexibility, and openness are of the essence in this process. As Hutten notes, science is "open at both ends," pushing forward the frontiers of knowledge through linking the new with the old and, at the same time, self-correcting its integrations, however well established, by its insistence that all its knowledge is tentative and open to revision.[59] It could be said, I believe, that such an understanding of knowledge is not only metaphorical—the linking of "this" with "that" in a tentative, open way—but also is a classic statement of such thinking.

The pressure in science in the high-view leans toward as complete an explanation as possible. This is what discovery signifies, as well as the excitement in seeing yet another connection in the network of relationships. In one sense, this impetus implies a desire to eliminate the surprising and the unfamiliar, to find, as Mary Hesse says, "a perfect metaphor" to explain everything.[60] She claims that while scientific models may initially be unexpected, their principal aim is not to shock; rather, "they are meant to be exploited energetically and often in extreme detail and in quite novel observational domains; they are meant to be internally tightly knit by logical and causal interrelations."[61] While such a statement may appear to lessen the tension that must always be present in a model lest it become literalized, such is not the case, for all the high-view people vehemently support an interactive, *tensive* view of metaphor. What Hesse insists on, and a point relevant to theological models, is that a good model can and should be exploited for its systematic potential and for its rich suggestiveness of relations and structures. In fact, she contends that a model will retain its interactive qualities as long as it continues to provide stimulation of this sort. It is when all the possibilities for further discovery have been exhausted in a model that it is most likely to become literalized. It is for this reason that Hesse stresses, as a principal component of a good model, the "neutral analogy"—the aspects of a model that have not yet been identified as either positive or negative, as either applying or not applying. A good model in science, and, we would add, in theology, is one with a large fund of neutral analogy, unexplored potentiality for connections. It is the neutral analogy that provides further possibilities for discovering new relations between the model and the modeled. As many commentators note, one of the ways the neutral analogy is enhanced is by using models sufficiently *different* from the principal subject so that insight is generated and tension retained.

In sum, the emphasis on *discovery* as one of the principal functions of models in science, discovery of a systematic interlocking network of models and theories for the purpose of explaining the way phenomena work in as comprehensive fashion as possible, provides a clue to the analogous function of models and theories in theology. Models and theories (called doctrines) in theology are similarly related so as to create a systematic network of explanation. The subject matter explained is, of course, different; it is not the natural phenomena but the basic phenomena of lived existence as understood within a religious tradition (such as the "paradigm" called Christianity). Moreover, the relative status of models and theories in science and religion differs; in science, theories are more permanent than models, while in religion models appear to be the more stable element. Frederick Ferré, for instance, notes that theories in science are abandoned only with the greatest reluctance since altering basic theory portends a scientific revolution, while models may be altered or replaced with less dire consequences. The reverse, he says, is true in theology, for theories tend to be abandoned or revised in the light of increasing knowledge, while the basic models remain:

And the highest level models, those at key positions within the overarching model of reality, are defended at all costs—defended most bitterly against the prophetic personalities who are usually the very ones who best succeed in altering the fundamental religious models—in the knowledge that a change in model signifies a religious revolution that may sweep away that which has received the devotion of multitudes over the ages.[62]

There appear to be two reasons for the enduring character of theological models in contrast to scientific models. Ferré mentions that theological models are of much broader scope; the dominant models of religious traditions are all-inclusive and hence can appear to be "above change."[63] Moreover, the liturgical use of theological models stamps them indelibly in peoples' minds as a permanent and necessary fixture of a religious tradition. The permanence of theological models has the value of providing continuity to a religious tradition; it has the liability, however, of turning certain models into idols and of sacrificing metaphorical openness to change, as well as reducing relevance to different peoples. When we turn to theological models and doctrines we will illustrate both of these points: models and theories as forming an explanatory network and the stability of major models.

When we ask, in regard to our second point, concerning the *content* of scientific models, the answer comes, interestingly, in terms of *form*. Science is concerned with the way things work, with the mechanism controlling the behavior of phenomena. Moreover, as our analysis of contemporary science showed, basic scientific phenomena are not considered to be substantial, static entities, but pulses of energy-related intricate structures and patterns. E. H. Hutten suggests an intriguing analogy between the increasing abstraction and loss of substance orientation in science and a similar development in modern art. In both cases structure, relations, and pattern are discovered rather than "matter" in science or realistic "objects" in art.

> The model is . . . very much what has occurred in modern art. We penetrate beyond the obvious likenesses of daily life to discover patterns—structures and functions—that exist in the world and, in particular, those that otherwise lie hidden in our inner "unconscious" world of feelings. The model is a picture which is non-figurative, or "abstract," since it shows relationships that are hidden to our ordinary view.[64]

Models in science do not picture any *thing* in a figurative way for there is nothing, in the common-sense view, there to picture! It is not the picturability of "objects" with which models are concerned, but the basic processes, relations, and structures that govern the world's phenomena. Since the seventeenth-century notion of "matter" as substantial entities has yielded to the twentieth-century notion of the primordial elements as pulses of energy, ever changing and related in structural ways, the identification of those changes and patterns of relationship is critical.

What we find in modern art and in physics, we also find in contemporary philosophy and should recognize as well in theology if theology is to be *au courant* and not anachronistic. In phenomenology, for instance, philosophers tell us that the basic unit is not the substantial self relating to an objective world as a neutral observer, but "the self-in-the-world." We *are* selves only in relationship—relationships with the world of which we are a part and with other selves who respond to us as well as influence us. Such phenomenologists as Edmund Husserl, Martin Heidegger, Maurice Merleau-Ponty, and Paul Ricoeur insist that the ancient subject-object dualism of self and world stemming from Greek philosophy is false to the actual experience of participation of the self in the world and the world in the self. The classical Western notion of the "individual" as a substantial entity over against the world (both cosmic and personal) is the correlate both of Aristotelian metaphysics and seventeenth-century science, and it is no surprise that the rise of the novel, which charts the destiny of the individual, occurred at approximately the same time as Cartesian philosophy, itself a product of seventeenth-century science. Similarly, process philosophers such as A. N. Whitehead and Charles Hartshorne as well as their theological disciples insist that reality, which includes the divine, human, and natural dimensions, is characterized by processes of growth, change, satisfaction, and loss. The relations among the various dimensions of reality are structural ones, obtaining throughout the entire system, and these patterns of relationship, rather than substantial entities, are what is most basic.

In significant ways the contemporary epistemology de-emphasizes isolated, substantial entities while stressing structures or networks of relationship as the context in which entities exist. Structuralism, as a hermeneutical method, is perhaps the most extreme example of this epistemology, but as we have noted, it is evident in diverse kinds of interpretive activity—in abstract art, modern physics, phenomenology, and process thought. It is also evident in the skepticism with which theologians speak of God's "nature," realizing that at most our talk of God can only be analogies from our experience of relating to God. The medieval doctrine of analogy, which relies on the relationship of the creator to creation, allows us to predicate attributes of God only to the extent that God is the cause of certain effects. What God is, apart from this relationship, we do not know. Luther was even more insistent that we can only know God *pro nobis*—God in relation to us or on our behalf; the hidden God, the *deus absconditus*, we do not know. Paul Tillich continues this tradition with his distinction between the symbol "God" and God as Being-Itself; the former is the God in relationship to us to whom our images refer, while the latter is beyond our knowing. Likewise, Gordon Kaufman's distinction between the "available" God and the "real" God underscores the same skepticism in regard to speaking of God apart from relating to God in experiences of worship, moral obligation, or limitation. Kaufman insists that *"all* concepts of God . . . , including that of scripture and faith, must be understood as creations of the human imagination; the 'real' God is never available to us or directly knowable by us."[65] This is not to say that the "real" God does not exist or is not like our constructs; it *is* to say that our images of God refer to the power with whom we are aware of being in a relationship.

In sum, the emphasis characteristic of contemporary epistemology on patterns of relationship in which entities exist is an emphasis which we also see in Christian theology's reticence to speak of God as an "object" available to us as "subjects." We know God *only* in relationship, only in experiences of relating to God: we do not know God's "nature."

The importance of this perspective for theological models cannot be overstated. It has long been the case that the subject-object pattern has dominated Christian piety, with the result that models and metaphors of God were considered to be "pictures" of the deity; thus, as the most ludicrous example, "God the father" was pictured as an old man with a white beard. Few people are that materialistic or realistic, but picturability and its concomitant, literalism, surfaces powerfully in the Western religious sensibility. Such literalism and naiveté has also contributed to the refusal to accept complementary and varying models for God: if, for instance, God *is* father, then God cannot be mother. The metaphorical "is and is not" should be sufficient to negate such identification; however, further insight and help is now available from the nonpicturability and structural orientation of scientific models.

It should come as support to theology in its attempt to model God, who is conceived of as nonpicturable but real, to turn to scientific models that focus on the structure of relationships among phenomena also considered nonpicturable but real. As we have emphasized, the content of scientific models consists of process, structure, and relationships, and this is also, as we have seen in the parables and Jesus as parable of God, what is critical in Christianity. If it is true, as I believe it is, that the heart of the Old Testament is the covenant between God and Israel—a structure or relationship of a particular kind emphasizing mutual commitment and trust—

and, if it is the case that the parabolic world of the kingdom of God is not a "place" but a way of being in the world characterized by a reversal of worldly expectations and a reorientation brought about by the unmerited graciousness of God to us, then models of this reality must focus on the relationships and processes involved. Thus, a model of God as father would in no way identify God as a father in an objective, substantial way, but would lift up the activity, processes, and relationships between fathers and children as one possible structure for interpreting the divine-human relationship. It should be obvious that if this understanding of model were accepted, an understanding centering on modes of relationship, there would be no cause to insist on *one* model or to exclude complementary models. This is surely the case with models such as "father" and "mother," both of which fall within the structure of parental relationships, though the commonplaces associated with each often vary and hence complement each other.

In sum, contemporary scientists insist that models are useful principally for projecting behavioral structures or modes of relationship from a known to an unknown area. Theological models following this lead will, I believe, not only reflect the basic biblical direction of concern with relations between God and the world rather than the picturability of divine and human entities, but also will avoid naive realism and the temptation to idolatry and irrelevance. The stress on structure rather than on picturability encourages, both in science and in religion, the use of multiple models. As E. H. Hutten notes, the more models projected for a particular theory, such as the theory of the atom, the better it is known, for each can give only a partial interpretation; auxiliary models usually overlap and are mutually compatible, but occasionally, he says, they become alternatives. The flexibility and tentativeness of scientific interpretation using models, evident in the following comment by Hutten, is an example of metaphorical thinking at its best.

> It has often been said that a theory is like a net we spread in order to catch the phenomena. If this is a picture that can be accepted, then it is clear that the size of the mesh may vary and that the net may be mended with pieces of different size; the net must also have a certain area, and so requires a good deal of material, before we can hope to catch anything. The net is held down only by a few anchors; but this is enough to make a catch. In other words, our interpretations are made up of many different models.[66]

If this is the case in science, should it not also be the case in theology? Do not our theories, the doctrines of the Church, which attempt to capture the mystery of the relationship between the divine and the human, require a good many "nets," with mesh of varying sizes, and some pieces mended here and there?

Are models in science a reflection of reality, or are they merely useful? Do they tell us anything about "the way things are" from a scientific perspective, or are they simply heuristic fictions which aid the scientist in the processes of discovery and predication? We come, finally, to the third point—that of ontological status—from our working definition of scientific models: a model aims at *discovering* that *set of relations or structure* in an unfamiliar area which is believed to be a genuine but partial *reflection of its reality*. Low-view supporters will range from saying that models are "disreputable understudies for mathematical formulas" or "props to feeble minds" to "a convenient way of thinking about the structure of a theory."[67] To be sure, these views, even the less enthusiastic ones, still save a place for models, but as *fictions* no commitment is being made about their ontological status. Some similarities are evident with theologians who see the parables of Jesus as illustrations of morality or doctrine, or who see religious metaphors and models as ways to communicate doctrinal truths.

It is evident that models will have a very different status in a profoundly metaphorical perspective. The metaphorical people, whether in science or theology, realize that they are permanently model-dependent, that there is no such thing as a value-free, neutral, direct route to reality and that if we are to have any knowledge of reality at all, it must be heavily dependent on models. It must be emphasized again that this confession of dependency does not mean that "everything is metaphor" or that relativism is so rampant that no distinctions can be made between better and worse, appropriate and inappropriate, ways of viewing reality. The issue is more complex in theology than in science, for theology is more dependent on its models and fewer opportunities for testing their isomorphism are available. Certainly in science models can be and are tested by investigating the properties one expects to be present and if the expectations prove to be correct, one concludes that the model *is* a description, albeit imperfect and partial, of reality. Models are possible explanations and theories are accepted explanations of phenomena. There is no such tight relationship between models and theories in theology, for many theories can be conceived from the same set of models, or as Paul Ricoeur says:

> . . . there is . . . more in the Parables taken together than in any conceptual system about God and his action among us. There is more to *think*

through the richness of the images than in the coherence of a simple concept. What confirms this feeling is the fact that we can draw from the Parables nearly all the kinds of theology which have divided Christianity through the centuries.[68]

Allowing for these differences between the relative status of models and theory in science and theology, however, it is still the case that a basic sensibility unites the metaphorical thinkers in both fields.

The further question that must be asked, however, is whether among high-view supporters, both scientific and theological, wishful thinking dominates. That is, given the fact that these people realize they are dependent on models, do they perhaps accord their models a higher status than can be defended? *Are* models a reflection of reality? Is not the "hermeneutics of suspicion" of the low view, both in science and theology, a wiser course than the more believing attitude of the high view? Is it the case that for high-view adherents, who realize they have no direct route to reality, models have become a strategy of desperation and are accorded more commitment than the evidence supports? Max Black says that the great physicists characteristically believe their models are existential: "Whether we consider Kelvin's 'rude mechanical models,' Rutherford's solar system, or Bohr's model of the atom, we can hardly avoid concluding that these physicists conceived themselves to be describing the atom *as it is*, and not merely offering mathematical formulas in fancy dress."[69] In science, the justification for supporting a view of models as referring to reality cannot, of course, be uniform; some models prove *not* to support this belief, or as Mary Hesse says, their isomorphism is purely "formal" similarity of structure lacking a "material" or actual similarity.[70] What makes the difference, what causes scientists to believe in certain models, is the explanatory power of the model. Does it, upon further investigation and experimentation, provide the mechanism or cause for the pattern of behavior of the phenomenon in question? If the purpose of science is to explain what makes things work, how phenomena behave, and if the structure of behavior from a familiar set of phenomena is used as a model for a set of phenomena whose mechanism is not yet understood, then, if this model proves to be fruitful (i.e., explains the behavior of the unknown area to the satisfaction of the scientific community), it can be accorded commitment as really describing the unfamiliar phenomena, although partially and inadequately. Rom Harré says that the function of all models "is to form the basis of a theory, and a theory is invited to explain some phenomena."[71] The only models that count in science as "existential hypotheses," he adds, are those that do not merely provide illuminating, descriptive metaphors such as "force," which is not necessary in order to understand the laws of mechanism, but those that explain the cause of something, such as "virus" as an explanation of certain diseases.[72]

It is evident, then, that scientists who believe that certain models reflect the way things are do not do so without evidence. The evidence need not be conclusive and it is never absolute; such models are not literal descriptions but they have been proven to carry explanatory power for the phenomena in question. Moreover, they are supported because they generate further discovery—the "neutral analogy" in such models is suggestive and as yet not fully exhausted. They also continue to provide connecting links with other theories and models in the overarching purpose of science to explain how phenomena work. Such an epistemological position on models may be called critical or modified realism and it owes its success, as Mary Hesse says, "both to fidelity to nature as revealed in experiments, and to the fertile imagination which selects appropriate analogies from familiar experiences and familiar types of language, and thus exhibits relations between one aspect of experience and another."[73] Both experimentation and imagination are ingredients of this perspective.

The status of theological models is more complex and problematic than that of scientific models, an issue with which we will deal in the next chapter. What is crucial, however, is that a form of critical realism can be defended as appropriate for both fields. While some might hold that scientific models are concerned only with "experimentation" and theological models only with "imagination," a metaphorical sensibility will insist that neither is the case. "Discovery" and "creation" are both involved in models of whatever field, and all knowledge is dependent, in some fashion and to varying degrees, on models, which both "are and are not" what they model. The *tension* of metaphorical thinking, its insistence on relativity and partiality while still supporting the possibility that some models "fit" reality better than others, appears to be at the heart of science, as it should also be at the heart of theology.

Our survey of models in science and other fields ranged from a glance at the power of archetypes or root-metaphors for both personal and public self-definition as understood in the human sciences, to the role of the imagination and paradigm-dependence in the natural sciences, and finally to a study of the nature and function of theoretical models in science, with an emphasis on the views of those who support the importance of models. Many specific insights relevant to the role of models in theology have emerged, insights which will be further developed in remaining chapters.

Several points should now be clear. First, models provide intelligibility for the unintelligible; they simplify and offer suggestive, concrete detail for expansion and exploitation. Second, models are not pictures of entities, but networks or structures of relationships, focused on behavior. Whether we take the example of a chess game for war, or waves and particles for the atom, or father for God, in each case we are dealing with a set of relationships that serve as an explanation of the way an unfamiliar phenomenon works in terms of the structure of a more familiar area. Third, models, in conjunction with theories, provide an ever widening panorama of explanation, allowing phenomena within a field and at times across fields to be linked in connecting networks. Hence, systems are constructed that provide intelligibility, not just to this or that phenomenon, but to reality as a whole. Fourth, models are paradigm-dependent, "created" as well as "discovered" by persons working within a set of assumptions that delimits the possibility of the innocent eye. Thus, they are always partial, even when deemed appropriate, necessitating both alternative and complementary models as well as eternal vigilance against their literalization, *against the loss of the metaphorical tension.*

4 Models in Theology

As we turn to models in theology, we recall Robert Funk's comment that the route between the parables of Jesus and systematic theology is a tortuous one. Models, as systematic and relatively permanent metaphors, are a critical link between parables, which are also metaphors, and conceptual language, which orders, analyzes, and criticizes the images of a tradition in a logical and comprehensive fashion. The distinctive goal of a metaphorical theology is to assess the ways in which the foundational language of parables and Jesus as parable—with their characteristics of openness, tension, relativity, indirection, and transformation—have been retained in the course of the various translation languages comprising theology. A metaphorical theology attempts to consider the relationships among metaphor, model, and concept for the purpose both of justifying dominant, founding models as true but not literal, *and* of discovering other appropriate models that for cultural, political, and social reasons have been suppressed. The focus of a metaphorical theology will be on *models*, for models, like metaphors, retain the tension at the heart of all religious language and, like concepts, order the images of a tradition so that they may become an intelligible pattern for life.

Differences Between Scientific and Theological Models

In the last chapter we suggested that certain insights from scientific models may prove helpful in understanding the function of models in theology. The emphasis, necessarily, was on the similarity between the two fields in an effort to see, as clearly as possible, the aid theology might receive from science. Now as we begin our study of theological models, it is imperative to note the substantial differences. In our comparison of science and religion we noted that while theories dominate more than models in science, the reverse is the case in theology. That point must now be underscored and expanded.

The broadest type of theological model—the metaphysical model of the relations between God, human being, and the world—is without limit and hence unfalsifiable. This is the root-metaphor or original model. In the Judeo-Christian tradition it is characteristically expressed in terms of personal relations. The biblical root-metaphor is that of a personal deity relating to the human and natural world as its source and its transformer— traditionally articulated in the models of "creation" and "redemption." This "model of models" is understood as a cosmic, metaphysical drama of relationships, of action and response, which includes everything that exists.[1] Whatever is, *is* only in relationship to God, both its hold in existence and the possible transformation of that existence toward fuller realization.

Nothing of this sort is present in science, and as Frederick Ferré notes, the basis for the conflict between science and religion is the false assumption that religion is advancing empirically testable assertions rather than metaphysical statements of unlimited scope, while science has been viewed, again falsely, as making metaphysical assertions rather than advancing limited empirical statements.[2] This difference does not mean that science makes no assertions about the way the world is, for as we know, many philosophers of science believe that scientific models are indirectly related to reality. Nor does this difference mean that theologians do not attempt to give evidence for supporting one model over another, for responsible theology must always provide such evidence. But scientists as scientists are not metaphysicians and even their paradigms, the assumptions within which normal science is conducted, undergo radical shifts of a sort uncommon to religious traditions. The difference is evident in the relative importance of history in science and religion. Past scientific theories constitute a minor body of evidence for contemporary scientists; the literature that counts is the ground-breaking work being published in the most progressive journals. The cumulative history of doctrine, however, is essential to contemporary theological construction. The basic assumptions and key models from the past continue not only to be influential but also to stand as the subject matter to be analyzed, criticized, and reinterpreted for the present day. Thus, while the ultimate goal of theology is *comprehension* of all reality by means of a root-metaphor and its dominant models, the ultimate goal of science is *discovery* of new phenomena and their mechanisms, which ideally will be integrated in ever-expanding patterns of intelligibility. But when this latter enterprise moves beyond the interrelations among scientific laws to overarching root-metaphors, it becomes metaphysics. For example, A. N. Whitehead, whose root-metaphor of "process" came from science, engaged in metaphysics when he used it as an explanation for all reality.

A second and critical difference between scientific and theological models is the crucial importance of models in theology. They are comprehensive and at base metaphysical, and a theologian is not able to operate without them. Many scientists, of course, insist that models are essential both for discovery and for making theory intelligible, although a narrow understanding of theory is possible by limiting explanation to mathematical formulas and the particular observation statements they entail and exclude. The resulting explanation will be intelligible only to the specialist, but even that option is not available to the theologian. Apart from models, theological theory would result in empty definitions which relate terms logically but meaninglessly. As one commentator notes, "while it is possible to say, 'A was in B relating C asymmetrically to A,' it is the models in the following translation that give it meaning: 'God was in Christ reconciling the world to Himself.'"[3] Since there are no empirical tests of the verifiability or falsifiability of theological statements of the order we find in science, it is models which provide the explanation of theological concepts, without which concepts would be empty and unintelligible.[4] A theologian, then, to a greater degree even than the scientist does not have the luxury of deciding between models and no models: the question is, which models?

This brings us to a third difference between models in science and religion: the quantity of models in theology and their mutual relations. There are fewer models in science (some classic ones such as "wave" and "particle" appear to function usefully in several fields) and they are not arranged hierarchically, as dominant and supporting models, as they are in theology. In a sense, it could be said that religious language consists of nothing but metaphors and models, and theological language is rife with them. One has only to think of christology to make this point. In the early Church, Jesus was seen as "Son of man," as "the Word made flesh," as "Son of God," as "the Second Adam," and as "Messiah." Similarly, the trinitarian controversy, while conducted in conceptual language, relied on the basic model of the relationships among "Father," "Son," and "Holy Spirit." Furthermore, the work of Jesus Christ, as elaborated in the atonement theories, has always been conceived in terms of models: models of "ransom," "sacrifice," "redemption," "substitution," and "moral influence." When theologians attempt to think in conceptual terms, free from models, they find, as Ferré suggests in this telling and amusing statement, that this effort is more difficult than it seems to be.

> Even the theologian's technical vocabulary is not so independent of his model as he might think. Is God's transcendence under discussion? An analyst need not look far before he finds the thinly disguised spatial metaphor that underlies this term. Everywhere the model peeps through, and it is more difficult than many realize to be rid of it and still *to say the same thing* that was intended before. "Transcendent? That means above the universe. Above? Well, not really above, but *beyond*. Beyond? No, not in space—but simply not exclusively in the universe. *In* . . . ?"[5]

Not only are metaphorical language and models ubiquitous in theology at a subconscious level, but many models have flourished and been encouraged at a conscious level because the complexity and richness of the divine-human relationship demand diversity *and* a multitude of models delimits the possibility of any one model becoming an idol. Diversity, says Ian Ramsey, is theology's lifeblood: "An endless number of metaphors and models . . . is 'no death by a thousand qualifications.' Rather, it is life by a thousand enrichments."[6] That enrichment, however, could result in chaos unless some structure were introduced into the panorama of images, and it is the task of dominant models—with complementary and supporting models—to provide the order. The dominant model in the Judeo-Christian tradition is that of a personal God relating to responsible and responsive beings. Within this model we find supporting and wide-ranging models of varying status: father/son, lord/servant, mother/child, lover/beloved, husband/wife, master/slave, companion/friend, and the like. We also find impersonal and natural models, which while less central, express feelings of awe, fear, exultation, and misery in ways which the more anthropocentric images do not. As we will see, the concepts arising out of the central models of this religious tradition are thoroughly infected by metaphor; that is, theological concepts are invariably models of a more inclusive and generalized sort—"creation," "redemption," "providence," "judgment," "grace." The attempt to isolate a "theory" untouched by the complex of various and diverse models from which doctrine arises is neither fruitful nor possible.

A fourth and final difference between scientific and theological models is, baldly stated, that scientific models refer to the quantitative dimension of the world while theological models refer to the qualitative dimension. This is not the old division between science as cognitive and religion as noncognitive, for knowledge is involved in both cases. The difference is between the *ways* the world is known: science knows the world from the perspective of its physical phenomena while theology knows the world from the perspective of human valuation. Science asks the question, "What is this phenomenon and how does it work?" while theology asks the question, "What is the meaning of life in the world?" Earl MacCormac notes that both religion and science "are conceptual explanations of human experience with the former stressing the personal dimension and the latter the external experience of man."[7] Hence, theological models have a valuational component lacking in scientific models. That is, theological models affect feelings and actions in the world; they often determine how we feel about ourselves and our world, and how we conduct ourselves in it. This is a critical difference between scientific and theological models, as should be evident from the parables of the New Testament. They not only tell us something about the world and how we should live in it, but a parable characteristically ends with an implicit finger pointing to the listener— "And what about *you?*" Ferré puts it graphically: "Beware of powerful metaphors. . . . They are influencing our attitudes and values and feelings —and even our ways of seeing ourselves and our world—more than we may know."[8] To say, however, that theological models are valuational does not mean that they are nonconfirmable. Not only are they emotive, but they are also cognitive—providing knowledge about the world and about how to live in the world. Therefore, some criteria must be advanced for appropriate theological models.

While scientific models often can be verified through empirical experiments, we have seen that increasingly (as in atomic physics) this is not always the case. Science also must often use indirect means of verification: heuristic fruitfulness, coherence and order, nonfalsification and approximate confirmation, and acceptance of anomalies provide support for the most acceptable theory rather than proof for the perfect theory. As we shall argue, responsible theology must also provide "evidence" in support of its dominant models or pay the price of having a ghetto truth unrelated to other truths people hold to be significant.

To sum up: we have noted four characteristic differences between scientific and theological models. The function of theological models is comprehensive ordering rather than discovery; they are a necessity for meaning and explanation in theology in a more pronounced way than in science; models are ubiquitous in theology and related hierarchically as they are not in science; theological models affect feelings and actions in ways scientific models do not.

It should be evident by now that models play a key role in theology:

they appear everywhere in theology and are central to the meaning, ordering, and living of the Christian faith. In the remainder of this chapter we shall attempt to chart the course of models in the Christian tradition from parables to systematic theology. The course charted will be little more than an outline, for it is indeed a "tortuous route." We shall begin where we left off in chapter 2 with the parables and Jesus as parable, attempting to understand the root-metaphor which emerges from that material. From there we shall delineate how this basic model influenced credal language, an early and interesting type of mixed metaphorical and conceptual language. Next, we shall reflect on relations between primary and secondary, or metaphorical and conceptual, language as the context for understanding models as a unique union of the two types of language. Finally, we shall turn to a consideration of the truth of and criteria for theological models.

Parable, Paradigm, and Root-Metaphor in Christianity

From the parables of the New Testament and Jesus as parable of God we concluded that the kingdom of God represents a way of being in the world—in permanent tension with accepted or conventional ways. The parables and Jesus as parable are metaphors that indirectly point to relational life characterized by disorientation and reorientation—disorientation toward life based on merit and reorientation based on the unmerited grace of God. What is critical here is a new quality of relationship, both toward God and toward other human beings. The content of the root-metaphor of Christianity, then, is a mode of personal relationship, exemplified in the parables and with its chief exemplar Jesus himself, a tensive relationship distinguished by trust in God's impossible way of love in contrast to the loveless ways of the world. This root-metaphor of Christianity occurs within the paradigm of the Jewish religion and its basic assumptions, which are partially affirmed and partially revolutionized by the introduction of the new metaphor.

We must now look more carefully at the nature of this paradigm and root-metaphor in order to understand their relationship and the transformations they undergo as they evolve conceptually. As we have already seen, a paradigm constitutes the most basic set of assumptions within which a tradition, in this instance, a religious tradition, functions. It is the unquestioned framework or context for its normal operations; it is its "world." The Jewish paradigm is distinguished by its monotheistic, personalistic character as well as by its profound sense of history. It manifests itself as a story of a people in a covenantal relationship with the one God of the universe, who created them and destined them to fulfill the divine purposes through their responsive activity of utter trust and loyalty to their creator and governor. An anomaly enters this paradigm in the person and activity of one of them, the man from Nazareth, who proclaimed that the search for total trust in God at the heart of the Jewish experience of God had been fulfilled in the kingdom which was at hand. Thus a revolution in the paradigm occurred, spearheaded by a new root-metaphor. The new root-metaphor, the kingdom of God, exemplified in Jesus' parables and in Jesus as parable of God, describes a mode of being in the world as the free gift of God. The hope of the Hebrews has been fulfilled, and in this transition, continuity and discontinuity are both evident. Jesus is inextricably linked with the new root-metaphor as both the proclaimer of the kingdom and the way to the kingdom. Its distinctive note is not a new view of God or a new image of human being; neither divine nor human *nature* is at its center, but a new quality of *relationship*, a way of being in the world under the rule of God. This way of being is highly metaphorical—abjuring identification, possession, absolutism, stasis, conventionality, and spiritualism. It is, to use John Dominic Crossan's phrase, "life on the edge of the raft," for it relies entirely on the security of relationship with God.

If this is an appropriate description of the root-metaphor of Christianity and if it has the metaphorical characteristics suggested, then that root-metaphor and its qualities should be evident in the various translation languages that emerge in an attempt to analyze and interpret it. This does not mean, of course, that the language must be the same or the metaphorical characteristics identical with those we have named, but the emphasis on *relationship* of a certain kind and on *tension* of a certain quality should be evident in all theological reflection. "Theological reflection," of course, takes place in creeds, liturgies, and ethics as well as in systematic theology.

Before we address such translation languages, and especially the creeds as a particularly interesting case of such language, it is necessary to consider in more detail the nature of root-metaphors, for, as we have seen, they are the guiding factor in a paradigm. If a paradigm is, as Ian Barbour suggests, the tradition that "sets the limits on the range of acceptable models,"[9] then root-metaphors are the content that specifies those limits. A change in root-metaphor signals a revolution in the paradigm, as David Tracy indicates when he says, "If it is true that every major religion's vision of human reality is grounded in certain root-metaphors, then an elimination of the metaphorical character of religious language is effectively a substitution of one set of meanings for another."[10] This is a critical comment, for it means that if the root-metaphor of a religion is lost, so is the religion: one does not have the same religion without its basic model. Tracy is saying two things here, both that a substitution of one root-metaphor for another results in a different religion and that the translation of the metaphor into conceptual language without bringing the metaphorical into the conceptual—funding it by means of the root-metaphor—changes the meaning of the religion. The importance of these points surfaces when changes are proposed within a tradition: what are the limits of change in basic models, brought about by anomalies, which will still preserve the character of the religion? When we deal with the anomaly posed to feminists by the model "God the father," we shall need to consider whether the proposed changes for that model affect the root-metaphor of Christianity. As should be evident, a root-metaphor does not stand alone in a religious tradition. Since theological models are hierarchically ordered and interrelated, changes in subordinate models have the potential both of enhancing and of endangering the status of the root-metaphor. As Paul Ricoeur says, "Root metaphors assemble and scatter. They assemble subordinate images together and they scatter concepts at a higher level. They are the dominant metaphors capable of both engendering and organizing a network."[11] The content of a religious tradition, then, is known through its root-metaphor and the subordinate models which support and enrich it.

More than content is involved here, however. If the content of the root-metaphor of Christianity is *relationship* of a certain kind that must be evident in subsequent theologies if they are to be metaphorical, of equal importance is the method of expressing this content in terms of its *tension.* Not only will Christianity be lost if another root-metaphor is substituted or if the model is absorbed by concept, but it will also be lost if the tensive qualities of the parables and Jesus as parable are forgotten.[12] Theology should be metaphorical both in content and in method, for if the main characteristic of metaphor—its tension—is lost, then Christianity's root-metaphor is lost as well, for it is precisely the inability to *possess* God's love which is at the heart of the relationship with God exemplified in the kingdom. "Justification through grace" can be understood either tensively as a translation of the root-metaphor of Christianity *or* descriptively as the possession of the Christian's new orientation. The first is metaphorical; the second verges on idolatry.

The root-metaphor of Christianity, then, is a relationship of a certain kind. The key exemplar of this relationship is Jesus of Nazareth: he not only tells us about it and demonstrates it in his own life, but he also is believed by his followers to be *the way* to it. He is its exemplar; hence, *he* is the root-metaphor of Christianity without which Christianity would not be the religion it is. While "the story of Jesus" is not the whole of the Christian paradigm by any means, it was and continues to be the principal way Christian faith is transmitted across generations. As Amos Wilder says, Christians confess their faith "just by telling a story or a series of stories."[13] In science as well as in religion, exemplars or accepted models are considered foundational. As Barbour suggests, "A religious tradition, like a scientific tradition, is transmitted more by *the memory of its exemplars* than by a set of explicit principles."[14] But the story of Jesus marks a beginning, not the whole; the relational model it exemplifies has undergone two thousand years of analysis and interpretation, starting with the first tellers of that story. We will by no means be able to follow that course of analysis and interpretation in any detail; at best we will stop at a few junctures to note changes that have occurred, attempting to see if the translations have been faithful to the metaphorical way. As we begin this journey, a summary of theology's task by Frederick Ferré reveals the complex, symbiotic interrelationships of models and concepts. Much of what follows will be an attempt to distinguish and to relate models and concepts as theology develops consistent, comprehensive orderings of reality.

> Theological speech projects a model of immense responsive significance, drawn from "the facts," as the key to its conceptual synthesis. This model, for theism, is made up of the "spiritual" characteristics of personality: will, purpose, wisdom, love and the like. For Christianity, more specifically, the conceptual model consists in the creative, self-giving, personal love of Jesus. In this model is found the only literal meaning which these terms, like "creative," "personal," and "love," can have in the Christian vocabulary. All the concepts of the Christians are organized and synthesized in relation to this model. The efforts of systematic theology are bent to explicating the consistency and coherence of the synthesis built on this model of "God" as the key concept.[15]

Creeds: Models or Dogmas?

The Apostles' Creed (and to a lesser extent, the Nicene Creed) is probably recited by more Christians with greater frequency than any other confession of faith. Sunday after Sunday it is repeated by Christians around the world, many of whom have little comprehension of its momentous assertions, let alone its power or its oddity. It is a majestic statement summing up the central beliefs of Christian faith in a narrative of amazing economy; in form it is trinitarian, its three articles specifying the work of the Father, Son, and Holy Spirit. All of heaven and earth is included in it, but it is neither general nor abstract; rather, it is comprised of concrete images and events that tell the story of the world in Christian perspective from beginning to end. Its power lies in the metaphors and models that people repeat over and over again: "God the Father Almighty maker of heaven and earth," "Jesus Christ his only Son our Lord," "descended into hell," "communion of saints," "forgiveness of sins," "resurrection of the body," and "life everlasting." These phrases have been the ones by which Christians describe and interpret their religious experience; moreover, they constitute the language *in* which Christians experience religiously, for the language is not only shaped by experience but shapes it as well. In fact, the language of the creed may become so ordinary and accepted that its oddity is forgotten: occasionally one is aware of its strangeness, but usually it is recited with the same equanimity with which one reads a newspaper.

When we notice some of the phrases from the Nicene Creed, the situation changes, for the form is less narrational and more abstract, the language less imagistic and more conceptual: "all things visible and invisible," "the only-begotten Son of God," "God of God, Light of Light, Very God of Very God, begotten, not made, being of one substance with the Father." We realize something new here, that a point is being emphasized concerning the relationship between the Father and the Son, and that this point is being pressed by means of concepts intended to be as precise as possible. We should also note, however, that while the key phrase, "being of one substance with the Father," is clearly philosophical, conceptual language, many of the other phrases are still metaphorical or contain metaphors. At the very least, then, the Church's main creeds are a fascinating mix of metaphorical and conceptual language in basically narrative form. The focus of their content, moreover, is *relationship*, not only the relationship of the Father to the Son and to the Holy Spirit, but also the relationship of God to the world, to its creation and salvation.

The evolution of these creeds and the controversies surrounding their development, most notably the trinitarian formula and the subsequent controversy ending in the Chalcedonian formula (A.D. 451), are incredibly complex and beyond our concern here. Suffice it to say that these controversies defined, as precisely as possible with available philosophical concepts, two key relationships: the relationship among the "persons" of the Godhead ("one substance, three persons") and the relationship between the divine and the human in Jesus Christ ("one person with or in two natures"). The overarching relationship of the creeds, and the reason for their concern with the above relations, is the one between God and humanity; the creeds were concerned with salvation above all else. Whether the credal understanding of this relationship is faithful to the root-metaphor of Christianity—the kingdom of God made known in the parables and Jesus as parable of God—is a highly complex question. We do not presume to answer that question definitely, although we must deal with it in attempting to analyze this translation language as emergent from and related to its metaphorical, parabolic base.

Are the creeds models or dogmas? Do they, as Augustine says, "fence a mystery," or do they pose as explanations of it and hence reduce it to literal statements? Is credal language open-ended, relative, tensive, iconoclastic, and indirect or is it absolutistic, possessive, static, literalistic, and idolatrous? The verdict is mixed. To be sure, many characteristics of models are evident in credal language. We notice immediately that two of the major images—"Father" and "Son"—are concrete, detailed models which simplify in an intelligible way what are otherwise impregnable mysteries, that is, God and Jesus of Nazareth. These models are well known, common ones with great potential for exploitation since we all have a vast network of commonplaces associated with paternal and filial behavior. Nescience immediately becomes knowledge, silence is broken, we can speak, *not* because we know now who God is or who Jesus is but because we know about fathers and sons. These models are also comprehensive and systematic: they provide a grid of interpretation for all of "heaven and earth." If God is Father, then he is "begetter" or creator of all that is, including human beings, who as creatures are "children"; he is also sustainer, provider, and governor of the world and, through his Son, he restores and reconciles his children when they fall away from him through sin and rebellion. An entire theology *in nuce* is present in these models. That these models are interrelated is evident: "Father" is the dominant model spawning subsidiary models of "Son" (not, the creeds insist, in subordination, but Father comes first, while Son comes second), "children," "creation," "rebellion," "reconciliation," as well as others. Many models emerge and they are related to one another intrinsically and naturally, creating a pattern of interpretation from the beginning of the world to its fulfillment. The models provide explanation for doctrine, or, more accurately, the theory emerging from the creeds of the relationships involved is exemplified in terms of models. The theory is not illustrated by the models but the models are exemplars of it: one does not have doctrine *and* models in the creeds, but doctrine *in* models. There is little attempt, even in the Nicene Creed, to expurgate models; rather, *conceptual and metaphorical language lie side by side.*

Above all else, the creeds focus not on describing human and divine natures, but on modeling relationships of various kinds: within the Godhead, between divinity and humanity in Jesus Christ, between God and humanity. This is a controversial assertion, since the creeds have been criticized as adopting the substance language of Greek philosophy, and by so doing, describing divine and human activity in terms of static, substantial divine and human natures. The criticism is valid to the extent that the conceptual framework does veer in this direction, but the form of the creeds is still narrational and hence dynamic. Moreover, and of greater significance, the conceptual language is, at base, relational because of the centrality of the models of father, son, and children—relationships, not natures.

Finally, the creeds powerfully shape feelings and attitudes due to their models, not to their conceptual elements.[16] It is no surprise that the central model of the creeds, the paternal one, has singularly influenced religious emotions and behavior, for, even if Freud had not told us so, we know from our own experience that relations with fathers embrace a highly complex mix of pleasure, pain, and guilt.

In sum, we can say, I believe, that credal language manifests many characteristics of interpretation by means of models. Serious questions must nevertheless be raised. While the creeds focus on relationships, the root-metaphor of Christianity—the kingdom of God and the relationship of reorientation based on security in God alone—appears in a somewhat skewed form. One does not expect it to appear in the same form in the creeds as in the parables (for translation languages necessarily change the form), but the critical marks of metaphorical theology—a relationship between God and humanity of a certain quality and tension of a certain kind—should be evident if continuity between the parabolic base and its interpretation is to be maintained.

While this issue is highly complex and undoubtedly involves many factors, one problem with the credal language appears to be the hegemony of the paternal model. In my opinion, it undercuts both the *content* and the *form* of metaphorical theology. It undercuts the *content* of the relationship with God as one based not on merit but on grace because paternal imagery alone is not capable of modeling this pattern. The commonplaces associated with paternal imagery move between the poles of domination and providence and, more often than not, tend toward reward through merit rather than toward acceptance through compassion. As we shall see, one of the advantages of including maternal models for the divine-human relationship is that traditionally maternal love has more frequently been associated with unmerited care than has paternal love.[17] Parental models alone of either a paternal or maternal cast are, however, not sufficient to serve as the only models in a metaphorical theology. The problem here, as in most areas where models are critical, is the reluctance or refusal to use many—complementary and varied—models.

It is this reluctance or refusal which also points to the way in which the paternal model undercuts the *form* of metaphorical theology. It is not this model in particular that is the problem but its hegemony, its status as *the* interpretive grid for Christian faith, which elevates it to an absolute, literalistic, and virtually idolatrous position. Credal language is both deceptive and powerful; hence, the temptations to idolatry are strong. It is deceptive because it looks like literal language: "I believe in God, the Father Almighty, maker of heaven and earth; And in Jesus Christ his only Son our Lord." It appears to be a straightforward assertion defining the nature of God as father and Jesus Christ as son, as well as the relationship between them. That "definition" is by means of *one model* and, as we have seen, it is a model carrying heavy emotional freight. The temptation to possess God in this language, to identify the relationships described as enclosed in this language, is almost irresistible. While Ian Ramsey's comment on Arius's literalization of the trinitarian formula may not be entirely fair to Arius, it does identify a tendency not only common among patristic theologians but among us moderns as well.

> In effect, Arius said: "Sons come after fathers," so that if we talk of Jesus in terms of worship, we cannot escape some degree of subordination if we are to use the words meaningfully. So did Arius idolize what is only a model, and run it to death. . . . Arius did not realize that words like "son" and "father" only provided models.[18]

While it is necessary to remember that creeds emerged in the fight against heresies and hence, understandably, tend in the direction of definiteness, it is even more necessary to recall their limitations. Augustine is not alone in his awareness of the inadequacy of all language to express divine reality. Karl Rahner has said that dogma is the beginning, not the end, of theological reflection and all sensitive users of religious language agree with him. J. F. Bethune-Baker, a patristics scholar, says that "all attempts to explain the nature and the relations of the Deity must largely depend on metaphor, and no one metaphor can exhaust those relations. Each metaphor can only describe one aspect of the nature of being of the Deity, and the inferences which can be drawn from it have their limits when they conflict with the inferences which can be truly drawn from other metaphors describing other aspects."[19] This obvious but often overlooked reminder lies at the base of our criticism of credal language as usually understood (whatever its intentions) as nonmetaphorical. Seldom is it recognized as tentative, open, relative, indirect, and tensive. The metaphorical "is and is not" is forgotten and identification takes place. God *is* Father, Jesus Christ *is* Son, and we *are* children. The appropriateness of these models as relative and helpful aids for interpreting the divine-human relationship is changed into an assertion of their literal and exclusive truth.

The verdict, then, on credal language is complex: credal language is a mix of models and concepts, in some ways a translation language in continuity with its parabolic base, but skewed due to its excessive reliance on *one* model, which is neither adequate to express the new relationship introduced by Jesus of Nazareth nor free from the idolatry which is the fate of any exclusive model. A central insight concerning the kingdom of God from the parables and Jesus as parable is that *it cannot be defined*, either imagistically or conceptually. It is a *relationship* modeled in the parables and in Jesus of Nazareth; hence, this relationship and not "God the father" (or "God the mother," or any other model) is the root-metaphor of Christianity. Many models will be necessary to intimate what it means to live in such a relationship with God and with others, but as an *event* which will take many forms at various times in different peoples' lives, it is not an "object" whose nature can be described.

By contrast, atonement theories have had quite a different history from that of credal statements on God and Christ. As we have mentioned earlier, there are several such theories and the four main ones—ransom, deification, satisfaction, and moral influence—all are models. In atonement theories, not only have the concepts never moved very far from the models in which they were first expressed, but, even more significantly, all the models have survived and some combination of two or more of them is often embraced together. Even here, though, when *one* model is absolutized—the prime example on the contemporary scene being the satisfaction model—the result has been as disastrous as in the creeds. Generally, however, with atonement theories the church has realized that its models incur inconsistencies and moral difficulties at the conceptual level; that the "negative analogy," that part of a model not meant to apply, enters at a particular point when the exploitation of details becomes overambitious. It is then necessary to pull back, to realize, for instance, that the appropriateness of interpreting Christ's work as "satisfaction" does not mean that something objective is done *to* us without internal transformation, and to balance that model with "moral influence," stressing change in heart as an intrinsic part of genuine reconciliation. Atonement theory has been, from one point of view, a "muddle" contrasted with the neatness of the Nicene and Chalcedonian formulas. From another point of view, atonement theory is a good illustration of metaphorical theology, for it has allowed for multiple and alternative models, an obvious admission of the relative, tensive, and indirect character of theological reflection.

Models and Concepts

Is theological language a "muddle"? It is certainly a mix of metaphorical and conceptual language, but what sort of mix is it? Is it possible to define more precisely the kind of relationship between primary and secondary language appropriate to theological language? These questions are crucial to an understanding of the special function models play in theology, for models are dominant metaphors with systematic, comprehensive, interpretive power. They *are* a mixture of metaphorical and conceptual language; hence, some understanding of the way these two languages are related should enable us to see how models are a peculiar and special operative form of primary and secondary language.

There are many examples of unfortunate relationships between metaphorical and conceptual languages. I will mention only two: one in which the two forms are opposites, the other in which they are identified. Arthur Koestler illustrates the first by the fate of imagistic language when it is translated into abstract academic jargon. From Ecclesiastes he quotes:

> I returned, and saw under the sun, that the race is not to the swift, nor the battle to the strong, neither yet bread to the wise, nor yet riches to men of understanding, not yet favor to men of skill; but time and chance happeneth to them all (Eccl. 9:11, KJV).

He then offers George Orwell's tongue-in-cheek conceptual translation of this passage:

> Objective considerations of contemporary phenomena compel the conclusion that success or failure in competitive activities exhibits no tendency to be commensurate with innate capacity, but that a considerable element of the unpredictable must invariably be taken into account.[20]

In addition to being amused by the juxtaposition of these two passages presumably "about the same thing," we are alternately enraged and disappointed: enraged that the powerful metaphors of Ecclesiastes have been reduced to trite generalizations and disappointed that the interpretation is so pretentious and unhelpful. Nothing significant from the first passage has survived its interpretation in the second; the second could have been written without the first, and better, we say, that it had been, leaving the poetry untouched by such insensitive, heavy hands.

Our second illustration moves in the opposite direction, suggesting that the quasi-concept "openness" can be substituted for the metaphor "light." The example is from John Macquarrie but Martin Heidegger's hand is obviously evident in it:

> The statement "God is light" could be translated into the language of openness by saying: "Openness is constitutive for being." The more openness, the fuller being and the more expansion in being; but where openness is obstructed, being is narrowed down and thinned away. Openness is the very law of being, so to speak, because Being itself or God is constituted by openness.[21]

The translation attempt here is obviously well intentioned, believing that "light" no longer speaks to contemporary people as a religious metaphor. The substitution, however, of "openness," which is general and vague, for "light," which is concrete and sensuous, has little to commend it. It is no accident that light has always been a primary metaphor in most religious traditions. Like other images such as food, water, blood, fire, and breath, it arises from the biological realities of birth, death, and the nurture of life between our beginning and our end. Such images are basic ones, serving as principal vehicles for spiritual experiences of rebirth and destruction. These images do not die or grow irrelevant, for they are rooted in the most basic patterns of creaturely existence. Therefore, while "openness" and "light" in Macquarrie's statement appear to be intimates— with the first the "natural" interpretation of the second—in fact much is sacrificed by the proposed substitution. Not only is the power of the light metaphor lost, but a proper task of conceptual thought—interpretation of primary language—is given up for mere translation into a more generalized and abstract vocabulary.

If metaphorical language and conceptual language should be neither the same nor totally different, what ought their relationship in theology be? It is important to note at the outset that any attempt to make a hard and fast division between primary and secondary language in religion will fail because of their *intrinsic interdependence*. While the beginnings of religious language lie in worship, in experiences of the presence (as well as the absence) of God, and it is these experiences, expressed in metaphorical language, which feed theological reflection, it is also the case that people within a theological tradition use that language to express their own religious experience. The relationship is a symbiotic one in which metaphors provide "food" for concepts and concepts provide "sight" for metaphors. Earl MacCormac says that in science observation statements are "theory-laden," for they occur within the paradigm of accepted assumptions and theories of a scientific tradition. Likewise, "statements describing religious experience are 'theology-laden' for theology provides the questions, context, and terminology for expressing religious experience."[22] MacCormac does not, however, mention the obverse relationship, the one emphasized by Paul Ricoeur, in which imagistic language, both symbol and metaphor, by its multivalency and ambiguity, gives rise to and insists upon interpretive, conceptual thought.[23]

Ricoeur identifies the problem involved in relating metaphorical and conceptual language: "Between the concept which kills the symbol and pure conceptual silence, there must be room for a *conceptual* language which preserves the *tensive* character of symbolic language."[24] Ricoeur does not solve the problem, but he has given some provocative hints of what he believes would constitute an appropriate answer.[25] These insights can be summed up in the following sentence: within the *continuity* of primary and secondary language there must be genuine *separation*, for the purpose of secondary language is *interpretation* in order to return us to the *event* that primary language seeks to express.

My summary of Ricoeur's position suggests several important points which we will try to sort out by focusing on each of the key words. We must first note, however, that in his overall perspective the purpose of theological language is finally a religious, existential one. Theological language must gain distance and be different from religious language *because* it is only in this way that modern people, deprived of a naive harmony with the sacred cosmos via symbols, can experience that connection—as a "second naiveté" through the indirect mediation of interpretation. Thus, the goal of conceptual language is not analysis or systemization for its own sake or even primarily for comprehensive ordering of all that is, but for a reoccurrence of the event which unites us to the ground of our being. While Ricoeur may be less than satisfactory in specifying one of the crucial functions of models—their ordering, systematic potential for comprehensive interpretation—he is, I believe, on the mark when he insists that the main task of theology is interpretation that returns us to the primary language of a tradition with fresh possibilities for it becoming a transforming reality in our lives. The kind of theologian Ricoeur supports is the hermeneut, the critic, whose main task is not to create completed, doctrinal systems but to interpret the multivalent, rich, ambiguous metaphors arising from the symbolic base of a tradition so that those symbols will once again speak to our existential situation. Just as a literary critic tries to interpret a poem or a novel in such a way as to return the reader to a deeper experience of the work of art, so the theologian tries to interpret an imagistic tradition in order to renew its religious potential.

These insights of Ricoeur's are especially helpful for understanding relations between primary and secondary language in theology. He insists that a basic *continuity* exists between the two languages. Interpretation is an intrinsic part of imagistic language; it is not tacked on but arises from within it. Thus, one can interpret properly only by living within the image: "Symbolic signs are opaque, because the first, literal, obvious meaning itself points analogically to a second meaning which is not given otherwise than in it."[26] This living within the symbol—symbols for Ricoeur being nonlinguistic bonds uniting us to the cosmos—results in linguistic (e.g., metaphorical) interpretations, redescribing the reality that the symbols embody but do not themselves interpret. Symbols need metaphors, for without them they are dumb; metaphors need symbols, for without them they lose their rootedness in life. Metaphor articulates symbolic richness, making distinctions, suggesting alternative interpretations, insisting on the tension in which we always exist in relation to reality. Thus, metaphor constitutes the first stage of interpretation and hence is intrinsically connected, on the one hand, to its depths in symbol and, on the other hand, to emerging conceptualization.

If there is continuity, however, between primary and secondary language there is also *separation,* for distance is necessary for *interpretation* to fulfill its proper task. Concepts are not worn-out metaphors to Ricoeur; he argues for a pluralism of discourse and wishes to avoid Heidegger's collapse of conceptual and poetic language. Otherwise, he insists, one loses the standpoint from which to criticize metaphors. To be sure, "the semantic shock [of metaphor] produces a conceptual need" and from the metaphorical proliferation of interpretation on the symbolic base many interpretations arise, but concepts are different from metaphors: "The discourse that attempts to *recover* the ontology implicit in the metaphorical statement is different discourse. In this sense, to *ground* what was called metaphorical truth is also to *limit* poetic discourse."[27] To take an example Ricoeur does not use, if we ask what it means to call God "father," we cannot answer this question by staying on the level of metaphors and models but must move to a level of broader and more comprehensive categories including not only "father" but also other metaphors as well as concepts which both limit and complement it. The conceptual level provides this distance without which we wander in a land of images that, while rich, is chaotic and unilluminated. Needless to say, such interpretation will always involve tension and never be complete, for metaphorical language suggests many possible meanings, and the meanings that emerge must always return to the images for revitalization and hence themselves always remain open and tentative. As Ricoeur sees it, interpretation exists at the intersection between metaphor and speculation:

> Interpretation is . . . a mode of discourse that functions at the intersection of two domains, metaphorical and speculative. It is a composite discourse, therefore, and as such cannot but feel the opposite pull of rival demands. On the one side, interpretation seeks the clarity of the concept; on the other, it hopes to preserve the dynamism of meaning that the concept holds and pins down.[28]

Finally, the end of interpretation for Ricoeur issues not in a total system, but rather in forms of interpretation that in different ways remain "under the control of the hermeneutical potential of the metaphor."[29] The overall goal of interpretation is *to return to the experience* the primary language expresses. In the case of Christianity, Ricoeur describes this experience as the parabolic redescription of reality—reorientation to the ways of the kingdom of God. But each of the translation languages that builds upon the parables ought, in some fashion, to perpetuate this experience; for instance, he notes that Paul's notion of justification by faith is intrinsically related to the parables' logic of superabundance.[30] Here the reliance, both on a certain kind of relationship between God and humanity and on tension within the language that expresses it, is evident. Even at the highest speculative level, at the level of philosophical conceptualization of the divine, Ricoeur believes in a limit to human pretensions and that the tension derived from the metaphorical "is and is not" should be fully operative. At the level of the most systematic reflection, he seems to be calling for continuity with the parabolic beginning in the sense of limit-concepts and indirect or figurative presentation of the Unconditioned.[31]

At the very least, then, Ricoeur is insisting on the hermeneutical circle: language is the mediation of raw experience (which we never have) and complete intelligibility (which we never have). Between these two unavailable poles we live, with intelligibility in the service of the experiential. In order to believe, we, exiled as children from the Eden of naiveté, must understand, but the function of understanding is to make it possible for us to believe once again.

All that Ricoeur says about metaphorical language applies to models, for he sees models as metaphors redescribing reality. The New Testament parables are models whose distinctive redescription of reality is the *tension* introduced between their perspective and our usual way of looking at things. A whole new way of looking at life—a way characterized by the logic of superabundance rather than of salvation by works—is introduced by the parables as models.[32] Ricoeur's interest, however, is not mainly in models as comprehensive ordering grids for theology. He does not deal with models above the level of parables. While his understanding of the relations between primary and secondary language, as well as his view of the theologian as hermeneut, are to my mind essentially right, he does not deal specifically with the function of models in detail.

The only theologian in recent times who has focused specifically on models as uniting metaphorical and conceptual language is Ian Ramsey. While he relies on scientific understandings of models and specifically on the work of Max Black, like Ricoeur, he sees the main function of models not at the systematic but at the experiential level. Unlike Ricoeur, he does not focus on parabolic models that redescribe reality in terms of a new way of being in the world, but on models of God-talk that bring God's presence near and give meaning to talk about God. For both Ricoeur and Ramsey, the emphasis is nonetheless on ways of experiencing, although for Ricoeur what matters is a relationship of a specific kind between the divine and the human, whereas for Ramsey what counts is empirically based meaningful talk about the divine. This is an important difference and each perspective contributes something critical to models as a special form of metaphorical and conceptual language. Ricoeur's contribution lies in his insistence that theological models focus on relationships; Ramsey's contribution in his insistence that theological models must both arise from empirical experience and be shown to be appropriate to it. Both of these elements are key factors in an adequate view of models, although what is lacking in both is movement from the experiential to the systematic level.

Ramsey's work is impressive and convincing, in part because he takes with utmost seriousness the contemporary problem of the absence of God and the seeming irrelevance of talk about God. In his analysis of the crisis of contemporary theology he writes: "First, there is the loss of a sense of God's presence; and secondly, there is a growing inability to see the point of theological discourse. We have become—for whatever reasons—insensitive to God; and theology—not God—has died on us. Theology seems often to the outsider just so much word-spinning, air-borne discourse which never touches down except disastrously."[33] It is precisely "word-spinning, air-borne discourse" that Ramsey wishes to abolish from theology, and models appear to him the way to do it. Models are principally ways of talking meaningfully and appropriately about God: God as First Cause, as infinitely wise, as infinitely good, as creator *ex nihilo*, as eternal purpose. In each of these phrases there is an empirical, concrete image such as cause, wise, or good (which is the metaphor or model, the grid or screen that licenses talk about God) and there is a conceptual qualifier such as "infinitely" or "eternal" that protects the model from anthropomorphism and idolatry. Such talk about God is meaningful, says Ramsey, because it is based in empirical experiences of goodness, wisdom, and causation which we understand *and* it is appropriate because the qualifiers keep our God-talk from reducing the divine to the level of our models. Hence, metaphor and concept work together to create both meaningful and appropriate language about God.

Ramsey believes, moreover, that models for God arise out of moments of cosmic disclosure in which we intuit the language to use for God through ordinary natural and personal events. For example, talk about God as Holy Spirit is anchored in concrete experiences of winds and gales which, through reflection and heightening, become revelatory occasions of a spirit that is both like and unlike winds and gales. The qualifier "holy" insures that "spirit" will not be merely a superwind, while the model "spirit" insures that "holy" will not render talk about God meaningless in terms of ordinary experience. Ramsey also insists that our models (with their qualifiers) be tested for empirical "fit" or appropriateness with other aspects of our experience, that they make sense in life and in the interpretation of life. Models of God arise from cosmic disclosures, which are mediated through natural, personal, conceptual, or moral experiences, and by transcending these experiences, one comes to a moment of insight where one sees something about God. Models of God return to ordinary life as appropriate forms for living a committed existence under the God who has been disclosed as infinitely wise, eternally good, First Cause, and so on. Ramsey's position on models forms an arc—from experience to language and back to experience. It begins in insight and ends in commitment, but the beginning and the ending are empirically based.

It is evident that there are significant similarities in his position with Thomas Aquinas's view of analogical predication of God. As one commentator says of Ramsey's models: "One is neither limited to talking about God in exclusively empirical terms (anthropomorphic univocation) nor forced to talk of Him in non-empirical terms (metaphysical equivocation)."[34] Aquinas as an Aristotelian was also an empiricist, believing divine predication must be based in concrete reality; since God is the cause of all that is, however, it is possible to predicate certain features from the creation of the creator, although *how* these qualities pertain to God we do not know. Aquinas insisted only that God realized them in the manner proportional to the divine being; thus, they were appropriately qualified and protected from idolatry. Ramsey, while not an Aristotelian or a Thomist, is, in his empiricism, brother to both, and it is his insistence that models be empirically anchored at their beginning in insight and at their ending in confirmation that is his greatest contribution.

We have arrived finally at the most difficult part of our attempt to see how models uniquely embody both metaphorical and conceptual language. It is time to take stock of the juncture at which we have arrived and where we have yet to go. It should be evident that metaphorical and conceptual languages in theology cannot be absorbed into each other or remain entirely distinct from one another: they are and always have been "colleagues," with both the mutual dependence and admiration, as well as slight suspicion and jealousy, characteristic of colleagues. Both Ricoeur and Ramsey have been helpful in stressing different aspects of this relationship, but neither of them gets to the heart of the matter. Ricoeur, in my opinion, comes closer than does Ramsey, for he understands models —the New Testament parables—as stories concerned with relationships between the divine and the human, while Ramsey understands models— qualified definitions of God—as descriptions of the divine nature. The first view is basically dynamic, process-oriented, relational; the second is more static, substance-oriented, descriptive.

One of the principal insights we gained from studying scientific models was that they focus not on picturing entities but on comparing and contrasting processes, relations, and structures. The contemporary assumption operative not only in science but in many other fields as well is that "entities," whether personal selves or physical phenomena, exist only in relationships and that the process or network of relationships is more basic than the "substantial individual." Or the individual achieves being, its ontological status, through its acts in relationship to the network in which it exists.[35] This is not to deny individuality or personhood (or, in scientific terms, the reality of physical phenomena), but only to emphasize that, as the existentialists would say, "we are what we do." Nor does the stress on relationship at the expense of "substance," whether divine or human, introduce a novelty into the Judeo-Christian tradition, for as we have seen, both the covenant in the Old Testament and the parables of the New Testament (as well as Jesus as parable) are relational at their core. Israel "existed" only in its loyalty to its covenant with God; the characters in the New Testament parables and Jesus himself "exist" only to the extent that they are responsive to the new way of being in the world that relies utterly on God's graciousness.

If this is the case, then the central role of models in theology is to provide grids or screens for interpreting this relationship between the divine and the human. Theological models are dominant metaphors with systematic, comprehensive potential for understanding the many facets of this relationship. Metaphors could not do this alone, for the relationship is a network or structure with too many intricate implications. In order to interpret this relationship, conceptual clarity and precision is necessary: the structure implied in the relationship must be sorted out and its implications for personal, historical, social, and political life made manifest. Concepts could not do this alone, for the relationship is too complex, rich, and multivalent for univocal concepts to define; it needs the simplification of complementary metaphors with their expansive detail to intimate this relationship. The attitudinal and behavioral influence of metaphors (which abstract concepts never have) is needed as well in order to express the power of this transforming relationship. Thus, metaphorical and conceptual language must participate in interpreting this relationship and we see this process occurring in a unique way in models.

It is the case, I believe, that models have been used principally this way in theology. While the common assumption may be that models are meant mainly, as in Thomas Aquinas or Ian Ramsey, for talking about the *nature* of God (a substance orientation), in fact, the critical models of the great theologians—their root-metaphors—are not about God or about human beings, but are concerned with the relationship between them. The basic insight in Paul's theology is justification through grace by faith; in Augustine's, it is the radical dependence of all that is on God alone; in Aquinas's, it is the analogy of being in which each creature participates in and glorifies God through realizing its own proper finite end; in Martin Luther's, it is Paul's once again; in John Calvin's, it is the sovereignty of God over all that lives and breathes; in Friedrich Schleiermacher's, it is the feeling of absolute dependence on God; in Karl Barth's, it is the election of all to salvation in the election of Jesus Christ; in Paul Tillich's, it is the ultimate concern hidden in all penultimate concerns. Each of these is a translation of the relationship between the divine and the human projected in the parabolic stories of the kingdom and in Jesus as parable of God. They do not use that language and all may not be appropriate translations, but the crucial point is that a form of that relationship as understood by each theologian is the central model, the root-metaphor, of his theology. My summaries of those models are in conceptual form, but the theologies themselves are a complex of metaphorical and conceptual language attempting to intimate the basic relationship which, as in the New Testament, *cannot be captured either in metaphors or concepts*, although both are necessary—the one to express its complexity and richness, the other to sort out its implications in the most comprehensive way possible.

Within this root-metaphor of the relationship between the divine and the human for which there can be no model or even any "super model," many models will develop, some with more dominant and permanent status than others. One enduring model in the Judeo-Christian tradition has been that of "person," since the heart of the root-metaphor is the relationship between the divine and the human. We imagine God in our image, even as Genesis says we were created in the divine image. This dominant model need not and ought not to be interpreted in a static, substantialist sense, in that the Bible sees personal life as relational from beginning to end. Hence, the traditional divine attributes of will, intellect, unity, love, and so on should be understood not as qualities of the divine being as such, but as conceptual abstractions from the relationship of God with the created order. Likewise, the trinitarian doctrine is a conceptual attempt not to circumscribe the divine being in an absolute, static formula (nor have theologians usually understood it to be that), but to delineate the implications of the relational root-metaphor with the help of some models, albeit usually paternal ones.

It is evident that if the function of models is to interpret relationships and not picture entities, two implications follow. First, models of different kinds will appear in theology—some very concrete and particular, others much more abstract and general. Thus, some will tend toward the metaphorical pole such as "friend," "liberator," "mother," while others will turn toward the conceptual pole such as "providence," "redemption," "creation." The behavior associated with the relational metaphors will be generalized by conceptual analysis into far-reaching models of divine and human activity. The potential for concrete, detailed expansion of the metaphorical models will be generalized into conceptual models. For example, the network of relations in the model of God as "healer" (disease, frailty, death, wholeness, and so on) will be exploited conceptually in a model of "salvation," with wide applicability for interpreting the human condition, but always dependent for its vitality and power on the metaphorical models that fund it. Theology, in a significant sense, is a hierarchy of interrelated models of varying degrees of concreteness and abstraction. Theology begins with a root-metaphor and ends in an ordering, comprehensive system, but even the system, while different from the metaphors that fund it, is or should be on a continuum with them. At the very least, theology should be concerned with the kind of relationship between God and humanity that distinguishes Christianity and it should retain the metaphorical tension that insists that all human constructions are relative, tentative, and indirect.

Second, and of great importance, *many* models will be necessary both to express and to interpret the complexity and richness of the divine-human relationship. We recall that in the New Testament no definition of the kingdom of God is given; what we have are models or exemplifications of it, none of which tells us what it is, but each of which shows us, by means of a brief drama, the way of the kingdom. No *one* of the parables is adequate alone, and even all together they do not add up to a definition of the kingdom. Rather, models of various human relationships—fathers and sons, judges and penitents, kings and subjects, employers and workers, landlords and tenants, rich and poor people, religious and non-religious individuals—are grids through which the new relationship of the kingdom is intimated. The relational metaphors of the parables are taken from the common life of the times; they complement one another in the sense that they are all partial ways of interpreting the relationship. The riot of metaphors in primary religious language is sorted out through dominant models that achieve ascendancy within the tradition, and in that process something is gained and something lost. The gain is interpretive consensus; the loss is expressive richness and variety.

As we have seen, the dominant model through which the church has interpreted the root-metaphor of life in relationship to God is a personal one, and specifically, a paternal one. If theology is to maintain continuity with its metaphorical base, however, then the question must be asked whether that model or any model should be allowed such status; that is, to put it positively, are not other models necessary both to interpret aspects of the relationship screened out by the paternal model, and to retain in theology the metaphorical tension that insists upon the relativity and tentativeness of all religious and theological language? A truly metaphorical theology will encourage a variety of interpretive models in order to be in continuity with its relational, tensive parabolic base. Life according to the rule of God is too complex, rich, and varied to be captured in any one model and any model so elevated is bound to become idolatrous. Since the root-metaphor of Christianity—the kingdom of God—is a *relationship*, models are not mutually exclusive or contradictory descriptions of divine and/or human *nature*. Many religious people are hesitant about several models or new models because they invariably think of them as picture models, as descriptions of God or human nature. One of the great advantages of seeing the root-metaphor of Christianity in relational terms is that it frees one from such inflexibility and potential idolatry. Thus if God is not seen *to be* "father," but "father" is understood as *one* model through which we interpret our relationship with God, then I suspect many people would feel comfortable about interpreting that relationship through other models as well, including a maternal model. That is to say, if the model is understood in relational rather than substantialist terms—that God acts toward us in a "fatherly way"—then many people could reconcile that model with God also acting toward us in a "motherly way." The network or structure of relationships involved in these models and the commonplaces associated with them are what is central, not the ontological assertion that God *is* "father" or "mother."

But even personal models, which are dominant both in the Bible and in the tradition, are not adequate to express the divine-human relationship. One of the great strengths of the Judeo-Christian tradition has been its interpretation of the God-world relationship in personalistic categories. A genuinely metaphorical theology, however, recognizes the limitations of *all* models and abjures a "super model," such as the personal one is often assumed to be in this tradition. God is not a "person" or "personal" as such; this model does not cease to be a metaphor merely because it is a more inclusive model than many others in the tradition. Nor can it escape relativism by the assertion that it is based on the life of a person, Jesus of Nazareth, the acknowledged focus of revelation for Christians. *No models are adequate.* Such "radical monotheism" ought to open Christians and Westerners to models of the God-world relationship from non-Christian and especially Eastern sources, where, for instance, both the immanence of the divine and relationship with the natural world are emphasized in a way that they are not in the West. In sum, the emphasis on *modeling relationships* rather than *defining natures* frees theology to entertain, interpret, and criticize many different models, some implicit but not dominant within the Christian tradition, as well as others that have not been part of the tradition.

Theological models, then, are a unique combination of metaphorical and conceptual language that provide grids or screens for interpreting the relationship between the divine and the human as manifest in the root-metaphor of Christianity. Given the nature of this root-metaphor as a relationship of a certain kind which can never be possessed, tension will qualify all modeling attempts. Thus, *many* models, both dominant and subsidiary, as well as many *kinds* of models (some more metaphorical and others more conceptual) will constitute a Christian theology. This summary points to a further characteristic of theology: its "theories" will always be wedded to models—there can be no absolute separation of the conceptual from the metaphorical. The reason for this should be self-evident: the unfamiliar and inexpressible can only be imaged in the familiar and expressible. Thus, theological concepts will always need metaphors and models.

The trinity is probably the most abstract and conceptual of Christian doctrines; it was hammered out with the aid of Greek philosophical concepts and much of its language tends toward the univocity of concepts in an attempt to be as precise as possible. This is as it should be, but it is noteworthy that the "persons" of the trinity (which is, of course, model language) are always expressed in one or another set of models: Father, Son, Holy Spirit, or Creator, Redeemer, Sustainer. Augustine's analysis of the trinity is especially interesting in this regard, for he realized that without the metaphors all one has is the abstract notion of "three-in-one." It is the metaphors involved in the processes of remembering and loving which provide explanation for that abstraction, which give it meaning. In a theological doctrine the model is not dispensable but is ingredient in the theory. For instance, in Karl Barth's doctrine of election it is not possible to separate the theory from the metaphor; rather, "election" is a model with both metaphorical and conceptual characteristics which provide a comprehensive ordering scheme for interpreting the relationship between the divine and the human.[36] One can and should analyze and criticize the model as well as sort out its many implications, but its emergent theoretical generalizations depend on the exploitable details of the model of election. The generalizations must, therefore, return frequently to the model for fresh insight as well as renewed power. This is not to say, of course, that concepts are the same as metaphors; on the contrary, it is only to remind ourselves that models combine *both* languages and that theology's special asset (as well as liability) is to be permanently and intrinsically linked to models.

The assets of this relationship are powerful: theology, when properly done, never becomes empty abstraction, never loses the thread that ties it to its metaphoric, parabolic base. Thus, theology, while becoming a system and ordering life in the world under God in as comprehensive a fashion as possible, undertakes its task through models of illuminating and persuasive power. It is not a concession to necessity alone that causes the theologian to wed concept to metaphor in the form of models, but also an awareness that this *kind* of conceptual thinking has a beauty, brings insight, and changes lives in ways abstractions alone cannot. Moreover, the great theologians are great because they know instinctively that their visions of Christianity—their root-metaphors—can be properly interpreted conceptually only by a continuous funding from a metaphorical base.

However, there are liabilities as well. When theology has gone astray it is usually not due to the root-metaphors but to the models that have been used to interpret the root-metaphors, especially when one model has become dominant—absolute or exclusive—at the expense of others. The model then moves in the direction of the univocity of the concept, forgetting its relativity and open-endedness as a metaphor. A model is a liability when it becomes an idol, when its ordering, comprehensive ability becomes identified with what it is modeling. While a model does have and ought to have more stability and permanency than a metaphor, it is still necessary to remember—even with the tradition's most favored models —the sensibility of the Hebrew poet who "sucked the juice out of each metaphor . . . and threw the skin away at once." Augustine had that sensibility when he said that our alternatives when speaking religiously were either to use our inadequate, limping language or be silent; Aquinas displays it when he said his entire theological work was as "straw"; Barth also illustrates it with his remark that doing theology is like trying to paint a bird in flight. The balancing act involved in proper theological reflection is a difficult one. The theologian must take his or her models with utmost seriousness, exploiting them for all their interpretive potential and yet, at the same time, realize they are little more than the babble of infants. The mystics, those to whom prayer is the center of life, know this, and as a consequence, their religious metaphors are the richest, least conventional, and most imaginative—and they never absolutize them.

The two most important safeguards against absolutizing models are the context in which theology must finally be carried on and the goal of theology. The most basic context (although not the working context) of theology ought to be worship, for the reason the mystics display. In prayer one knows the inadequacy of all one's images; as Simone Weil says in *Waiting for God*, "I am quite sure there is no God in the sense that I am sure there is nothing which resembles what I can conceive when I say that word." Prayer also is the source of new metaphors, as Augustine's prayer life and the rich religious imagery that emerged from it in the *Confessions* amply illustrate. The goal of theology also serves as a safeguard against the liabilities of models, for with Ricoeur and Ramsey, I would see the point of Christian theological interpretation as not the creation of a complete conceptual system for its own sake, but helping people to encounter more fully and perceptively the new way of being in the world exemplified in the parables and Jesus as parable. This is not to say that the theologian's working goal is religious encounter. But when theologians reflect on *why* they are involved in such reflection, the answer ought to come close to Anselm of Canterbury's aphorism that we understand in order to believe (the hermeneutical circle, of course, demands the obverse as well). Theologians are not preachers, but in different ways both would properly claim that intelligibility is in the service of experience and not for its own sake. The new way of being in the world—the way of the kingdom—is the final goal of all workers in the church.

The Truth of Theological Models

Underlying our discussion of models, both in science and theology, two unanswered questions remain. We must consider the hesitations that all users of models have and finally must face: Everything said about models may be fine and interesting but are they *true*? Are models merely desperate attempts to say *something* when we do not know what else to say, or do they in some sense refer to the way things are? Also, why choose some models over others? What makes some models better than others—are there objective criteria or are models a matter of taste? These questions, however, do not take us by surprise, for we have said from the beginning that the outstanding characteristic of metaphor is its tensive "is and is not." Metaphor has a positive as well as a negative pole and the positive pole is an assertion, albeit an indirect one, of reference to reality. That reference is, however, not only indirect but redescriptive; that is, metaphorical construction refers to reality both in the sense of creation as well as discovery. The epistemology that lies behind this statement is, of course, "critical realism," and it is, as we recall, the view not only of high-view supporters of models in science but also of Ian Ramsey and Paul Ricoeur.[37] Constructive thinkers in any field (poetry, religion, philosophy, science, political theory, and so forth) are critical realists to the extent they believe that all perception and interpretation is metaphorical—that is, indirect (seeing or interpreting "this" as "that")—and who also hold that their constructions are not heuristic fictions but discoveries of some aspect of the structure of reality. Moreover, all critical realists will claim that their metaphors and models are not merely a matter of personal preference, but can be better substantiated than the alternatives. These bold assertions must now be supported if the status of theological models is to be secured.

Philosopher of science Max Wartofsky suggests that there is an implied truth claim in all models.

> If the argument runs: "I don't really take the entities in the model to exist, but it is useful to think of them that way . . . ," then I would raise the question as to what makes it useful to think of it that way at all, if there were not some sense in which the model mirrored some aspect of what it is taken to be a model of. In short, the existence claim of a model may be limited in scope or applicability . . . but to deny it such a claim makes a mystery of its significance altogether.[38]

The physicist Max Born supports this view when he writes: "All great discoveries in experimental physics have been due to the intuition of men who made free use of models which were for them not mere products of the imagination but representations of real things."[39]

Not all scientists, however, are critical realists, nor are all theologians. A brief survey of other options on the status of models in science by Ian Barbour will help to place critical realism in perspective; the types are as appropriate for theology as they are for science.[40] Barbour notes four options: naive realism, positivism, instrumentalism, and critical realism. In *naive realism,* theories (doctrines in theology) are accurate descriptions of the world in itself with the consequence that models are taken literally as replicas of the world. Theological fundamentalists would be covered by this type. In *positivism* observation alone counts, while theoretical concepts are merely convenient categories for classifying observations. Hence, models can be dismissed since theories can be inferred directly from observations by inductive generalization. Biblical literalists resemble positivists in their reliance on "empirical data"—biblical texts—and their disregard for interpretive categories, whether conceptual or metaphorical. *Instrumentalists* hold that theories and models are not to be judged either as true or false but merely as useful or not useful. In this view models are heuristic fictions, useful in limited ways as temporary psychological aids in the formation of a theory, but finally dispensable. This position, supported by Richard Braithwaite and at one time by Stephen Toulmin, is widespread in science; it gives a place for models, but adheres fairly rigorously to the importance of both theories and observation statements in contrast to models. I am aware of no direct correlate in theology for instrumentalism, although the widespread skepticism in some forms of liberal theology— the turn to experience and ethical behavior—as seen in different ways in such theologians as Friedrich Schleiermacher and Albrecht Ritschl as well as in evangelical pietism, is evidence of a sensibility that is reluctant to make ontological claims for the models and doctrines of Christian faith. Finally, *critical realists* claim that while all theories and models are partial and inadequate, the scientist discovers as well as creates: "They hold that there are entities in the world something like those described in the model; they believe there is some isomorphism between the model and the real structures of the world."[41] Critical realists, whether scientific or theological, will claim that while all constructs (models) are human and indirect and hence relative, nature (for the scientists) and the divine-human relationship (for the theologian) "is such as to bear description in some ways and not others."[42]

This, however, is only a beginning. If we grant that all serious users of models believe, at least to some degree, that their models refer to reality, we must also ask in what *way* do they refer? The clue is in the indirection of models—their reference through what Max Black calls a grid or screen. That is, they *redescribe* reality; the reference is not to reality as ordinarily or conventionally understood, but, both in science and theology (as well as in poetry and other fields), something *new* is being said about reality which the user of the model believes describes it better, more appropriately, than the accepted views. We recall, and this point must be strongly emphasized, that a metaphorical view insists that there is no uninterpreted access to reality; hence, we are not dealing, on the one hand, with "reality as it is" and, on the other hand, with views of it; but solely with the latter. We are dealing with old and new, accepted and unconventional, views of reality.

We also recall that models, whether scientific or theological, are not concerned with picturing objects but with interpreting an unfamiliar structure of relationships in terms of a more familiar network. Therefore, to see basic atomic units as "waves" is to interpret their behavior in terms characteristic to the activity of waves; likewise, to see the kingdom through a parable is to interpret life in the kingdom in terms of the structure of relationships we discern in the parable. The emphasis on relationship is critical at this point because metaphorical reference, whether scientific or theological, is not concerned with picturing objects but with understanding modes or patterns of relationship. For science, these patterns are the ones which are pertinent to relations intrinsic to physicial phenomena; for theology, they are ones pertinent to ways of being in the world.

If we say, then, that theological models are redescriptions of reality in the sense that they offer new ways of being in the world, let us examine how this mode of reference operates. Paul Ricoeur is helpful when he compares the way models refer with the way Aristotle understood poetic reference.[43] Poetry, according to Aristotle, is an imitation of human actions, but only through its own tale, its own *mythos*. It, like a model, organizes and redescribes human reality: "This metaphoricity consists in describing a less-known domain—human reality—in the light of relationships within a fictitious but better-known domain—the tragic tale—utilizing all the strengths of 'systematic deployability' contained in that tale."[44] The story functions as a model, creating a new world which, while not a copy of the conventional world, is related to it in the sense of being a redescription of it. The new world of the work of art is tested for its truth by a number of criteria, some internal and some external, among them its coherence, comprehensiveness, and consistency; its fruitfulness for living; its fit with experience; its profundity; its compatibility with other models of human life, and so forth.

The heart of metaphorical reference, as Ricoeur insists, is summarized in the aphorism "is and is not."[45] Models do not refer directly to reality; they are not copies of it. Yet they do refer indirectly through their own interpretive glasses, and the reality to which they refer is concerned with relationship, with ways of being in the world. To see how this process of re-description works in a theological model, let us look at Psalm 23.

> The Lord is my shepherd; I shall want nothing.
>> He makes me lie down in green pastures,
> and he leads me beside waters of peace;
>> he renews life within me,
> and for his name's sake guides me in the right path.
> Even though I walk through a valley dark as death
> I fear no evil, for thou art with me,
> thy staff and thy crook are my comfort.
>
> Thou spreadest a table for me in the sight of my enemies;
>> thou has richly bathed my head with oil,
>> and my cup runs over.
> Goodness and love unfailing, these will follow me
>> all the days of my life,
>> and I shall dwell in the house of the Lord
>> my whole life long.
>> —*The New English Bible*

While the choice of this particular Psalm for illustrating how models rede-scribe life in the world, given its archaic and, to our minds, demeaning metaphor of "sheep" for human existence, may appear unfortunate if not counterproductive, I believe it has much to commend it. For one thing, the Psalm presents a sustained, extended metaphor with great economy and thus will illustrate metaphorical reference in brief compass. Moreover, the tone of the entire Psalm is not one of sheeplike ineptitude, but rather of profound gratitude for divine solicitude and comfort. The principal model is the Lord as "shepherd," not people as "sheep." It is also note-worthy that the characteristics associated with shepherding are very similar to those associated with maternal imagery for God in the Old Testament: renewal, comfort, physical nurture, care, guidance, compassion. Hence, the shepherd model joins with maternal imagery as part of a suppressed tradi-tion in Scripture over against the dominant patriarchal, monarchical imagery. It also has obvious links with the liberator model in Luke 4:31–44 in its concern for relief of suffering to the downtrodden: "To proclaim release for prisoners and recovery of sight for the blind; to let the broken victims go free." For these reasons it seems to be an excellent example for our purposes; in any event, it presents only *one model* for expressing cer-tain aspects of relating to God—many others are needed as well.

Obviously the Psalm is a redescription. The Lord is seen through the screen of "shepherd" and life with the Lord is interpreted by means of commonplaces associated with activities of shepherds toward their charges: adequate food and water, guidance for the strays, protection from danger. The principal model of shepherding and the supporting metaphors are not meant to be taken literally (the Lord is not a shepherd and life with the Lord is not really being cared for as sheep are), and yet the Lord *is* being described as a shepherd here and that interpretation presents to the reader a possible new way of envisioning life with the Lord. That the description does not merely refer to shepherd and sheep but to a redescription of life in the world is evident from the multivalency of the supporting metaphors —"waters of peace," "renews life," "the right path," "valley dark as death," "thy staff and thy crook are my comfort." On one level, the images are concrete and literal. The reader must grasp the conventional, commonplace meaning of water, life, path, valley, staff, green pastures, and so forth in order to appreciate the rich detail of shepherding as a model for life with the Lord. One has to say both that the model "is and is not": one must both acknowledge the literal reference and suspend it, for the primary reference here is to a new way of being in the world with the Lord, but this way is available to us *through* the model of shepherding. Douglas Berggren describes the tension of the metaphorical "is and is not" as "stereo-scopic vision," and Ricoeur explains this double vision when he says: "In the same way as the metaphorical sense not only abolishes but preserves the literal sense, the metaphorical reference maintains the ordinary vision in tension with the new one it suggests."[46] This view of metaphors and models as interactive means, of course, that both parties are affected; not only is the Lord and life with the Lord redescribed through the model of shepherding, but shepherding is changed, elevated, and enhanced by being the model for life with the Lord.

The important point that Ricoeur is making when he insists that tensive, interactive metaphors and models are critical to all forms of constructive interpretation, whether scientific or theological, is that such metaphors and models *do* refer to reality, but as redescriptions of it. That redescription depends upon being conscious of the literal reference of the models but always in tension with their primary reference that provides the reinterpretation. Thus, in the Twenty-third Psalm one does not have a new interpretation apart from the model of shepherding, yet the interpretation cannot be reduced in a literal way to shepherding. A transformation has occurred through the stereoscopic vision of the model which looks in two directions, both back to the literal reference and forward to the new reference. One sees life with the Lord *through* the model of shepherding but never identifies the two; one redescribes reality now in these terms but knows it is not a literal description.

It is obvious that the redescription of reality by models in science and in theology is of a different sort. While both may be said finally to refer to a common world, the world of ordinary experience, the interpretations via scientific models refer to the deep structures—the networks of relationship —of that world in one way, while theological models refer to the deep structures of that world in another way. To see atomic particles as "waves" is one way to penetrate beneath conventional reality; to see life under the rule of God is another way to envision the structure of reality beneath our common world. Both are redescriptions of reality, one concerned with the basic structures of physical phenomena, the other with the basic structures of human existence. Critical realists in both science and theology would claim that their models which interpret these relational networks are both discovered and created. As Ricoeur says, "It would seem that the enigma of metaphorical discourse is that it 'invents' in both senses of the word: what it creates, it discovers; and what it finds, it invents."[47]

Criteria for Theological Models

It should be evident that no *one* model, whether scientific or theological, is able to interpret adequately the networks of relationships that constitute the world, whether these be the structures intrinsic to physical phenomena or to human existence. The complexity of the subject matter makes such pretension impossible: metaphorical thinking is an acknowledgement of multiple interpretations and relativism in dealing with our world at this level. Therefore, the criteria for our choice of models, for adequate and inadequate models, for dominant models, for the criticism of models, for the introduction of new models, are the critical issue. Our concerns, both with the idolatry of some theological models and with the irrelevance of others, demand that we deal with these criteria very seriously.

The dialectic of discovery and creation in models means that when we turn to our final question, the issue of criteria for theological models, we confront a complex situation in which both empirical and systematic categories are involved. That is to say, as Ian Barbour notes when one judges the adequacy of models, one moves both "from the bottom up" and "from the top down," although in theology, unlike science, greater influence comes from the top down. Nonetheless, "evidence" is advanced for theological models, for as Barbour insists, "one cannot prove one's most fundamental beliefs, but one can try to show how they function in the interpretation of experience."[48] We will try to trace these two movements from the top down and the bottom up, but as we begin we must recall that no model, whether in science or religion, is ever evaluated by itself apart from the network in which it appears. Models are paradigm-dependent—there is no innocent eye; hence, the principal criterion for judging a model, even in science, is not whether it corresponds with the "facts," but whether it fits in the schema of "facts" as understood by a given paradigm. In other words, the pattern predominates over the facts, for it is the only way that facts are accessible to us. Barbour's statement on this point, while it refers to concepts, would also include models in theology because of the intrinsic relationship between theological doctrines and models.

> It was stated that science is not primarily a search for facts, *but a search for pattern:* scientific theories order experience intelligibly. Religious concepts also result in an intelligible ordering of experience, though the relevant experience is more closely related to the personal lives of subjects. It will be recalled that scientific concepts and theories can be *tested only in networks.* Webs of interdependent constructs are evaluated as total systems. The fabric of interlocking religious beliefs must also be contextually tested; ideas of God, self, society and nature are not independent. An interpretive scheme is evaluated indirectly by the convergence of many lines of inquiry.[49]

We start, then, from the top down, with the network of interrelated models that makes up the Christian paradigm and the theologies that have emerged from it. The first and most basic thing to say about this network is that it breaks the silence; it allows us to speak; it makes us articulate about the mysterious. This is nothing more than a gesture of appreciation toward models, for their fecundity and their complex extensions which allow us, as the metaphors of the psalmists allowed them, to talk about the divine-human relationship endlessly, richly, exuberantly. Whatever criticisms one may level against particular models, it would be small-minded and ungrateful not to praise models as loosening our tongues to express, however inadequately, the inexpressible.

The Christian paradigm, we have suggested, derives from the root-metaphor of the kingdom or rule of God, a relationship between the divine and the human characterized by disorientation toward conventional securities and reorientation toward security in God alone. Such a relationship is intrinsically tensive and it is, we contend, based in the parables and in Jesus as parable of God. The Bible is the classic text modeling this relationship and as such is the foundational text for Christians. It is authoritative because it models this relationship; Christians have given it authority and continue to do so because the divine-human relationship it models impinges in profound ways upon their experience of being in the world. Once again we see the inevitability of the hermeneutical circle: we believe in order to understand and we understand in order to believe. The translations of this root-metaphor from Scripture which surface in theologies ranging over two thousand years are far too complex and varied for us to comment on here. As we have noted several times, however, the dominant model of Christianity is a personal, relational one: the divine and the human have been envisioned in terms of responsible interaction. Personal models of all sorts, although principally hierarchical, monarchical, and patriarchal ones, have predominated and have formed a comprehensive explanatory system that constitutes the Christian paradigm.

In the next chapter we criticize this paradigm in detail, but now we are concerned with general criteria for assessing models that constitute such a system, in other words, criteria "from the top down." One reason the great theologians are great—in addition to their faithfulness to the root-metaphor of the classic text of Christianity—is that they offer total, well-integrated, aesthetically satisfying systems derived from expanding the implications of that root-metaphor. For example, the traditional *loci* or doctrines of Christianity (creation, sin, salvation, God, anthropology, church, and so forth) deal with dimensions of the divine-human relationship and they deal with these issues in a connected way that makes sense of them internally. Models are critical in this process for it is models, to a large extent, that provide the unity. In the hierarchical, patriarchal, monarchical model—God relating to human beings as father, lord, or king—we can readily see how a pattern of interlocking models is formed: how multimodel discourse can emerge, how models can be cross-plotted, how models can mutually qualify each other, how dominant models covering a wider range of language subsume other models under them.[50] The major models of a theology provide the framework for envisioning the whole network with supporting models which lend substance and detail to the total system. A theology is indeed a network, principally a network of dominant and subsidiary models, and it is this network as a whole that must finally be judged adequate or inadequate.

The need for such internal consistency and comprehensiveness suggest two criteria for a theological system which are especially appropriate from the perspective of metaphorical theology. First, the models in a theology must be of a similar or complementary type. The major models of a theology and, in fact, of an entire theological tradition, must share characteristics which identify them as belonging to the same syndrome. The models of the divine-human relationship in the Western theological tradition are largely personal and positive. They emerge from central human experiences of healing, restoration, guidance, protection, liberation, and so on. Thus, the models of God as father, protector, healer, savior, and their theological elaboration into the doctrines of creation and redemption are of a piece. They "fit together" in such a way that one could not imagine also calling God jailer, destroyer, or devil. Hence, diametrically opposed or contrary models cannot be introduced into a theological system, but complementary models can and should be. Yet, as we have seen, the Christian theological and liturgical traditions have tended to narrow the syndrome of acceptable models in comparison with the much richer and more varied Hebrew base. As a consequence, they have moved toward an idolization of certain models. The Western theological tradition need not cling to its narrow base of modeling God as father, lord, and king in order to fulfill the criterion of similar or complementary models. Models of God as mother, lover, liberator, and friend (to name but four relational models of primary importance to human beings) *complement* the traditional models in ways that are needed in order to express dimensions of the divine-human relationship *not* expressed in the model of God as father.

A second criterion suggested by the requirements of consistency and comprehensiveness is the ability of models to cope with anomalies, with "contra-factors."[51] Are there events, factors, experiences with which the models cannot deal, or can speak to only superficially and with considerable strain? Is the theology skewed because of its reliance on one model or on a defective model, and does the evidence for this inadequacy emerge because of the hegemony of a model that is being forced beyond its limit? A classic example of this situation is Calvin's attempt to stretch the model of election into the doctrine of double predestination in order to explain the fact that not all human beings respond to the gift of salvation. Barth rightly criticizes this position, insisting that the model of election cannot explain human perversity. The Jewish Holocaust is another event that has placed considerable strain on traditional models of evil, creating anomalies for the Christian paradigm which have no systematic, comprehensive answers. The feminist critique, with its insistence that Christianity excludes the experience of women and images of women, also presents a current serious anomaly for that tradition.

Anomalies—events, factors, and experiences which strain a theology beyond its ability to cope—are, perhaps, the most serious criteria for assessing a system. Theologies, like scientific paradigms, will continue to function and gain support as long as the anomalies can be endured. In fact, the scientific community will accept fairly serious anomalies in its central paradigm, if the system is otherwise comprehensive and fruitful. One gives up the ordering pattern, whether scientific or theological, very reluctantly, and then only when another pattern is available which can deal with the contrafactors more adequately. A critical difference, however, between science and theology is that science operates with only *one* central paradigm at a time (i.e., the scientific community does not accept Newtonian and quantum physics simultaneously), whereas many religions (and their theological systems) flourish concurrently. Buddhism is not necessarily "wrong" nor Christianity "right," nor is Thomism passé in relation to process theology. Nonetheless, unless the major theological traditions of whatever religious origin can deal with the most significant perennial as well as contemporary human events and experiences, they prove themselves to be inadequate.

The discussion of anomalies has moved us subtly into external criteria and illustrates clearly that systematic and empirical criteria cannot be kept in separate compartments. Moreover, as important as continuity with Christianity's classic text and internal criteria are, external criteria or criteria "from the bottom up" are just as critical, although they have not usually been so considered. A metaphorical theology, however—one that realizes that all interpretation is relative, tentative, and open-ended—must take all of these criteria into consideration with utmost seriousness. Metaphorical theology cannot assume that it is absolute; its concern both to avoid idolatry and to promote relevance demands careful attention to what Ian Ramsey calls "empirical fit." Models must "fit" with "data," not scientific but human data. Ian Barbour says it succinctly: "One of the functions of models in science is to suggest theories which correlate patterns of observational data. One of the functions of models in religion . . . is to suggest beliefs which correlate patterns in human experience." He suggests further that "religious models . . . serve an 'attention-getting' function, accentuating the patterns we see in the facts."[52] Hence, the broadest and most basic thing to say about the empirical fit of a network of models is that it is illuminating. That is, the language the model gives us—its license for articulation—is not just *any* language, but one that lights up our experience in the world in profound ways. It provides something similar to "the shock of recognition" we get from reading a fine poem or seeing a good play: "Yes," we say, "life is like that"—not life as conventionally lived or usually understood, but at its deepest level, or as it could be, ought to be, might have been. The basic structure of experience is illuminated and we feel the transformation that is the secret of the linkage between discovery and creation at the heart of great poetry and at the heart of great religious traditions.

Such illumination in theology is not just a passing insight, as, for instance, one may derive from a good poetic metaphor. Rather, it provides opportunity for an illuminating system, a pattern of increasing insight that makes sense out of life as a whole. In science one judges such insight in terms of its "epistemic success"; that is, a model or theory is used and continues to be used as long as it keeps providing information about the world, as long as it is fruitful. This is admittedly a pragmatic or quasi-pragmatic criterion, but since no model or concept (if one accepts paradigm-dependence) "pictures" reality, and even scientific facts are tested in networks, there is no alternative to testing models for their illuminating potential. As Frederick Ferré perceptively suggests, however, such illumination carries an implied reality commitment with it.

> But if language literally based on certain models of great religious responsive depth found within human experience is capable not only of synthesizing our concepts in a coherent manner but also of illuminating our experience—moral experience, sense experience, aesthetic experience, religious experience—we may ask *why* this happens to be the case. And if some models are capable of providing greater coherence and adequacy than others, we may begin to suspect that this tells us something not only about the models but also about what reality is like: reality is of such a character that a metaphysical system based on model X is more capable of interpreting our experience and unifying our ideas than a metaphysical system based on model Y.[53]

As this statement illustrates, "illumination" is not principally an aesthetic criterion. When we find that the models of a theological tradition illuminate our experience, we are claiming that they interpret, explain, make sense of that experience. More important still, we are making a judgment that they can make sense of it *because* they refer to reality, because in their own way—that is, partially and indirectly—they are a redescription of it. They are not reality, but a construct or interpretation of it, which must, however, be in some sense isomorphic with reality *or* they would not be able to make much sense out of life as lived.

The isomorphism between scientific models and the reality to which they refer is capable of much more careful testing than is the case with theological models. But even for theology such testing is not totally absent. The isomorphism, or similarity of structure, between our models and the divine-human relationship can certainly never be direct. We do not *know* that our models of father and mother, of liberator and friend, of creator and redeemer, really reflect the structure of the divine-human relationship. At most, we can say that, given our experiences of healing, of liberation, of renewal, and so on, they appear to be apt or appropriate to the most profound dimensions of human existence. Such a statement is, of course, finally a statement of faith, and it can only be made responsibly and convincingly in light of the anomalies, especially the experience of evil in ourselves and in the world, which often, and for some people constantly, appear more real than experiences supporting belief in God. It is no accident and certainly no surprise that most theologies founder on the question of evil, for it is the most constant and serious anomaly to religious belief. Ferré provides a fine summary statement to this brief treatment of criteria for judging the adequacy of theological models:

> As organizing images through which we see ourselves and all things, the powerful images of religion should bring certain aspects of our experience into prominence, should minimize the importance of other aspects, and should throughout function to illuminate our total environment by discovering to us otherwise unnoticed parallelism, analogies, and patterns among our data. They are reliable, and thus candidates for reasonable adoption, to the extent that our experience of life as a whole (not, remember, just specific bits and pieces of experience) is open to organization in this manner without distortion, forcing, or ill fit; and to the extent that the total account of things that they suggest is consistent, unified, and free from uninterpreted disconnections.[54]

In sum, the choice of theological models is neither arbitrary nor absolute; models are selected and survive because they make sense out of human experience. Certainly, they are required to "fit" with our experiences of God, but their range, since they deal with the divine-human relationship in its many implications, goes far beyond any narrow view of that relationship. Major theological models are not merely "religious" but encompass all dimensions of life in the world. Thus, we must demand, if we are to reject a "ghetto Christianity," that these models also fit with and illuminate all ways of looking at the world and all "truths" about life we hold to be significant.

Moreover, a metaphorical theology, which is nonidolatrous but relevant, seeks to see how Christian theological models both differ from and can be illuminated by the models of existence in other religious traditions. Such theology is intrinsically open to other perspectives, aware that none is absolute, but that each may well illuminate aspects of the divine-human relationship that the dominant Christian models screen out. An obvious distortion and inadequacy of the personalistic model of Christianity is its tendency toward supernatural transcendence at the expense of the immanence of God both in human life and in the natural world.[55] The price paid for the hegemony of the hierarchical, monarchical model in this regard is a heavy one indeed: not only has God been removed from us as a distant being in some other world but, also, apparent license has been arrogated by "man" to dominate and destroy the natural environment.

The evidence, then, that one advances for a network of models is of a very broad sort. It does not only include what a believer finds personally illuminating, but also how this network squares with other interpretations of life in the world, such as scientific, political, cultural, and religious views. Of course, one is not seeking to divert all these streams into "the great river of truth," but one does look for points of contact and mutual illumination, because there is no *one* model able to encompass the richness and complexity of the divine-human relationship. Metaphorical theology, in continuity with the prophetic rather than the priestly tradition, believes unity does exist but will be realized only in the future. Here and now there is no certainty, no "closure"; hence, we live intellectually as we live personally, on "the edge of the raft," knowing that our models are *only* models, and while we advance evidence energetically to support them over against other models, we should do so in the spirit of passionate nonchalance, that is, in the spirit of prayer.

5 God the Father: Model or Idol?

Among the criteria advanced for theological models are two of special significance for the issues of idolatry and irrelevance. The first is the necessity for many complementary models to intimate the richness and complexity of the divine-human relationship. If this criterion is not accepted, idolatry results. The second is the ability of the major models of a tradition to cope with anomalies. If this criterion cannot be met, irrelevance occurs. The issues of idolatry and irrelevance come together in the image of God as father, for more than any other dominant model in Christianity, this one has been both absolutized by some and, in recent times, found meaningless by others. The feminist critique of God as father centers on the *dominance* of this one model to the exclusion of others, and on the *failure* of this model to deal with the anomaly presented by those whose experience is not included by this model. It is, therefore, an excellent test case for a metaphorical theology, since its task is to envision ways of talking about the divine-human relationship which, in continuity with the parables and Jesus as parable, are nonidolatrous but relevant. A metaphorical theology, guided by the Protestant sensibility, insists that we will not relinquish our idolatry in religious language unless we are freed from the myth that in order for images to be true they must be literal. It also insists that we will not find religious language relevant unless we are freed from the myth that in order for images to be meaningful they must be traditional.

Much has been written on this model in recent years and it is not our intention to repeat that material here;[1] rather, we wish to assess both the power and the limitations of the model from the perspective of a metaphorical theology as an example of a good model gone astray. In the feminist critique of the model of God as father an anomaly has entered the Christian paradigm, a serious rupture has appeared, and the question is posed whether the paradigm can weather the storm. As we recall, a change in the root-metaphor of a paradigm is a basic change; in a religious tradition such a change, David Tracy suggests, means a new religion.[2] Is the feminist critique of this sort? Does it reach to the root-metaphor of Christianity? Or is the root-metaphor of Christianity not the model of God the father, and are there resources within the Christian paradigm both for limiting that model and for permitting complementary models? These questions will be central ones as we look at the possibilities within Christianity for dealing with one of the most serious and far-reaching criticisms of a dominant model in the history of Christianity. Whether there is revolution or reformation—a new paradigm or a change in the existing paradigm—depends both on the profundity of the basic models of a tradition and a tradition's flexibility in admitting limitations and new options.

It has been the contention of this essay that the root-metaphor of Christianity is not God the father but the kingdom or rule of God, a relationship between the divine and the human that *no* model can encompass. The divine-human relationship, therefore, demands both the limitation of the fatherhood model and the introduction of other models. A theology based in the parables and Jesus as parable does not merely allow many models—models relevant to many different peoples—but *insists* on them. In this way the tension at the heart of metaphorical theology is retained, and only in this way can the unity in which we believe, but do not now possess, be protected against idolatry. What revolutionary feminists have done in their critique of the hegemony of the patriarchal model is to open once again the gates of the religious imagination which for too long have been locked against interpreting the divine-human relationship except in one dominant mode. Like the Christian Gnostics and mystics, their images are sometimes bizarre and sometimes frightening in their unconventionality, for they disrupt our usual ways of seeing. They are radically metaphorical, making connections most people do not make and that many find uncomfortable. The serious anomaly they pose to the tradition and the depths to which they probe it demand careful attention, not only to ask where it may be amiss but also to acknowledge where it is on the mark. At the very least, it seems evident that their insistence both on the limitations of the patriarchal model and the need for other models is a service to Christianity. But even more important, the revolutionary models they imagine can help to remove blinders and widen the field of vision. Few reformations occur without the revolutionaries: they are the visionaries who imagine futures seldom if ever realized, but necessary for any decent present.

In order to assess the patriarchal model along the lines sketched above, we shall first look at the power of this model and reasons for the feminist critique of it. We shall then address the radical feminist alternatives to the model, alternatives which, we shall discover, constitute a paradigm change as well as materials for reformation of the Christian paradigm. We shall also consider resources within the Christian tradition—some of them repressed, some overlooked—that could constitute a significant reformation of the paradigm, a reformation both meaningful to feminists and in continuity with the root-metaphor of Christianity. Finally, we shall suggest a model which appears only marginally in the tradition—God as friend—as a complement to other and more dominant models as well as one relevant to our times.

Patriarchy in Perspective

Mary Daly has written with characteristic economy and force, "If God is male, then the male is God."[3] In spite of its elliptical form, this assertion makes two critical points: God has been modeled in masculine images (excluding feminine ones), and, as a consequence, the notion has arisen that men have godlike attributes. The first point underscores the dominance of such imagery as lord, judge, father, king, master in the Christian tradition, while the second point emphasizes the interactive character of models, that is, the way in which the model and the modeled mutually influence one another.

The substance of the feminist critique of the patriarchal tradition of Christianity has pressed the first point. It can be summed up by two conclusions from Donald Schon in his discussion of tendencies of all dominant metaphors: the "law of maximum expansion" and the "law of least change."[4] By the first he means that dominant metaphors have a tendency to expand to cover as much ground as possible; this is in fact *why* they are dominant—they have the ability to provide comprehensive structure. By the second he means that dominant metaphors have a tendency to resist revision; this is their permanency and stability, an outstanding characteristic of theological models as we have noted. The patriarchal model displays both of these tendencies to a remarkable degree and it is the reason why the model is both so inclusive (as well as exclusive) and long-lasting.

It is therefore a mistake to focus on God the father as a limited model for talk about God; rather, it is patriarchalism—the expanded, intransigent model radical feminists take to be the root-metaphor of Christianity—

that is at issue. As Sheila Collins says, patriarchalism is "a metaphysical world view, a mind-set, a whole way of ordering reality."[5] This root-metaphor refers to "the whole complex of sentiments, the patterns of cognition and behavior, and the assumptions about human nature and the nature of the cosmos that have grown out of a culture in which men have dominated women."[6] At the heart of patriarchalism as root-metaphor is a subject-object split in which man is envisioned over against God and vice versa.[7] God, as transcendent being, is man's superior Other and woman in this hierarchy becomes man's inferior other. From the basic dualism of a righteous God and sinful man, other dualisms develop—mind/body, spirituality/carnality, truth/appearance, life/death—which are projected upon men and women as their "natures," with the feminine becoming "the symbol of the repressed, subjugated and dreaded 'abysmal' side of 'man'."[8] Thus a whole series of "orders of creation," hierarchically arranged, developed in Christianity, a pattern of superior and inferior in which men stood below God, Jesus, and the angels but above women, children, and the beasts. That "superior-subordinate paradigm" is still with us, Collins insists, in relations between husband and wife, boss and employee, priest and parishioner, white and black, affluent and poor; at best, she says, it is paternalism, and at worst, tyranny.[9] Rosemary Ruether agrees when she sums up the subject-object, superior-inferior hierarchical pattern of Western society as rooted in "God as transcendent Father."

> . . . the ultimate theological rationale for the hierarchical symbolism of masculinity and femininity is the image of God as transcendent Father. Creation becomes the wife or bride of the "sky Father." Most images of God in religions are modelled after the ruling class of society. In biblical religion the image of God is that of patriarchal Father above the visible created world, who relates to Israel as his "wife" and "children" in the sense of creatures totally dependent on his will, owing him unquestioning obedience. This image allows the king and patriarchal class to relate to women, children, and servants through the same model of domination and dependency.[10]

It is important to note in this analysis of patriarchy as a root-metaphor that it is not being asserted merely that through historical accident or brute strength men have oppressed women. Rather, the analysis pertains to the alienated consciousness of Western religion in which man, alienated from God, has projected the pattern of subject-object dualism down the line with woman—as man's most significant human "other"—the chief repository of his alienation. Thus, it is not whimsy, cruelty, or arbitrariness that causes men to oppress women, but a desperate attempt to overcome their own self-alienation. It is a matter, then, not at the level of an amusing "war between the sexes" or even of cultural conditioning, but at the level of man's *being*: it is ontological warfare in which women are the first victims. It is in this spirit that Ruether says, "Women are the first and oldest oppressed, subjugated people."[11] This does not mean that economically, politically, or personally women are more oppressed than, say, black males or the poor, but that in the struggle for self-integration, woman is the prime inheritor of man's alienation.

Feminists who have analyzed the patriarchal model have only brought into sharp relief the pattern that, from at least the time of Augustine, has been the dominant one in the Christian understanding of relations between God and humanity, as well as people with each other.[12] It reached its apotheosis in the Thomistic synthesis. According to the philosopher Dorothy Emmet we see the same structure of relationships in the middle ages between God and man (and man and woman) that the feminists have noted. The difference is that for the people of that time it was taken to be the "natural" order while for feminists it is taken to be an alienated, perverted order: "The structure of the family was taken to be the patriarchal family, exhibiting relations of monarchical justice (father to children), aristocratic justice (husband to wife) and democratic justice (brothers to brothers). . . . Such an order reflected the 'natural justice' of the world."[13]

The assertion that patriarchy reflects the "natural justice" of the world leads directly into the second point in the feminist criticism of patriarchy: the interactive character of models means that men not only model God but God, in return, bestows divine qualities on men. We have already seen evidence of this, but the point needs to be sharpened because it is a critical one. The way to make it most sharply is to state the obverse: women do not model God and, hence, do not become "named" by God. Their existence, unlike that of men, is not elevated and defined; they live, quite literally, in "no man's land," where their biological and traditional functions as wife, mother, sister, housekeeper, and so on have not received idealization and standard setting as have men's functions as husband, father, brother, master. George Caird, the biblical scholar, underscores this point when he remarks that metaphors for God derived from human relationships tend themselves to "two-way traffic in ideas," that the metaphors such as judge, king, father, and husband used in the Bible for God return to man as the ideal standard for his conduct in these roles. "Man," says Caird, "is created to become like God, and the ultimate justification of anthropomorphic imagery lies in the contribution it makes to the attainment of that goal."[14] This means, of course, that men have a "role-model" in God, a model for defining their self-identity, in a way that women do not. The Virgin Mary, as mother and as embodiment of traditional feminine qualities of compassion, nurture, purity, and humility, has served as a surrogate model for many Catholic women, but since even Mary is an inferior in the patriarchal hierarchy, her influence has served not to liberate women but to confirm women's position as inferior and subservient.[15]

The power of the patriarchal model is both its inclusiveness and its exclusiveness. It expands to include all of heaven and earth, and in so doing orders all of reality in a hierarchy in which women are always subordinate and invariably identified with the inferior or bodily dimensions of life. In this inclusive model woman is defined only in relationship to man—as man's "other," as that part of man from which he is alienated and which both fascinates and disgusts him. But the model excludes women as well by not naming them, by refusing to include their functions and occupations as metaphors for God that will return to them as models for their own self-identity. The patriarchal model oppresses women as much by what it does *not* say about woman as by what it *does* say. What it does say defines her as inferior; what it does not say leaves her without alternatives.

It remains only to remind ourselves that major models that become world views have subliminal, pervasive power to protect them against criticism. Such models constitute our "world" and their basic assumptions are buried deep within our consciousness, within our language. We, like the citizens of Oz who did not know that it was the glasses they wore that made Oz green, can see reality only "patriarchally." As Peter Berger and other sociologists have pointed out, we human beings, unfinished at birth, construct our world, which is then objectified over against us as "reality."[16] We forget that these constructions are *ours*, partly because, as protection against the terrors of chaos, they serve to provide permanent order to life and hence are valuable to us. By reifying our constructions into objective realities, however, we make them resistant to change and we become prisoners of our own creations. Religion is one of the most powerful legitimators of our social constructions because it grounds our precarious creations in ultimate reality. It provides them, as Berger puts it, with "an ultimately valid ontological status, that is, by *locating* them within a sacred and cosmic frame of reference."[17] That the patriarchal model has received such legitimation needs no elaboration; it is in many ways the epitome of Berger's point. The androcentric metaphors that form the principal imagery for God in the Western religious tradition return to us with divine sanction to legitimate the patriarchal world in which we live. Austin Farrer, the sensitive analyst of religious imagery, nonetheless reveals his "false consciousness" in the following statement in which he appears to recognize neither his masculine bias nor the human construction of social realities: "Perhaps only a father with supernatural awe to clothe him could have created the civilizing patriarchal family."[18] From a feminist perspective the creation of the patriarchal family is man's work and it has not proved "civilizing" for either men or women.

At this point, however, we might ask the question, whatever perversions have occurred in the patriarchal model, is not the metaphor of "father" a critical one in the Christian tradition? Is it not the most typical address used by Jesus for God? Is it not classic in the sense of being foundational and perennially relevant to Christians over the ages? We will deal with the possibility of a reconstructed father model later in this chapter, but it is important now to indicate that the Bible as a whole, including the New Testament, does not clearly support the patriarchal model in the form in which it developed. While Hebraic family patterns were clearly patriarchal long before the time of Jesus as well as during his lifetime, the idea of the covenant between God and Israel in the Old Testament and the notions of adoption into the community and the new birth in the Spirit in the New Testament tended to undercut the blood ties of the natural, patriarchal family.[19] In a similar vein, Rosemary Ruether claims that Jesus' way of referring to God as father undermines the patriarchal pattern in which ruling-class males identify with divine fatherhood so as to put themselves in a hierarchical relationship to women and lower classes. She refers especially to Matt. 23:8–11 as characteristic of Jesus' admonitions against the rise of Christian leaders who associate themselves with divine titles such as father in order to gain power over other Christians: "But you must not be called 'rabbi'; for you have one Rabbi, and you are all brothers. Do not call any man on earth 'father'; for you have one Father and he is in heaven. Nor must you be called 'teacher'; you have one Teacher, the Messiah." Ruether concludes with a statement that if this teaching had been maintained "the fatherhood of God could not have been understood as establishing male ruling-class power over subjugated groups in the Church or Christian society, but as that equal fatherhood that makes all Christians equals, brothers and sisters."[20] At the very least, this statement suggests that patriarchalism as it developed is not necessarily based on Jesus' teaching. That it did develop, and very quickly as we see in Paul's theology, is unfortunately the case and the situation with which we must deal.

Revolutionary Feminist Theology: A New Paradigm and a New Model

Feminist theologians agree on at least one issue; the patriarchal model, developed and maintained over almost two thousand years, can no longer be tolerated. Strategies for dealing with this model vary widely since feminist theology, a new phenomenon with few traditions, is characterized by diversity rather than schools or movements. It does seem fair to say, however, that, broadly speaking, feminist theologians fall into two groups—revolutionary and reformist.[21] The revolutionists maintain that the main resource for feminist theology should be women's experience, while the reformers believe that Christianity contains untapped possibilities for revision of traditional theology. Revolutionists do not usually identify themselves as Christians, while reformers do; the former take as their primary criterion what fits with and enhances woman's life, while the latter take as their prime criterion the potential within the Christian tradition for liberating human life, both female and male. Philosopher Marcia Keller, in an analysis of recent feminism in the United States, notes that "commitment to ending male domination is a value shared by all feminists but that feminists may be divided into those who favor full equality between the sexes and those who favor temporary or permanent ascendency of women and the female principle."[22] While a division of this sort is always risky, it does appear to hold for feminist theology and to make it even sharper we could say that for revolutionists women's liberation is the key category, while for reformers human liberation is central. The dangers of both positions are obvious: those who focus on women's liberation can be accused of merely "turning the tables," advocating a matriarchy to replace the patriarchy, while those who focus on human liberation can be accused of being "co-opted by the establishment," engaging in softheaded reform which can do little to undermine the power of patriarchy.

It is important as we look at revolutionary and reformist feminist theology to appreciate why these stands are taken and what each has to offer. Revolutionary feminist theologians are certainly not opposed to human liberation; rather, they despair of achieving it within the patriarchal model

—and, hence, within Christianity. As a consequence of their movement outside conventional models and modes of thinking, they achieve something that reformers cannot: they play with possibilities, they see peripherally, they think "to one side." In a way similar to fantasy writers, they imagine what, from the perspective of convention, is unimaginable. Reformist feminist theologians are certainly not opposed to women's liberation; rather, they believe such liberation can happen only as it occurs for all people and they interpret the root-metaphor of Christianity in liberationist, not patriarchal, terms. As a result of their position inside the Christian paradigm they have the possibility of tapping dormant sources that may have power for genuine revision. At this point in history, one cannot say that either position is correct or incorrect; only time will tell whether reform is possible or whether the patriarchal model is indeed an idol resisting all attempts at deliteralization. As one who identifies herself as a reformer, I believe that the root-metaphor of Christianity is not patriarchy and that, with new models—from the revolutionaries as well as from suppressed models within the tradition—to express its genuine root-metaphor, the Christian paradigm can name women's experience as it has named men's. Nevertheless, a genuine metaphorical theology always hears that whisper, "and it is not," even of the Christian paradigm if it has become absolute and irrelevant.

As we turn now to the positions and contributions of revolutionary feminist theology, some interpretive context for understanding and appreciating this novel phenomenon is in order. To many people this theology appears bizarre if not wrongheaded, and while it would certainly be inappropriate to try to explain it in terms that would make it more credible or palatable, it is not without analogies to other phenomena which might illuminate it.

A central tenet of the revolutionary perspective is its reliance on women's experience. What is novel in this assertion is the qualifying adjective, for experience is scarcely a new idea in religion. In fact, it could be said that religion is the interpretation of the meaning of experience at its most profound level. We recall that one of the basic differences between religion and science is that the former deals with the world in a qualitative, valuational way while the latter deals with the world in a quantitative, functional way. Religion is concerned with the meaning of life, science with how phenomena work, or, as Earl MacCormac reminds us, while both are explanations of experience, religion focuses on the personal dimension and science on the external dimension.[23] We remember also that for both Ian Ramsey and Paul Ricoeur, it is experience of the sacred from which all religious metaphors arise and to which all theological models finally return.

But we need not look only to these sources to make the point that experience is central to religion, for it is clearly evident in all reformations of religious traditions. In fact, the reason that religious traditions are reformed is that they are not proving to be relevant to the most profound levels of experience for "liminal" thinkers or groups—those persons or communities who become conscious of an anomaly in a religious paradigm, something in their experience that does not fit into the conventions of a tradition.[24] One way to view Jesus of Nazareth is as a liminal thinker whose own experience of God did not fit the conditions and expectations of Judaism. The anomaly he preached and lived created a new paradigm, Christianity. A stunning example of a disciple whose experience was revolutionized by this liminal thinker is Paul of Tarsus, whose conversion marks a radical transition from one paradigm to another. Throughout the history of Christianity, whenever reformations have occurred—as in the Protestant Reformation of the sixteenth century or Vatican II in the twentieth—a return to experience has been the critical factor. This can be clearly seen in Luther's major doctrine of "justification by grace through faith," which emerged from his own profound personal and fruitless attempts to be righteous in the eyes of God.[25]

When revolutionary feminists return to experience, then, they are following the classic pattern of liminal thinkers who, having discovered an anomaly the religious paradigm does not address, are attempting a radical transformation as many have done before them. In the case of these feminists, the claim is being made that the experience of half the human race has not been acknowledged by the Judeo-Christian tradition, that this religious tradition, pretending to speak of the *human* experience of God, has in fact been created by and for men and speaks to them, not to women. By "experience," as Carol Christ and Judith Plaskow say, the radical feminists mean several things, the simplest of which is "the fabric of life as it is lived"—by women.[26] Because their experience has been so deeply submerged by the structure created for them by men—in other words, by the patriarchal model—it is necessary to raise women's experience to consciousness. Hence, the first step is "consciousness-raising," which helps women to uncover the dimensions of their own experience of life as lived beneath the layers of male formation, interpretation, and domination. These dimensions include both liberation and traditional experiences; that is, women need to recognize oppression and move beyond it into freedom as well as to appreciate female experiences of embodiment and characteristics such as intuition, feeling, and concern for the personal dimensions of relationships, which have been denigrated in the patriarchal model.[27] In essence, the radical feminist theologians are claiming that women's experience, which in significant ways is different from men's both because of different bodily experiences and because of oppressive political structures, has been overlooked and repressed by Western religion. One of the first attempts at feminist theology—an essay by Valerie Saiving published in 1960—points out that the traditional interpretation of the doctrine of sin as pride and will-to-power are the temptations of men, not women; rather, the sin to which women are tempted is "underdevelopment or negation of self."[28]

In a number of ways, then, women's experience, say the radical feminists, has been submerged or negated. It has not been "named." It is not part of the language and hence not part of the paradigm, the assumptions of Western religion. In our terms, such experience has not informed the basic metaphors and models of Christianity. And this is the key point. The revolutionary feminists insist that "language" and "world" are synonymous and that those who name the world own the world. Mary Daly expresses it well when she says, "To exist humanly is to name the self, the world and God. . . . The liberation of language is rooted in the liberation of ourselves."[29] Feminists agree widely on this point. Revolutionary feminists, however, propose that women's experience is the major source for "naming" new religious metaphors and models that will be commensurate with that experience, a view not shared by the reformers. Revolutionary feminists are primarily concerned with the search for self-identity—the becoming of women—and for movement from nonbeing within the patriarchal model to a new naming of the self and the divine. This defines what is acceptable religion and acceptable models for the divine-human relationship, and not what can be salvaged from tradition. The central theme, then, is the search for self-identity: the metaphors and models unabashedly arise from women's experience, from female experience. The religion that emerges, as we shall see, is strongly immanental and designed, first of all, to be relevant to women, two features the radical feminists believe are notably lacking in the tradition.

Can an immanental, exclusively feminist perspective be absorbed into the Christian paradigm? It is doubtful, in my opinion, that it can be, nor is revolutionary feminist theology interested in making it commensurate with the tradition. The critical act, at least from a reformist perspective, is to see the genuine insights it offers for needed revision in that paradigm. While there are several varieties of revolutionary feminist theology, one of the most interesting from the point of view of models is "Goddess religion." Again we must note that among the several feminist theologians who write about Goddess religion, there are significant differences and nothing that could be called a school or a movement. Such theologians as Naomi Goldenberg, Carol Christ, and Mary Daly, however, are united in their belief that a female deity or divine principle is necessary if women's experience is to be included in a religious world view. What must be mentioned at the outset is that, in spite of the novelty of such an assertion in the Judeo-Christian paradigm, it is conventional from the perspective of other religions since the Western religious tradition, including Islam, is alone in its transcendent monotheism modeled only in masculine images. Whether one looks at primitive religions such as Native American, Eskimo, Aboriginal, or Pygmy where androgynous images are evident; or at the early Goddess cults such as the Greek Demeter, Egyptian Isis, Mesopotamian Ishtar, or Canaanite Anath; or at major living religions that include a female deity or principle such as Hinduism or Taoism—one sees female personification or characteristics as part of the way divinity is understood. E. O. James in his classic study, *The Cult of the Mother-Goddess*, notes "whether or not the Mother-Goddess was the earliest manifestation of the concept of Deity, her symbolism unquestionably has been the most persistent feature of the archeological record of the ancient world."[30] In agrarian cultures, Ruether argues that the Mother-Goddess is the dominant figure as the center of fertility, with the male god as consort who reigns at her pleasure: "All power, generative and political, is based on the maternal. Men exercise power by basing themselves upon the Great Mother. Men see themselves as children of the nature mother, created by her, exercising power through worshipping her, rather than transcendent or prior to her."[31] The characteristics stressed in such religions are regeneration and renewal, nurture and care, compassion and acceptance.

It is this pattern of an ascendent female divinity with the associated qualities which contemporary feminists have revived as a model for a religion based on women's experience. To Naomi Goldenberg the ancient myth of the superiority of the Mother-Goddess to her male consort is important, as it gives women a higher place in the power structure. The myth sees men as helpful sons and lovers but, as the year waxes, the son becomes the lover of the Mother-Goddess and then dies to appear again as son when she gives birth to her new consort. The matriarchal principle is dominant throughout, for the Mother-Goddess is the principle of life, with the male connection to life only through the role of son and lover of the Goddess.[32] However, Goldenberg, who is a Jungian, is not interested in personifying or literalizing the Goddess or in restricting divine symbols solely to female ones. She supports a pluralism of deities, both male and female, which are not "beings" but symbols of the divine within human beings. Her perspective is not allegiance to any religious tradition but whatever helps women define themselves; hence, it is the "feminine life-force," in whatever symbols or models it may usefully appear, that is critical. She, like others interested in Goddess religion, supports witchcraft as one of the few ancient religious traditions controlled by women. In Goldenberg's description of contemporary witchcraft covens, the important notes are individualism, immanentalism, pluralism, relativism: "In feminist witchcraft . . . since each woman is considered a Goddess, all of her creations are in a sense holy. No one has the right to put another person's feelings into categories of sacred and profane, religious or secular. . . . Each is the priestess of her own religion. Celebrant and Shaman are identical."[33] She notes further that the main points of modern witchcraft include not only female deities, but the end of body/soul dualism, division between good and evil, reliance on sacred texts, as well as appreciation for nature as sacred, the body as good, and time as cyclical. She sums up her position with a comment that "witchcraft is the first modern theistic religion to conceive of its deity mainly as an internal set of images and attitudes."[34]

What is critical in Goldenberg's position as well as typical of the position of two other radical feminist theologians—Carol Christ and Mary Daly—is the stress on immanentalism and on female power. These notes are the determinative ones in a statement by a contemporary practicing witch named Starhawk:

> The craft is earth religion, and our basic orientation is to the earth, to life, to nature. There is no dichotomy between spirit and flesh, no split between Godhead and the world. The Goddess is manifest in the world; she brings life into being, *is* nature, *is* flesh. Union is not sought outside the world in some heavenly sphere or through dissolution of the self into the void beyond the senses. Spiritual union is found in life, within nature, passion, sensuality—through being fully human, fully one's self. . . . Thou art Goddess. I am Goddess. All that lives (and all that is, lives), all that serves life, is Goddess.[35]

A somewhat more pragmatic approach to these themes of immanentalism and female power is found in the work of Carol Christ. Her position, influenced by Clifford Geertz and Peter Berger, stresses the profound psychological, cultural, and political power of the patriarchal model on women's self-esteem. Such a model legitimates male political and social authority over women while Goddess religion frees women to look to the female principle in herself and in other women as the sustaining and saving power: "The simplest and most basic meaning of the symbol of Goddess is the acknowledgment of the legitimacy of female power as a beneficent and independent power. A women who echoes Ntosake Shange's dramatic statement, 'I found God in myself and I loved her fiercely,' is saying 'Female power is strong and creative.' "[36] Christ's pragmatic position is illustrated by her lack of concern whether the Goddess is entirely immanent or also transcendent; what matters is the power for self-definition that it gives to women, its focus as a unifying symbol of female power. As such, says Christ, it serves to affirm the female body not only as the giver of physical life but also as the nurturer of the arts of civilization against the denigration of the body and nature by Western religion. Moreover, the symbol of Goddess supports the initiative of women, not as a will to power but in harmony with the wills of other beings and the energy of nature.

Finally, in the most radical of the feminist theologians Mary Daly, the notes of immanentalism and female power are taken to their logical extremes. Daly's position has neither the pluralism of Goldenberg's nor the pragmatism of Christ's, for hers is an ontology solely by and for women. Her most recent book, *Gyn/Ecology: The Metaphysics of Radical Feminism*, strains English usage as she attempts to find a new language in which to express her radical vision of a journey into the inner being of women to discover the source of life and power. Her book, she says, "is about dis-covering, developing the complex web/of living/loving relationships *of our own kind*. It is about women living, loving, creating our selves, our cosmos. It *is* dispossessing our Selves, inspiriting our Selves, hearing the call of the wild, naming our wisdom, spinning and weaving world tapestries out of genesis and demise."[37] She "names" the world anew, now only a women's world, taking ancient and despised images of women—crone, hag, witch, spinster—as symbols of female power exorcising male evil, of female intuitive wisdom in contrast to rational intellection of males, of female creativity in body and spirit in contrast to male necrophilia in war and the destruction of nature. Like Goldenberg and

Christ, Daly sees the Goddess as the immanent power of "the life-loving be-ing of women and nature" in contrast to the transcendent male God, but she sets them apart as polar opposites, with the Goddess symbolizing life, nurture, creation, intuition and the God symbolizing death, pollution, destruction, logic. It is difficult to assess Daly's book fairly, for, as with many highly creative, angry works, it verges on madness at times. It is also unsettling and allows for no compromises; its value lies in its unrelenting analysis (which contains some powerful insights and some gross overstatements) of the misogyny of Western religion, as well as in its reinterpretation of the most despised images for women as symbols of power rather than of denigration for women.

It needs to be pointed out, however, that Daly's extreme position suggests two significant problems with contemporary Goddess religion in general: its embrace of stereotypical feminine virtues, which becomes a new form of "biology is destiny," and its lack of a critical dimension in its elevation of women as savior of self and world. The latter point is of particular concern to us, for one of the primary emphases of a metaphorical theology is the distance, the negative "and it is not," which insists that no metaphor or model of the divine can be identified with what it models. If the Goddess *is* woman, every woman, then the idolization of woman follows as it clearly does in Daly's work, although not in Goldenberg's or Christ's because of their pluralism and pragmatism. While Goddess religion rightly criticizes the Western tradition for its overriding transcendence and its masculine models, the solution does not lie in a total immanence or in identification of women as divine. Nor does an elevation of female qualities, either biological or culturally stereotypical, aid the liberation of women. While the appreciation of the body and its functions, as well as of the qualities of nurture, compassion, and concern for the natural environment, is clearly needed as an antidote to the suppression of the body and lack of attention to these qualities, the identification of woman as source and repository of what should be seen as *human* qualities places her once again in the role she has had since the demise of the fertility cults—in the role of inferior.

One of the basic difficulties with contemporary Goddess religion is that it is anachronistic: as Ruether and James among others point out, Goddess religion is agrarian religion, thriving in cultures prior to the time when human beings were fully cognizant of the role played by the male in generation. Once civilization became urbanized and the male generative role was known, the power of the Goddess waned, never to be ascendant again. The "Sky-God," sometimes with a subordinate female partner and sometimes without, took over, and even in those religions where a female principle is evident, she is always inferior, usually connected with evil, and at the most a support for women only in their role as mothers.[38] In these religions we see attitudes similar to those in the Judeo-Christian tradition: ambivalence toward women, extolling them as mother, fearing them as temptress; identification of femaleness with the dark side, symbolized by taboos on menstrual blood; suppression of women socially and educationally; denial of access for women to religious leadership.

The limitations of Goddess religion, however, should not blind us to its insights. At the very least, it is a cry in the wilderness, a cry of pain and anger against the patriarchal model as oppressive to women, not just as irrelevant to them but as destructive of their being at every level—physical, emotional, spiritual, political, cultural. Its radicalness is part of its value, for in its unconventionality, its uncompromising vision of novel models alien to Western religion, it forces a reassessment both of the absolutism of the patriarchal model as well as its irrelevance to many women. Like fantasy writing, it paints a new world—a world radically different from the one we know, giving us alternatives, some of which are dark, while others pose possibilities for a richer, more humane life. Although the Goddess theologians do not identify themselves as fantasy writers, it seems to me that such a context provides a helpful analogy for appreciating their contribution to a reformist perspective. To suggest that radical feminist religious models, specifically the Goddess model, be seen as fantasy writing in no way undercuts their importance. On the contrary, as Robert Scholes says of such writing, "fabulation . . . is fiction that offers us a world clearly and radically discontinuous from the one we know, and yet returns us to confront that world in some cognitive way."[39] He notes that fabulation has been a favorite vehicle of religious thinkers because they know that the common-sense view of reality is not the "really real," that another reality which upsets and criticizes conventional reality touches a deeper level of the truth of human existence.

We saw this pattern clearly in the parables and Jesus as parable, modeling the divine-human relationship by disorientation to conventional expectations and reorientation to the way of the kingdom. Scholes claims that it is no surprise that science fiction and religious fictions such as parables are of the same league, for they are both prophetic forms: they question the present in the light of future possibilities. Leander Keck agrees when he claims that the kingdom of God in the New Testament is not the fulfillment but the critique of the present, and as such, is not a support for the status quo but a threat to it: "By allowing the future-leaning, future-grasping, expectant Jesus to be the model by which we think of God we are led away from the understanding of God to be only the Ground of what is and what is presently experienced, and we are brought to understand God to be the One who is free to restructure the present by impinging upon it."[40] A metaphorical theology, we have suggested, finds its unity not in the past nor in the present, but only in the unity of the new rule of God which is not yet. It is open-ended theology, realizing the relativity of all models of the divine-human relationship and, with this sensibility, ready both to question traditional models and entertain new possibilities which may overcome the limitations of present models.

Thus fabulation, as Scholes defines it, is an obvious resource for metaphorical theology, for it opens the imagination to think what has not yet been thought. In significant ways, the Goddess feminists are thinking what has not yet been thought—at least not in the Judeo-Christian tradition—and for that reason alone they deserve a serious hearing. They are asking their readers, at the very least, to engage in an imaginative exercise: What would it be like if the divine-human relationship were seen in terms of feminine rather than masculine models? How would that change our images of ourselves, our world, and our relation to the divine? C. S. Lewis, who militantly opposed anything except divinely-inspired masculine religious images, made the point in derision which feminist theologians wish to affirm: "A child who has been taught to pray to a Mother in Heaven would have a religious life radically different from that of a Christian child."[41] Yes, say the feminist theologians, that is indeed the case, and let us imagine that possibility and the changes it would entail.

One of the critical insights, then, of radical feminist theology comes in its willingness to think, as Arthur Koestler says, "bisociatively" rather than "associatively." Bisociative is revolutionary thinking that destroys the conventional, habitual patterns of associative thought and by so doing has the singular possibility of allowing others *to see differently*. To see differently, says Koestler, is extraordinarily difficult because "the mind likes a strange idea as little as the body likes a strange protein and resists it with similar energy."[42] Koestler insists that the only way to cut through the prejudices of conventional vision and allow people to see differently is to substitute another universe of discourse for the given one, for, he says, "the rules of the game . . . cannot be altered by playing that game."[43] This is what the radical feminists have done—changed the rules of the game from the patriarchal to a matriarchal model—and by so doing they have raised the possibility, at least as a thought experiment, of what a feminine aspect to the divine-human relationship involves.

As an illustration of such a thought experiment and one which I believe sheds significant light not only on the male-female relationship but also on the nature of opposition and love in all human relations, let us look at a work by one of the most interesting of contemporary science fiction writers Ursula LeGuin, whose book *The Left Hand of Darkness* is a fine example of bisociative, revolutionary thinking. A comment by her on the function of science fiction is also an appropriate statement on her own book, for she sees it as a "kind of question-asking; reversals of a habitual way of thinking, metaphors for what our language has no words for as yet, experiments in imagination."[44] In *The Left Hand of Darkness* she imagines a world in which everyone is at some time male and female and at all times exhibits characteristics we attribute to both. There are no "men" and "women" but all persons not only have the option at various times in their lives of being both mothers and fathers, but all share what we call masculine and feminine virtues. While one may regret, as I do, LeGuin's use of the male pronoun for these people, as it not only follows the conventions of sexism, but decreases the shock value of her thought experiment, nonetheless she is successful in her portrayal of them "as man and woman, familiar and different, alien and utterly human."[45] The leading character in the book, a male from earth named Genly Ai, is initially unnerved by this phenomenon, especially as he becomes close to one of them named Therem Harth: "A friend. What is a friend, in a world where any friend may be a lover at a new phase of the moon? Not I, locked in my virility: no friend to Therem Harth, or any other of his race. Neither man nor woman, neither and both, cyclic, lunar, metamorphising under the hand's touch, changelings in the human cradle, they were no flesh of mine, no friends, no love between us."[46] When forced to make an eight-hundred-mile journey together by ice sled across a frozen wilderness, Genly Ai learns to appreciate both the man and the woman in his comrade and, of equal importance, to accept and love Therem Harth: "And I saw then again, and for good, what I had always been afraid to see, and had pretended not to see in him: that he was a woman as well as a man. Any need to explain the sources of that fear vanished with the fear; what I was left with was, at last, acceptance of him as he was."[47] In short, Genly Ai experiences a revolution in consciousness, a profound expansion in his understanding of human relationships, an expansion that depends not on suppressing the male or the female in his friend, but appreciating each, as well as his difference from Therem Harth.

This parable—for it surely is a parable, an extended metaphor that suggests a new way of being in the world at odds with the conventional way— portrays a revolution in consciousness for readers who, along with Genly Ai, must relate to characters in the story not as males or females but as both. Some critics have questioned the biological workability of the scheme, but that is beside the point, for good science fiction is not predictive of the future but descriptive of the present. As LeGuin comments in her introduction to the book, she is not predicting that people will some day be androgynous, but that "if you look at us at certain odd times of the day in certain weathers, we already are."[48] Hence, the book does not present a utopia, a practical alternative for life in the future, but an alternative to the conventional point of view for seeing life now. She is saying that men and women are not aliens and that both hold within themselves charactcristics of the other, characteristics such as initiative, compassion, courage, nurture, pride, and care, which are more basically *human* than they are sexually differentiated. Of equal importance, she is saying that all human contact involves opposition and it is *with* that difference from others appreciated and acknowledged that love thrives. Hers is a complex "statement" which, because it is a parable, cannot be fully conceptualized. She is dealing with sameness and otherness, similarity and difference, opposition and love, fear and friendship, by means of the metaphor of sexuality. In and through her story of an earthling for whom sexual differences are dualistic and absolute—one who meets a world in which the differences are patterned in an alternative way—she upsets the conventions of our world and allows us to imagine new possibilities for overcoming alienation of many kinds between people.

When a fantasy writer asks, "What if things were very different from the way we are accustomed to seeing them?" she is asking a serious question. Speculative fiction is not necessarily frivolous or unrelated to "reality." Fantasy can be seen as the creative negativity of dialectical questioning in the search for understanding, the radical openness on the part of the interpreter who finds the tradition in which she stands in need of change. One of the most powerful ways to question a tradition is to imagine new worlds that challenge it. Speculative fiction, with more tenuous ties to everyday life than "realistic" fiction, creates a world in sharp contrast to our conventional one and hence, simply by juxtaposition questions and criticizes it. What is imagined in fantasy writing is often less important than the inventiveness, radicalness, and openness of the imagining. It is in this sense, in the sense of opening up the conventions of a culture, its paradigms which are unquestioned, its models which have become absolutized and irrelevant, that LeGuin's remark that "the truth is a matter of the imagination" is indeed true.

It seems to me that one can fairly and profitably interpret the radical vision of the Goddess theologians as a serious questioning of the patriarchal model by juxtaposing it with a very different model. The shock of this model causes initial resistance if not fear in many persons; it appears radically opposed to the traditional understanding of the divine-human relationship in Christianity. But were we to understand the Goddess theologians not as predicting an alternative future for religion, but as presenting an alternative way of seeing our tradition and its possibilities, perhaps their radical vision could be appreciated, as parables and science fiction are, for making us think in new ways, see new things, which can only be thought and seen through the shock that undercuts our conventional, comfortable ways. I am not suggesting that the Goddess theologians see their work in this light; they have little interest in reforming the tradition and, for most of them, Goddess religion is a new paradigm utterly opposed to the Christian paradigm. Moreover, we have already noted the inherent problems of matriarchal absolutism as well as sexual determinism in the revolutionary perspective. Nonetheless, from the reformers' point of view, the greatest contribution of the revolutionary feminist theologians lies in asking the question: whether a feminine model for the divine-human relationship is not only needed but also desirable, not just for women or for adherents to a new religion, but for all people and for Christianity? The revolutionaries have posed the question; it will be up to the reformers to see if the Christian paradigm has any resources for answering it.

Reformist Feminist Theology: The Search for New Models

Reformers believe that the root-metaphor of Christianity is human liberation, not patriarchy, and that liberation for women can occur within the Christian paradigm. This is a bold faith, for as we have seen, there is little surface evidence to support it and much to refute it. By "liberation," reformers do not mean merely freedom from male domination or freedom for self-expression, although these are important motifs in any genuine, concrete understanding of freedom. Christian liberation at its most profound level must address human bondage to the conventions and expectations of the ways of the world in contrast to the freedom of life according to the way of God's new rule. This is the heart of Jesus' announcement. In line with Luke 4 we have seen that the root-metaphor of Christianity is modeled in the parables and Jesus as parable of God. Human liberation consists of a new divine-human relationship characterized by unmerited love and qualified by tension as one lives within this relationship. If the root-metaphor of Christianity is a particular kind of relationship between God and human beings, then it is an event, an alive, moving, and changing occurrence, which *no* metaphors or models can capture and pin down. The form of the parables as stories and the interpretation of the life of Jesus as a parable attest to the dramatic, eventful character of the root-metaphor of Christian faith. As a feminist reformer, I believe we must start with this paradigm as the Gospel for all peoples, and not just for women, or for men, or for any other division of the human community.

But having said this, what is there in it which is liberating *for women?* In its inclusion of all peoples does it not ignore our insistence that there is no "innocent eye," that all understandings are interpretations from particular points of view and interests? Does it not forget that this very Gospel is the one that spawned the patriarchal model which has been oppressive, not liberating, for women? The answers to these questions could take several forms, but the one we wish to focus on concerns the possibilities for a feminine model in which to understand the divine-human relationship. Before turning to the issue, however, it is important to note that the relationship as modeled in the parables and in Jesus as parable of God is intrinsically destructive of conventional power arrangements and hence liberating to those who are oppressed, whether by their sex, race, economic situation, or other factors. Rosemary Ruether makes this point for the Bible as a whole when she claims that the liberating element in both testaments is the prophetic messianic tradition that assumes the perspective of the disadvantaged. This tradition understands God as the One who sides with the oppressed: "It means that the God-language of the Bible tends to be judgmental and destabilizing toward the existing social order and its hierarchies of power; religious, social, and economic."[49] While the vision of a new age of justice versus the present age of injustice is not specifically applied to women, says Ruether, it is the basic perspective of the Bible and *can* be applied to women. The biblical writers "have been responding to the fears of death, estrangement and oppression and the hopes for life, reconciliation and liberation of humanity. They have been doing this on male terms. But women can discover this critical element and apply it to themselves. In so doing, they will not leave it as it was, but transform it in profound ways. They will make it say things it never said before."[50] What counts, then, for Ruether and other feminist reformers is not particular statements in the Bible that oppress women, such as we find in Paul's letters, but the overall liberating perspective of our classic text. While this text is the product of patriarchy and has the bias of patriarchy as do all our cultural artifacts, nonetheless it contains a perspective undercutting patriarchy and all other worldly hierarchies. It is in this light that Paul's enigmatic words on the revolutionary power of the Gospel in contrast to the law should be read: "There is no such thing as Jew or Greek, slave or freeman, male or female; for you are all one person in Jesus Christ" (Gal. 3:28).

When we turn to the more specific question of feminine imagery for God we find that the possibility of answering this question affirmatively also rests in the nature of the new relationship with God which lies at the center of Christianity. It rests in understanding the root-metaphor of Christianity as a relationship, not a state of affairs, between God and human beings, and as a relationship, many models from many experiences of that relationship are appropriate as well as necessary. There is no possibility of exhausting or petrifying that relationship, for it is necessarily concrete and plural, particular and universal. The experience of people relating to God as the One who frees them from the particular chains that bind their bodies and spirits issues in metaphors too various to enumerate: liberator, comrade, creator, mother, friend, rock, father, thunder, lover, brother, teacher, sister, light, fire, defender, sustainer, nurturer, advocate, and so on. The images which tumble from the mouths of those experiencing the liberating love of God are not meant *to describe* God so much as *to suggest the new quality of relationship* being offered to them. Hence, religious metaphors and the models that emerge from them are not pictures of God but images of a relationship; as such, they are nonrestrictive and highly particular. The freedom and flexibility of this approach should be immediately evident; since one is not describing God but expressing the quality of a relationship, all kinds of metaphors will be appropriate which genuinely reflect some aspect of that relationship.[51] Certain images emerge as significant to the experiences of many peoples' relationships to God; these metaphors become dominant models of a tradition, the comprehensive structures through which relationship to God is understood and expanded to include all dimensions of life. What begins, then, as a nonrestrictive and highly particular fund of metaphors becomes increasingly restrictive and generalized, and this is surely the history of patriarchalism, which began as *one* good model of relating to God as "father." In almost all religions "father" is, for good reasons, a dominant model, and given Jesus' reliance on it as an expression of his own experience of God, it is bound to be central in Christianity. Its growth, however, into patriarchalism, a system fostering male superiority at all levels of personal and public life, is a serious perversion of Jesus' understanding of the father model and utterly opposed to the root-metaphor of Christianity, which is against all worldly hierarchies. Moreover, its exclusion of other models is restrictive of the plurality of ways people experience the liberating love of God, as well as idolatrous toward one model of what *no* model can ever capture.

Therefore, I advance the thesis that by attending to the relationship between God and human beings rather than to descriptions of God, it is possible to find sources within the Christian paradigm for religious models liberating to women. A similar possibility, of course, is open to other groups of persons—racial, cultural, economic—who have also felt excluded by the patriarchal model. While we will be focusing mainly on one kind of imagery—the imagery emerging from experiencing the relationship with God in feminine terms—this focus should be understood illustratively rather than restrictively. The case can certainly be made that just as "father" is a natural dominant model in religion and especially in Christianity, so "mother" is as well, but it should be obvious that a relational perspective cannot absolutize any model, whether it be feminine, masculine, parental, personal, or impersonal.

As we turn to the Christian tradition to support this thesis, we will rely on the work of reformist feminist theologians, those who have found, in biblical texts and other sources, support for feminine metaphors for the divine-human relationship. The point of this exercise is not to suggest that since feminine imagery can be found in the Bible and the tradition, it is therefore legitimate; such an approach would be contrary to the basic openness and relativity of a metaphorical theology. Even if the Christian tradition gave no support for images from women's experience, they might still be appropriate. The critical criterion is not whether the Bible and the tradition contain such metaphors, but whether they are appropriate ones in which to suggest dimensions of the new divine-human relationship intrinsic to this religious tradition. Since women have been excluded *as women* from that tradition, it comes as no surprise that feminine imagery is not central. The fact, however, that it is present at all in spite of patriarchalism is witness to its importance for expressing experiences of the new way of being in the world which other metaphors are unable to express as well. The goal of our analysis of Christian sources, therefore, is to show both that feminine images are not only there but also have been suppressed. More importantly, we will show that feminine images are highly desirable and necessary in order to express certain profound dimensions of the experiences of relating to God as the gracious giver of a new way of being in the world. As we shall also see, feminine images for God are important to men as well as to women, as both attempt to express the depths of what this new relationship means to them.

We begin with the Old Testament since it provided the material for the Christian patriarchal model in significant ways. Phyllis Trible, in her impressive exegesis of the Old Testament in relation both to feminine imagery of God and to the position of women, insists that "the patriarchal stamp is permanent" but nonetheless "a feminist perspective enlightened the Bible."[52] This perspective is, however, unlike that of the Goddess religions, for while God is imagined in masculine as well as in feminine metaphors, the divine is neither male nor female but embraces and transcends both.[53] This is a critical point, for it means that the sexual difference is not absolutized by its projection onto the deity as in the case of many world religions, including the Goddess religions. As we recall, we imagine God in our image, but that image returns to us authorized and legitimated with sacred power. One of the special if not unique features of the Judeo-Christian tradition has been its refusal to absolutize the sexual difference into a dualistic opposition. This refusal allows for the possibility that just as God transcends sexuality, so we, created in that image, are not determined by our sex; in other words, the sexual difference is not more basic than the common humanity shared by men and women.

Trible makes this point with her fine exegesis of Gen. 1:26–30, the key text being 1:27: "And God created humankind in his image; in the image of God created he him; male and female created he them." Trible sees this verse as a metaphor, with "male and female" the vehicle and "the image of God" the tenor. Thus, humankind, which is not an androgynous creature but two equal creatures in harmony but differentiated, is the model not for God but for "the image of God." Trible is making at least two important points here. First, the original unity of humankind embraces sexual differentiation, not sexual identicalness, but that differentiation suggests no hierarchy or subordination. "The human creation . . . is not delineated by sexual relationships, roles, characteristics, attitudes, or emotions."[54] Both sexes share equally in the two functions given to humankind: procreation and dominion over the earth. Second, while "male and female" is a metaphor for the divine, it is not a description of God, for the distinction between "the image of God" and "God" suggests that God transcends all images. A metaphor is "like a finger pointing to the moon"; however, "the moon . . . can be seen but not possessed."[55]

> God is neither male nor female, nor a combination of the two. And yet, detecting divine transcendence in human reality requires human clues. Unique among them, according to our poem, is sexuality. God creates, in the image of God, male and female. To describe male and female, then, is to perceive the image of God; to perceive the image of God is to glimpse the transcendence of God.[56]

In sum, sexual differentiation is a basic and appropriate metaphor for pointing to the divine-human relationship, but even as God transcends "the image of God," so we, created in that image, are not determined by the sexual difference. Trible's exegesis licenses male and female imagery for God with the qualification that such imagery neither describes God nor legitimates any hierarchical masculine/feminine stereotypes for human beings.

This is a radical perspective with profound implications for feminine models of God within the Judeo-Christian tradition. Trible believes that the Old Testament contains such metaphors in abundance, and while not as frequent as male imagery, they form an important suppressed tradition. Feminine imagery is widely used, not as descriptions of God, but of Israel's experience of relating to God as the One who conceives and brings the people to birth, suckles and feeds them, comforts them as a mother, and provides clothes to cover their nakedness. These female metaphors accomplish something male metaphors cannot: the image of God carrying Israel and giving birth in pain, of suckling Israel at the breast, are profound expressions for both men and women of the experience of relating to a deeply compassionate God. Trible makes this point explicitly clear in an in-depth exegesis of the metaphor of womb as an expression of God as compassionate, merciful, and loving.[57] Short of saying that God possesses a womb, the Bible does say that "Yahweh bears Israel from its conception to old age":

> God conceives in the womb, God fashions in the womb; God judges in the womb, God destines in the womb; and God carries from the womb to gray hairs. From this uterine perspective, then, Yahweh molds life for individuals

and for the nation Israel. Accordingly, in biblical traditions an organ unique to the female becomes a vehicle pointing to the compassion of God.[58]

Trible's work is especially important in light of the fact that she has unearthed a tradition of female imagery in Scripture neglected by most male exegetes. It is noteworthy, by contrast, that in an otherwise fine book by George Caird, *The Language and Imagery of the Bible,* published in 1980, no mention is made of feminine images at all. In giving a list of parts of the body used as images of God, Caird does not mention "breasts" or "womb." Moreover, while he writes in detail of father imagery, he says nothing of mother imagery: "As father God is the source of life (Deut. 32:6), of parental care (Matt. 7:9–11) and affection (Hos. 11:3–4), of discipline (Heb. 12:9) and authority (Mal. 1:6), of family unity (Eph. 3:14) and mutual love (John 15:9–12); and on those who claim to be his children he lays the obligation to take after their father (Matt. 5:45)."[59] We see here what readers have been led to believe, namely, that the only tradition in the Bible is the paternal one—with the added admonition that they should "take after their father." Women rightly feel excluded from such a tradition; Trible and other feminist exegetes have allowed women to see in the Bible the possibility that they *can* "take after their mother."

The New Testament does not contain specific maternal imagery of God, although attempts have been made to try to accommodate Jesus' understanding of God as father with the Goddess of radical feminist spirituality. For instance, Elisabeth Schüssler Fiorenza claims that in the New Testament images of life, love, light, compassion, mercy, care, peace, service, and community we can see similarities with motifs from Goddess religion such as enabling power rather than hierarchical power, wholeness and healing love, noncompetitive community: the Goddess "brings us in touch with the creative, healing, life-giving power at the heart of the world."[60] Such, she suggests, could be said also of Jesus' image of God as father.

This is an intriguing suggestion, but it rests on the complex issue of Jesus' understanding of the fatherhood of God, a question that appears to contain more than is immediately apparent. On the one hand, some scholars such as Joachim Jeremias and more recently Robert Hamerton-Kelly, have attempted to accommodate Jesus' teaching on the fatherhood of God to a maternal model. Hamerton-Kelly claims that Jesus' address to God as "Abba" portrays intimacy not expressed by other Jews of Jesus' time. The characteristics of the father to whom Jesus prays, says Hamerton-

Kelly, are not those that contribute to the patriarchal model; on the contrary, they are ones of profound parental care and compassion, traditionally more related to maternal than to paternal love. It is not the stern, judgmental autocrat of the patriarchal Jewish family who emerges as the model for Jesus' father; it is, rather, the parent who, as in the parable of the Prodigal Son, agonizes over the lost child and runs to meet him with joy at his return. Such a parent could, Hamerton-Kelly asserts, be mother as well as father. He quotes approvingly from Jeremias: "From the earliest time the word 'Father' when applied to God included for the Orientals something of what 'mother' means to us."[61] Jesus, says Hamerton-Kelly, was such an Oriental.

On the other hand, a scholar such as Edward Schillebeeckx, while agreeing on the centrality of Jesus' use of "Abba," does not see that centrality as accommodating a maternal model but rather as expressing Jesus' intimacy and identification with the God whose liberating mission was also his own. Schillebeeckx bases his argument on paternal authority at the time of Jesus: ". . . in Jesus' time what the *Abba* signified for his son was authority and instruction: the father is the authority and teacher."[62] Calling God "Abba," then, meant doing God's will and this, Schillebeeckx claims, is what Jesus did totally in his entire ministry and praxis. Jesus is *the* obedient son of the father and thus his intimacy is not primarily a reinterpretation of patriarchalism or an inclusion of maternal qualities in the paternal model, but an indication of his radical openness to fulfilling God's mission of salvation to all. Hence, Schillebeeckx understands the Jesus who addresses God as "Abba" to be *also* the one who proclaims the kingdom of God, for the obedience of Jesus as son is precisely to preach the rule of God to the suffering, the oppressed, the excluded. Thus, on this reading, eating with tax collectors and sinners is a direct implication of calling God "Abba."

On the face of it, this interpretation of Jesus' understanding of God as father appears less immediately relevant to feminists than does the accommodation of the model of father to include mother. It does not provide us with a maternal model and in fact does not even undercut patriarchal characteristics of the paternal model, for Schillebeeckx understands Jesus' mission to be obedience to the father's will. What it does do, however, is raise the question of why, contrary to Jewish expectations, Jesus proclaimed salvation to all, and especially to the rejected, the excluded, and the oppressed. Schillebeeckx says that the answer lies in Jesus' profound experience of oneness with God's will expressed by addressing God as "Abba."

> Thus the *Abba* experience of Jesus, although meaningful in itself, is not a self-subsistent religious experience, but is also an experience of God as "Father," caring for and offering a future to his children, a God, Father, who gives a future to the man who from a mundane viewpoint can be vouchsafed no future at all.[63]

We have in no way escaped the model of God as father; what surfaces, however, is an understanding of God as the One who is, as Schillebeeckx says, "bent upon humanity"—One who wills the liberation of the abandoned and rejected. In sum, Jesus was a Jew of his time, a time of powerful patriarchal authoritarianism. His "Abba" address suggests radical obedience as son to his heavenly father, but this obedience was to a God whose reign was a reversal of expectations, offering liberation to the excluded. Just as the prophetic tradition of the Old Testament can be seen as undercutting oppression and hence as liberating to women and other excluded peoples, so also Jesus' proclamation of the new rule of God can be seen as of crucial significance to reformist feminists attempting to find resources within the Christian tradition for relevant ways of speaking of God.

If we do not find strong support for maternal models in the New Testament, neither do we find them, except marginally, in later materials. Apart from the cult of Mary, feminine models for the relationship between God and human beings are found in the tradition only in the heretics, in the mystics, and in minor sects. It is not possible or appropriate here to mention all the sources; two illustrations from Gnosticism and mysticism will suffice to make it clear that feminine imagery both persists at the fringes of the tradition and is neglected by it.

Elaine Pagels in her work on Gnosticism says that while the earliest teachings of Jesus could have resulted in the Gnostic Christian egalitarian ministry of men and women as well as in its female imagery for God, neither came about. The hierarchical, male, authoritarian pattern both in ecclesiology and in imagery triumphed, and with that victory a feminine ministry and imagery was lost to the church.[64] Whatever one might think of some of the Gnostic imagery for God—its dyadic, androgynous nature as well as its esoteric complexities—it was an attempt to retain a critical place for female power, both divine and human. Moreover, the diversity and richness of the Gnostic texts on the nature of the female aspect of the Godhead provide sources the tradition has militantly refused to consider in spite of the fact that, as Pagels points out, they emerged not from Goddess religions but from the Hebraic Wisdom tradition and the New Testament tradition of the Holy Spirit. For instance, in one Gnostic source, the *Secret Book of John*, where the phrase appears "I am the Father; I am the Mother; I am the Son," John's interpretation of the trinity as including a feminine component rests on the Hebrew term for spirit, *ruah*—a feminine word—and he then describes Spirit as Mother: "the image of the invisible virginal perfect spirit. . . . She became the mother of all, for she existed before all, the mother-father [matropater]."[65] Or in the *Gospel of Thomas* Jesus contrasts his earthly parents Joseph and Mary with his divine Father and his divine Mother, the Holy Spirit.[66] Elsewhere in the *Gospel of Thomas* we read that "whoever does not love his father and mother in my way cannot be my disciple; for my [earthly] mother gave me death but my true Mother gave me Life."[67] The reason for mentioning this material here is principally to suggest that some of it appears as consonant with our classic text as does material which is considered orthodox, for it continues the suppressed tradition of openness to female imagery and characteristics for God which we have seen in the Old Testament.

In an interesting attempt to refute the relationship between trinitarian doctrine and patriarchalism, Jürgen Moltmann insists that trinitarianism, for reasons different from Christian Gnosticism but with similar results, supports a "bisexual or transsexual" image of God. For, he says, if the Son comes from the Father alone as trinitarian language claims, then the Father both begets and gives birth. Such a father, says Moltmann, is no mere male father, but a "motherly-father."

> Whatever this declaration may be supposed to be saying about the gynaecology of the Father, these bisexual affirmations imply a radical denial of patriarchal monotheism. *Monotheism* was and is the religion of the *patriarchism* just as we may suppose, pantheism ("Mother Earth") was the religion of the earlier *matriarchism*. The Christian doctrine of the Trinity, with its affirmations about the motherly Father, represents a first step towards limiting the use of masculine terminology to express the idea of God, without, however, changing over to matriarchal conceptions. It really points to a fellowship of women and men in which there is no subordination and no privilege. . . . Only a human fellowship free from sexism and class rule can become like the triune God.[68]

While I must admit reluctance to basing feminine imagery for God on the logic of trinitarianism, the attempt does at least suggest that even within the orthodox doctrine of God, possibilities are present for denying the hegemony of masculine imagery. I am inclined toward a more modest proposal: if we were to consider this material not as a literal description of God—a picture of God—but as expressing experiences of relating to God as giver and renewer of life, as compassionate creator and renewer of existence, then we could imagine that maternal imagery is not only appropriate but necessary for intimating some of the most profound dimensions of such experiences.

We notice a similar pattern when we turn to medieval mystics. In the contemplative tradition, as another reformist theologian Eleanor McLaughlin mentions, there is enormous metaphorical freedom. No images of the divine-human relationship are inappropriate which will express the intimacy of the mystical experience of God. Where one knows that God cannot be contained by one's metaphors, as the contemplative tradition knows, one feels free to use *all* images that will help to intimate the profound renewal occasioned by life with God. Naturally, therefore, maternal images are central, not merely as rhetorical devices, but as pertaining to the very being of God as creator of our physical and spiritual selves: "God is really our Mother as he is our Father."[69] Not only women mystics such as Julian of Norwich, Christina of Markgate, and St. Birgitta of Sweden used such metaphors, but Anselm of Canterbury and Bernard of Clairvaux also speak of the motherhood of God.

The value of medieval mystical imagery for God rests, in part, on its revolutionary, radical character when placed against the orthodox, patriarchal tradition. In ways similar to the metaphors of contemporary radical feminists, this thinking is bisociative, imagining possibilities the tradition excludes. It shocks conventionality, helps us to break habitual ways of interpreting, juxtaposes other possibilities with accepted ways, and hence allows us to question their adequacy. Many of the ways of speaking about the experience of relating to God and Christ in the mystical tradition are as radical and unconventional as anything to be found in the Goddess religion; yet, these metaphors come not only from Christians but from those whose entire existence was dedicated to experiencing God in the most total and intimate ways. Thus Anselm speaks of Jesus as Mother because he gives birth to souls and because he nourishes and nurses the newborn Christian.[70] Mechthild of Hackeborn, aware that no *one* metaphor can encompass the totality of God's relation to us, speaks of God as Father in creation, Mother in salvation, Brother in dividing up the kingdom, Sister in sweet companionship.[71] Julian of Norwich sees the ontological dependence of human beings on God as best conveyed through the model of God as Mother: "We owe our being to him, and this is the essence of motherhood."[72] A favorite passage of the mystics is Matt. 23:37 where Jesus is likened to a hen gathering chicks under his wing. In McLaughlin's words, the mother hen "comforts, gentles the frightened, revives the despairing, gives life through her warmth to the dead, consoles the terrified."[73] In sum, the profound experience of total dependence on God, both for natural and spiritual birth as well as for the nurturing of the new life in God, found expression for the mystics in maternal imagery of giving birth, nursing, comforting, and caring.

While these metaphors are radical in relationship to the tradition of patriarchal language, they are not only entirely appropriate for expressing profound experiences of renewal and solicitude, but are also the best metaphors available to human beings to convey such aspects of relating to God. Moreover, these modes of relating to God—as creator and nurturer of a new way of being in the world—are not marginal addenda to Christian existence, but central to it. The freedom for female imagery in relation to God stems in part, claims McLaughlin, from the belief in medieval culture that men and women are also both male and female, from the belief that all souls are female before God. As we have seen before, divine and human images are interrelated, and a culture such as ours that denies what Ursula LeGuin calls the androgyny existing in all of us ("if you look at us at certain odd times of the day in certain weathers") will also deny both masculine and feminine imagery for God. The medieval mystics are a rich source of divine imagery that is deeply personal as well as contemporary, with little regard for sex—mother, sister, nurse, knight, lover, brother, friend. The imagery came from what mattered most in human life; this imagery, they surmised, was the best and most appropriate for expressing their love and gratitude to God.

It is important to note also that the mystics were not restricted to personal images: God is not a "person." In many ways natural images can express the immanence of God and the pervasive presence of God in a believer's life more profoundly than can personal ones. Thus, fire, oceans, rain, springs, food, sun, moon, and so forth all appear frequently in mystical literature. The tendency to personify and literalize God is qualified by such powerful natural images. Finally, and of great importance to our contemporary situation, McLaughlin notes that the metaphor of God as "friend" to the soul is a recurring theme, especially in the later middle ages.[74] As a nonfamilial, non-gender-related image, "friend," a suppressed image in the tradition, is one that deserves a prominent place in Christian models. McLaughlin notes, however, that the gains made in the middle ages towards flexibility in metaphors for the divine-human relationship—gains towards female, natural, non-gender-related images—were to die out with the Reformation's turn from contemplative, immanental piety to an emphasis on the transcendence of God. Masculine imagery has traditionally been linked with divine transcendence and it was clearly to be so in Protestantism.

This development can be clearly seen in the rise and fall of the cult of Mary. As many commentators have noted, Mary served as the feminine side of God in the Catholic tradition, for while not herself divine, she symbolized characteristics of compassion, nurture, acceptance, purity, and motherhood, which in other religions have been associated with the female deity. E. O. James sees Goddess religion entering Christianity, not first in Mary, but in Christ's marital relationship to the church.[75] By the fifth century, however, the Goddess influence can be seen in the naming of Mary as "Mother of God" proclaimed at the council of Ephesus in A.D. 431. By the height of devotion to Mary in the Middle Ages, almost every aspect of the Goddess cult is evident, claims James, although the status of Mary was not that of fertility Goddess but that of one critical to the incarnation.

> She is nothing less than the Mother of God, the Queen of Heaven, the Woman clothed with the sun, having the moon under her feet and a crown of twelve stars above her head; and on earth the immaculate ever-virgin, the Lily of Eden, the Second Eve, the Star of the Sea, the co-redemptress, the compassionate Mother, the bestower of grace, the giver of good counsel, Our Lady of Victory, and now at Notre Dame de Lourdes she has been hailed as the bestower of not a few medically attested miraculous cures at her world-renowned Phrenaean shrine.[76]

In spite of Mary's elevation, along with all the characteristics of the Goddess, feminists have not found her cult a contribution to the liberation of women. On the contrary, she has served as the repository of stereotypical female virtues of passivity, receptivity, and acceptance, as well as promoter of contradictory impulses towards sexual asceticism and motherhood. Ruether notes that while Protestantism rejected Mariology, Protestant theologians from Luther and Calvin to Barth have seen Mary as the symbol of humanity's absolute dependence on God:

> Thus, in Protestantism more than ever, the super- and sub-ordination between God and creatures, Christ and the Church, is represented by a hierarchical, omnipotent "masculine" God and a passive, self-abnegating "feminine" humanity. The symbolic relations between Christ and the Father,

Christ and the Church, pastor and people continue to enshrine this rigid hierarchical complementarity of male over female.[77]

Thus we see that the cult of Mary, both within the Catholic tradition as well as transformed by Protestantism—the only form of female imagery orthodox Christianity has allowed—has contributed not to models supportive of women or to a feminine dimension of the divine-human relationship, but rather to the enemy of feminism, the patriarchal model.

In our study of sources in quest of a feminine model for expressing the divine-human relationship, we are led to the conclusion that given the nature of that relationship—one which disorients conventional standards and expectations and reorients us to a new way of being in the world characterized by God's gracious love to all peoples—feminine models for God are not only appropriate but also required, for men as well as for women, in order that they might express certain dimensions of experiencing that relationship.[78] Specifically, the critical experiences expressed most adequately in these models are ones of rebirth, nurture, unmerited love, security in God alone, compassion, forgiveness, service. If we eliminate these experiences from the Christian relationship with God or substitute nonfeminine metaphors for expressing them, we will lose, I believe, essential aspects of that relationship. For these experiences are *central* to Christian faith and it is difficult if not impossible to find better metaphors than the feminine ones for embodying them.

Moreover, as we have seen, a suppressed but by no means insignificant tradition of feminine imagery within the Judeo-Christian paradigm supports its use. In fact, masculine imagery in this suppressed tradition gives credence not to a patriarchal, but to a parental model with shared characteristics of motherhood and fatherhood. The patriarchal model should be seen as a perversion both of the relationship between God and Israel implied in the covenant as well as of the relationship between God and human beings implied in the kingdom, with its radical reliance on the unmerited love of God. Hierarchy, subordinationism, and patriarchal authoritarianism do not model this relationship; parental images, both maternal and paternal, with their notes of compassion, acceptance, discipline, forgiveness, nurture, and guidance do so more appropriately.

God the Friend

Parental models alone, however, whether maternal or paternal, are obviously insufficient. They screen out certain critical aspects of the divine-human relationship. For instance, by their elevation and absolutizing of divine compassion, guidance, and security for the individual, they neglect the public and political dimensions of that relationship, those dimensions concerned with what one critic of parental imagery calls "the contemporary world-wide struggle for the humanisation and self-assertion of the masses."[79] Thus, parental images need to be balanced, as the medieval mystics clearly illustrate, by many other metaphors. Certainly our time of desecration of the natural environment desperately needs immanental, natural metaphors which will help to address the imbalance that centuries of the Judeo-Christian emphasis on humanity's "dominion over the earth" have brought about. This is not the place to engage in a diatribe against Western religion's contribution to the pollution of the atmosphere, the decline of natural resources, the proliferation of nuclear weapons, and so forth. At the very least, however, it must be mentioned that an open and appreciative attitude toward Eastern models, which portray the divine presence as immanent not only in human beings but also in nature, is mandatory.

In addition, maternal and paternal models need to be balanced by nonfamilial, non-gender-related ones. One such metaphor, although by no means the only one, is God as "friend," a metaphor with potential for becoming a model. It is found here and there in the Bible: in the sweeping inclusion of all Israel as friends of God in Isaiah—"But you, Israel my servant, you Jacob whom I have chosen, race of Abraham my friend" (Isa. 41:18); in Jesus' saying that there is no greater love than laying down one's life for one's friends (John 15:13); in Jesus' reference to the Son of man as the friend of tax collectors and sinners (Matt. 11:19). Friendship with God is also suggested in biblical passages referring to companionship or fellowship with God (Josh. 1:5, 1 John 1:3, John 17:21) and partnership with God (Hos. 2:23, 1 Cor. 3:9). It is found in the tradition, though sparingly: in Irenaeus of Lyons for whom the friendship of God for humanity is a powerful metaphor; in the medieval mystics; and a variation of it in A. N. Whitehead's metaphor for God as "fellow-sufferer."

As a balance to parental models, the model of friendship has much to offer. First, female and male experience is not exhausted by parenthood; many people are not parents today, have no intention of becoming parents, and rightfully resent femininity and masculinity being linked to the ability or desire to produce children. In our society, parent-child relationships are not as central as they have been in former times, and it is unnecessarily restrictive to interpret personal models only in parental terms. Second, parental images stress the characteristics of compassion and acceptance as well as guidance and discipline, but they cannot express mutuality, maturity, cooperation, responsibility, or reciprocity. The metaphor of friendship is ideally suited to express certain dimensions of a mature relationship with God. Third, in a time such as ours when at both the personal and political levels all kinds of people are working together for common causes, friendship expresses that ideal of relationship among peoples of all ages, both sexes, and whatever color or religion. It is an increasingly important metaphor for us on the human level. Hence, following the logic of all religious imagery that what matters most to us is the way to model our relationship with God, it is also an appropriate religious model.

By "friendship" we do not of course mean easy empathy for one's own kind to be found in clubs, secret societies, and unfortunately, churches all over the world. Genuine friendship does not negate differences but can thrive on them, as the old adage, "opposites attract," suggests. But even beyond the personal level, the ideal of friendship to the stranger, to the alien both as individual and as nation or culture, suggests a model. Like Dante's vision of the harmony in paradise where the saints hold hands and dance in a circle, the friendship model is one for the future on our increasingly small and beleaguered planet, where, if people do not become friends, they will not survive. Rosemary Ruether suggests a similar model when she writes: "Women seek a re-construction of relationships for which we have neither words nor models. . . . We seek a new concept of relationships between persons, groups, life systems, a relationship which is not competitive or hierarchical but mutually enhancing."[80] She calls this new concept "communal personhood"; I prefer the model of friendship, for it is as old as human beings are, and it runs deep in our history and in our blood, and now, after centuries of hierarchical, polarized models, it is especially appropriate for us.

In Ursula LeGuin's fantasy of two people separated by all that can separate human beings—not only the usual matters of race, culture, religion, and sex, but the extraordinary one of being citizens of different planets—it is *friendship* that describes the relationship developing between them. In notes on *The Left Hand of Darkness*, LeGuin says that the real subject of the book is not gender or sexual difference but betrayal and fidelity. And it is for this reason, she says, that the dominant image in the book is an extended metaphor of a winter journey through ice, cold, and snow.[81] Her two characters, opposed in so many ways, are put to the test of achieving friendship through the trials of an incredible journey, the success of which depends entirely on their fidelity to each other. Their sexual difference is a metaphor for all their differences, differences which might have led to betrayal, but instead lead to friendship. Genly Ali says: "For it seemed to me, and I think to him, that it was from that sexual tension between us, admitted now and understood, but not assuaged, that the great and sudden assurance of friendship between us arose: a friendship so much needed by us both in our exile, and already so well proved in the days and nights of our bitter journey, that it might as well be called, now as later, love."[82]

The model of friendship for our relationship with God and its ramifications for our relationship with other human beings, however, suggest more than the overcoming of differences. If one of the most meaningful contemporary understandings of the atonement is the suffering of God for and with the pain and oppression of the world, then the model of God as friend takes on special significance. Jesus, in his identification with the sufferings of others throughout his life and especially at his death, is a parable of God's friendship with us at the most profound level.

We see this identification in parables such as the Lost Sheep, the Prodigal Son, the Good Samaritan, and the Great Supper where the outcasts are welcomed and the conventionally righteous turned aside. We see it also in the Beatitudes and in Jesus' reading in Luke 4 from Isaiah 61:1–2 proclaiming good news to the poor, release to the captives, and liberty for the oppressed. But we see it even more dramatically, as many New Testament scholars have suggested, in Jesus' table-fellowship with "sinners and tax collectors." Joachim Jeremias, Günther Bornkamm, and Norman Perrin, for instance, agree that Jesus' practice of eating with the outcasts of his society was both the central feature and the central scandal of his ministry.[83] The passage in Matthew—"the Son of man came eating and drinking, and they say, 'Behold, a glutton and a drunkard, a friend of tax collectors and sinners'" (11:19)—is not only one of the best-authenticated sayings in the New Testament but also what could be called "an enacted parable." Bornkamm states this directly when he writes, "what the parables say actually happens in Jesus' fellowship with other people" and Perrin claims that Jesus' table-fellowship "is not a proclamation in words at all, but an acted parable."[84] Jesus' table-fellowship both shocked his enemies and impressed his followers because eating with others was the closest form of intimacy for Jews of that time and conveyed honor to those chosen. One did not eat with the ritually unclean, with Gentiles, with those in despised trades; hence, for Jesus to eat with such peoples, to be called the "friend" of such people, was a scandal to most people as well as a form of radical acceptance for his friends at table. Jeremias and Perrin agree that such a practice alone was sufficient cause for his being put to death on a cross, for it shattered the Jews' attempt to close ranks against the Roman enemy by keeping the community pure. Jeremias states: "For the offence after Easter was Jesus' accursed death on the cross—his table-fellowship with sinners was the pre-Easter scandal."[85]

The acceptance of the outcasts and the oppressed at table is a concrete enactment of forgiveness of sins. Here Jesus is not just expressing God's love but, as Bornkamm says, doing what God alone can do—forgiving sins, extending salvation to the outcasts.[86] If, as seems to be generally agreed by New Testament scholars, the fellowship of the table for the early Christian community is a symbol of the messianic banquet (as well as a precursor of the Eucharist),[87] then Jesus, in his friendship with outcasts and sinners, is a model of friendship with God. Jesus as parable enacts God's friendship with humanity. The God of Jesus is the One who invites us to table to eat together as friends.

If Jesus is the friend who identifies with the sufferings of the oppressed in his table-fellowship against all expectations and conventions, so also is he the one who in his death, as John says, lays down his life for his friends (15:12–15). The Johannine passage is of a piece with the table-fellowship, although no claims have been advanced for its authenticity as it is probably a postresurrection tradition. What is critical, however, as Raymond Brown points out, is that "the model of the disciples' love is Jesus' supreme act of love, his laying down his life."[88] His way of expressing his love for his friends also must be our way of expressing gratitude for such love—we too must lay down our lives. Thus, we are no longer called "servants" but "friends," doing for others what our friend did for us.

The life and death of Jesus as friend, are, then, of a piece: as parable of God they reveal, as Jürgen Moltmann says, a God who suffers for us and, by so doing, invites us into a fellowship of suffering with God and for others. Such a relationship, says Moltmann, is "friendship with God": "The friend of God does not live any longer 'under God', but with and in God." Such a person shares in the grief and the joy of God; such a person has become "one" with God.[89]

The model of friend for God, as is evident from the foregoing analysis, moves away from hierarchism and toward egalitarianism. It also has strong immanental tendencies: we are no longer under but with and in God. Initially, many people in the Western religious tradition may be wary of such a model for it raises difficult questions: What is the authority of God as friend? Can such a God protect and save individuals and the world? How do we worship a God who is our friend? These are large and important questions that cannot be fully answered here. But some attempt can be made.

THE AUTHORITY OF GOD AS FRIEND

The issue of authority between friends is far more complex than between superiors and subordinates. If we look first and very briefly at Jesus as friend both in his teaching and his acts, one can at least say that he was an "extraordinary" friend, that the relationship between him and his disciples, let alone between him and the outcasts at table, was scarcely one of equality. To be sure, he appears in the synoptic Gospels, especially in some of the Son of man sayings, to be a person in need of friends both for physical and moral support and comfort. Yet, the relationship is not one of equality: he gave more than he received. The classical Greek understanding of friendship demands that it can occur only between equals— a factor, among others, in the presumption that friendship was possible only between men, not between men and women. But the mode of Jesus' friendship with others does not suggest that equality is its main characteristic; rather, identification with the needs and sufferings of others, regardless of difference of class, race, gender, nationality seems far more critical. Friends bear one another's burdens—if need be, to the point of death.

But what sort of authority *can* there be between friends, even if one takes into account inequalities and differences? One helpful exercise for us as we try to think "experimentally" about this issue is to meditate on what Max Black calls the "associated commonplaces" of our model. What characteristics does one associate with the give-and-take between friends? My list is only suggestive and not meant to be inclusive: mutuality, respect, acceptance of differences, cooperation, solidarity, attraction, perseverance, tolerance, gift-giving, delight, sacrifice, constructive criticism. Some of these commonplaces are egalitarian, while others, especially attraction, criticism, and respect, suggest authority of some sort for one friend in relation to the other. At times we are aware of the attractive power of the other calling forth goodness in us; at other times, one friend assumes a position over against the other in criticism; at all times friends respect the independence of each other.

I would suggest that the principal overriding characteristic of friendship as a mode of relating to another is "maturity"—it is a way of relating that is pertinent to adults. We often say that we are glad when children become adults because then we have the possibility of being friends with them. The authority that parents have over children is markedly different from the authority that can exist between friends. For instance, one takes the criticism of a friend very differently than one takes the criticism of a superior. Between friends, there is the desire to please the other, to stand well in the friend's estimation; hence, criticism is taken very seriously. Such criticism is assumed to be "meant well," to be for one's growth; it is also assumed that the friend will be honest and not tell one merely what one wants to hear. Friends, however, are not totally dependent on one another; they are adults and cannot give over entirely to another's opinion. Each must take responsibility for his or her own life. One cannot *tell* a friend what to do, for decision finally belongs to each alone.

As another example, the kind of reconciliation and gratitude that can occur between friends after a rupture in the relationship is substantially different than that between parents and children.[90] Children *expect* parents to forgive them, while parents *expect* children to confess their wrongdoings; the reconciliation that results tends to be tainted with lingering notes of duty and/or resentment. But friends, lacking as they do that primordial bond of expectation on both sides, experience genuine grief at the rupture (and an awareness of its seriousness) as well as honest surprise and joy that the bond can nevertheless be renewed and in fact strengthened. Such reconciliation is not simply a restoration to things as they were, but a step into a new dimension of relationship. It is perhaps no accident that Irenaeus, one of the few theologians who has used the model of friendship between God and humanity, also believed that the fall was "fortunate"; that is, reconciliation for us is not just a return to the obedient behavior of Eden, but is a fulfillment of our potential to become friends with God.

The Scottish theologian Ruth Page suggests that a meaningful contemporary understanding of God's transcendence is not the God "above" but "alongside"—a horizontal rather than a vertical relationship.[91] The most appropriate image for such a horizontal relationship is God as companion, one who travels with us and shares our experience. She notes three motifs in this relationship which speak directly to the issue of authority between companions. First, in companionship there are elements of both dependence and independence; it is "the kind of dependence we have on those whose opinions and experience we value and whose company we enjoy," but it is not pathological overdependence, such as children have on parents.[92] Second, companionship reshapes our view of power, because "companionship . . . works by attraction unlike lordship which works by subjection. God has our attention and devotion by the lure of his goodness rather than by the command of his sovereignty."[93] Power, therefore, between companions does not assault and subdue but attracts; it does not constrain the freedom of the other. Third, companionship reshapes our view of service, for one does not serve a companion but one wants to be well-thought-of by one's companion. "One endeavours in a sense to please them and similarly one seeks to be well-pleasing to God. For companionship to be a reality there must be a communality of ideas, aims and behaviour to a considerable extent, and the pleasure this brings God takes the place of service in the older models."[94] As Page notes, while the rationale has altered, the result in practice is likely to be the same. This is not a minor point, for if the authority of God has traditionally been concerned with stipulating the appropriate service that we as creatures owe to our creator, then a model of God which is psychologically more effective for the contemporary world and, yet, still brings about that end has much in its favor. As twentieth-century Christians, the model of God as the companion whom we wish to please and who attracts our cooperation may be a more powerful model for us than the model of God as father or king who commands us to be obedient children or servants.

THE SAVING ACTIVITY OF GOD AS FRIEND

Can God as friend protect and save individuals and the world? If the issue of authority in regard to the model of God as friend gives pause, the issue of salvation does even more so. The God of Christianity has been the all-powerful protector, comforter, and savior, solving all problems for the individual and for society. The traditional understandings of the atoning work of Jesus Christ, for the most part, have been the objective, mighty acts of God. Whether one understands atonement as a redemption from the powers of evil, or a substitutionary sacrifice, or a reunification with the source of life, it has been seen as *God's act alone* and one which brings about a new state of affairs in reality. Western theology has relied on models of salvation with powerful objective images: we are enslaved by demonic powers and must be ransomed by Jesus Christ in order to be set free; we are guilty before the tribunal of the almighty judge and must either be punished or a righteous man—Jesus Christ—found to stand in our place; we are alienated from the source of our being and thus doomed to death and only life itself in the Word made flesh can reunite us to life. These models permit no cooperation on our part; in fact, any view of the saving work of God which significantly involves our participation has been considered heretical, for it appears not to take seriously our status as sinners totally dependent on the graciousness of God.

Nevertheless, the result of this view of salvation has been pernicious in several ways. It projects an image of human life as infantile, individualistic, and isolated. It has tended to stress an all-powerful father of helpless children, some of whom, as favored, are rescued individually from a sinful world. To be sure this is a caricature, but like most caricatures it contains a truth, especially for popular piety. Since we live within our models unconsciously, the way we model our relationship with God has significant impact on our understanding of human existence. If the traditional model of God's saving activity contributes to a view of human life as infantile, individualistic, and isolated, then it is deeply in need of substantial revision, for human life cannot responsibly be seen in those terms. Nor, I would suggest, does Jesus as parable of God, either in his teaching or his activity, support such a view.

Our major thesis is that, whether we look at the contemporary epistemology operating in science and philosophy, or at the covenant in the Old Testament, or at the parables in the New Testament, or at Jesus as parable of God, we see *relationship* as the central motif. We cannot know things in isolation, and we do not live as individuals apart from other beings and apart from our world. The shift from Newtonian to quantum physics, for example, reflects this understanding, as does the contemporary ecological sensibility that the universe is a total, interrelated system. We see it as well in contemporary liberationist movements which insist that solidarity is the key to freedom. We are not alone and cannot exist alone or be saved alone. The imminence of nuclear warfare, the desecration of the natural environment, and the scarcity of food to support the world's increasing population lend irrefutable credence to this reality. Moreover, it appears increasingly to be the case that our health and well-being, which is to say, our "salvation," depends in part on ourselves, on our willingness and ability to work cooperatively and with all our intelligence and strength. Any notion of salvation which presumes that individuals can be rescued *from* the world; that does not take seriously our necessary efforts to participate in the struggle against oppression and for well-being; or that allows us to abjure our responsibility by appealing as children to a father who will alone protect and save—any such notion must be seen as immoral, irrelevant, and destructive. At the very least, it cannot be a model for adults; moreover, it is, I believe, contrary to Christian faith.

Such a model is contrary certainly to the image of Jesus as the friend of outcasts and the one who gives his life for his friends. The dominant motif in these images is one of unconventional and radical identification with the needs and suffering of others. If Jesus' mode of friendship were to be taken as a parable of God's saving activity, salvation could in no way be called infantile, individualistic, or isolated. Nor would this be the case if we look at the commonplaces associated with that friendship: solidarity, gift-giving, sacrifice, suffering, and the acceptance of differences. Rather than stressing the protection, comfort, and redemption of individuals *apart* from others and the world, a friendship model emphasizes sacrifice, support, and solidarity *with* others and the world. God's saving activity is seen in an "adult" not a "father/child" mode. God is our friend who suffers with us as we work with God to bring about a better existence for suffering humanity.

This view of salvation lacks the "objectivity," certainty, and sense of absoluteness found in traditional views. It does not stress what God does *for* us apart from our participation, and it does not claim that "God's in his heaven/All's right with the world." In a time when we have "come of age," have become adults, as Dietrich Bonhoeffer insisted, that kind of certainty and objectivity is no longer appropriate. Moreover, we realize increasingly that our decisions, not God's will, cause most of the oppression of other human beings; that we, not God, have polluted and desecrated the ecosphere; that if nuclear disaster comes it will be our doing, not God's. At the most, a *credible* view of salvation can only be that God is *with us*—on our side—as we suffer through and work towards overcoming these evils and the perversity of our hearts from which they come. In this view God as savior, with Jesus as parable of God, is the One who, in radical and total solidarity with us, wills our salvation and works through us for its realization. God is the friend who sacrifices on our behalf; who cooperates with gifts of power, perseverance, and insight; who accepts our differing talents and efforts on behalf of the well-being of all; and when, as is bound to happen, we fail through weakness, perversity, fear, or selfishness, who forgives us—us, the "outcasts." The friend who accepts the outcasts is not a God who does everything *for* others, but the One who empowers others to join together to overcome oppression of all kinds. Friends do not and cannot "save" one another; rather, they work together for common goals in such a way that each is encouraged, empowered, and enlivened to do what each is able to do for the good of the whole.

Such a view of salvation does not ensure its outcome. If we understand salvation as the well-being and fulfillment of all that lives, it is certain that *we* cannot bring that about, but it is also certain that *God* cannot bring it about apart from our participation. If we are not puppets or children but adults, then we must be part of the process, even if the outcome is uncertain. That realization is unsettling, especially in a tradition which has understood God's power as total and the salvatory act as an objective event that occurred two thousand years ago. On the model of friend, however, God's power is persuasive, attractive, cooperating, and salvation is not a once-for-all act but a relationship to us and our world that grows as we respond to our friend's desire to befriend us.

Jesus as the friend of sinners and outcasts is the one who shows us concretely in word and act that God *is* this way, always has been this way, and always will be this way. As parable of God, Jesus does not bring about a new situation, a change in God's attitude toward us, but, in actually befriending us sinners and outcasts, he models God the friend. Rather than being a "low christology," this view presents a "high christology," for he is Emmanuel—God with us.

Yet, God as friend does not entail equality with us. Friends are not necessarily equals, for differences in ability, economic and social class, race, and sex can exist between friends. God as friend is not "reduced" to our level, although the model does suggest a different form of egalitarianism than the conventional view. The kind of egalitarianism between friends is based on common interests and goals while recognizing and appreciating different roles and functions as they work together. We as God's friends receive more than we give, but God as our friend receives also: God is not "everything" and we "nothing."

God as friend, moreover, involves a modification in the traditional understanding of God's transcendence. God as friend is not above, apart, over us in an absolute sense; rather, just as friends participate in each other's lives, so God is part of our being as the source of power, of love, of endurance, of insight. But God is also the source of our life. The model becomes strained at this point, for friends are not the source of each others' lives. The "thought experiment" on the model of friend falters at the point of the gift of life, and other models—those of creator and sustainer—are needed to complement it. Nevertheless, the model of friend is a rich one for illuminating the notion of God's immanence in our ongoing lives. Friends, over a long period of time, become more and more intimately involved with each other. Friendship does not happen all at once, but grows with mutual dependence, support, suffering, and delight. People who have been friends for many years become part of each others' identity. Those who have been friends with God for many years become, as Moltmann says, "one" with God.[95]

In sum, the model of God as friend offers us a view of salvation substantially different from traditional views in which God redeems and protects individuals. Rather, it supports an "adult" view of shared responsibility with God as our friend, identifying with us in our suffering and working with us toward overcoming the oppression brought about in large part by our own perversity and selfishness. And as we are able to forgive our friends for failure, and at times even for betrayal and treachery, so much the more, as we know from Jesus as parable of God, does God forgive us—the outcasts and sinners.

WORSHIPING GOD AS FRIEND

The thought of praying to a friend probably seems odd if not inappropriate to most of us. As Ruth Page says, one may proliferate many models of God which are theologically fruitful, but unless they work in practice—unless they mediate God—they will be seriously inadequate. Her comment on prayer to God as companion is therefore an interesting one.

> Prayer as a session with a companion has changed the felt quality of the practice. Confession, for instance, becomes startlingly existential precisely because I can imagine what it is to confess to companions or colleagues. God as Companion therefore does not simply underwrite complacent personhood.[96]

The comment is especially pertinent in that it underscores again the adult quality of the friend model. Once we pass childhood most of us more often ask forgiveness and acceptance from colleagues and friends than from parents. The vast majority of people today, women as well as men, work outside the home; hence many of the tensions, conflicts, and failures in our lives occur with companions and colleagues.

More than confession, however, is involved in worship. How intimate can one be with God as friend? Can one feel thankful to God as friend? Can one ask God as friend for aid and support? The friend model appears especially suggestive in regard to feeling close to God, thanking God, and asking for help. It is no accident that the friendship model appears in the immanental tradition within Christianity—in the Gospel of John, in Irenaeus, in the medieval mystics. This tradition stresses our union with God through Jesus Christ and as a consequence the oneness of all people with each other. A powerful model for expressing this sense of union has been friendship, for as a nonfamilial, non-gender-related image, it crosses the boundaries separating people of different classes, sexes, races, ages, and religions. One *can* be friends with *anyone*, including, in mystical thought, God.[97] The friendship model is in part eschatological: it projects a possibility of a time when all peoples *shall* be one with God and with each other. It models not only what we are now in part but what we hope to be. As an eschatological model, it offers us a standard or perspective from which to see our present alienation more clearly and to criticize, in prophetic fashion, that alienation more perceptively. It suggests that the adequate and appropriate worship of God is not a solitary affair between the soul and God but, as Dante envisioned in the *Paradisio*, a dance in which all will join together accompanied by the music of the spheres. Friendship is an intimation of the unification of all that is, the natural as well as the human, joined together in harmony with God.

In addition, the intimacy intrinsic to friendship makes the model a good one for worship. Friends are deeply thankful to one another for all the gifts, both material and spiritual, that pass between them. They feel free to ask for help when it is needed and take pleasure in supporting each other. Thankfulness and requests for help between friends do not carry the notes of duty or expectation conventionally found in parent/ child relationships. While parents and children are expected to give gifts to one another and to help when needed, a gift from a friend or an offer of aid is suggestive of grace, of unworthiness, of surprise. Hence, the friend model balances the parental model: our experiences of relating to God include both comforting expectation of acceptance as well as amazement for the many gifts and aid we receive.

The intimacy with God intrinsic to the friendship model is not, however, one of cozy relaxation. The mystical tradition, which more than any other has emphasized *oneness* with God, also insists on *distance* from God. The closer one becomes to a friend the more one realizes the mystery of the other. Acquaintances do not seem particularly mysterious, but friends, who have shared much over a long time, seldom feel they know the other completely. The mystics witness to this paradox of intimacy and distance—the dark night of the soul comes not to those who do *not* know

God but to those who *do*. Because of the blood ties in families, this sense of distance is often less pronounced. Parents can see their children as extensions of themselves, and children can imagine they have grown beyond their parents' more simple worlds. Friends rarely reduce each other in such fashion, for differences in backgrounds and experience create a sense of otherness between them. To be friends with God is to be friends with ultimate mystery—the paradox remains.

THE LIMITATIONS OF THE MODEL OF GOD AS FRIEND

No one model is adequate and indeed, all models together are not adequate to express our experiences of relating to God. We have attempted a "thought experiment" with the model of God as friend, but like any model, it has its limitations. Friendship and its associated commonplaces—mutual respect, listening, sharing of joy and suffering, reciprocity, forgiveness, solidarity, reconciliation, sacrifice, fidelity—are all appropriate motifs for modeling certain aspects of the parabolic understanding of life with God. The model of friendship does not, it seems to me, have the potential for becoming a root-metaphor in the way that the partriarchal model presumably has, but so much the better, for the basic problem with the patriarchal model has been its expansion, its inclusiveness, its hegemony, its elevation to an idol. The root-metaphor of Christianity is not *any one* model but a relationship that occurs between God and human beings. Many models are needed to intimate what that relationship is like; none can capture it.[98] "Friendship" is but one suggestion; a model perhaps particularly relevant to women in their relations with each other and with men, but to all people as well, a model for a common humanity in which differences will be the occasion, not for alienation, but for that love based on mutual respect, on reciprocity, on shared suffering and joy. Since we model God in the significant images of our time, the friendship we seek in the human community causes us also to look at God as our friend.

The model of God as friend, however, needs to be balanced by other models, for friendship is deficient in several respects. First, it can appear to be too individualistic. Letty Russell prefers the model of "partner," for it is a social image suggesting commitment to a common struggle: "Partnership may be described as a new focus of relationship in which there is continuing commitment and common struggle in interaction with a wider community context."[99] Just as the trinitarian God is a *relationship*—a partnership of mutual love between the persons and toward creation—so we too are partners with God.[100] We share in the work of the economic trinity—"the work of caring for creation, setting the captives free, and standing as witness for and with those who need an advocate."[101] The model of partner, as a variation and expansion of the model of friend, is appropriate. To me, however, it has connotations of contracts, of business affairs, of casual relations. It lacks the ancient, deep roots in human experience of "friend" and has less personally significant associations. "Friend" is comparable in depth to "father," "mother," and "lover" as basic bonds in the experience of all peoples from our beginnings. Therefore, I did not choose "partner" as the model for my experiment, although I accept its socializing associations as a necessary balance to friendship.

Second, the model of God as friend needs to be complemented by models which differentiate between the status of the friends. These need not be hierarchical models such as father, king, lord, and master, but should be ones intimating guidance, leadership, protection, governance, preeminence. It is difficult in a democratic society to suggest models which possess these characteristics intrinsically, since democracies choose officials to *function* in these ways. Thus, president, prime minister, or governor are too extrinsic to serve as models of God's preeminent status as guide and protector. It seems to me that the search for models of *intrinsic* leadership is one of the most difficult issues of our time. We do not trust our leaders and have few contemporary models of guidance with integrity and widespread acceptance. It may simply have to be acknowledged that *we do not know* how to model God in this respect in terms of current images from our society and will not know until our own patterns of governance prove more viable and successful. Yet, it would be a mistake, I believe, to revert to anachronistic models or to return to hierarchical models which give all power to a determining, controlling God who alone is in charge of human affairs. The *via negativa* is an old tradition when one does not know *how* to speak to God and perhaps the most honest response is to evoke it on the issue of divine guidance.

Third, the model of God as friend is unable to express experiences of awe, ecstasy, fear, and silence in relating to God. In fact, none of the anthropocentric images can convey these experiences. Again, the mystics are instructive for not only have they produced novel anthropocentric images but they are also rich in images from nature suggestive of the emotional heights and depths of relating to the cosmic God. Such images need not be abstract or impersonal, for as Eleanor McLaughlin points out, many were extraordinarily intimate.[102] One medieval mystic speaks of God as follows:

> Thou art an immense ocean of all sweetness . . . lose myself in the flood of thy living love as a drop of sea water . . . let me die in the torrent of thy infinite compassion as a burning spark dies in the rushing current of the river. Let the rain of thy boundless love fall round about me.[103]

The nature imagery of the mystics is, of course, hardly new for one recalls the rich natural imagery of the Hebrew Psalms. The variety and depth of such imagery should undercut any pretensions to idolatry of the major anthropocentric models. God cannot be imaged in any *one* model, for the whole cosmos is God's "body." "The world is charged with the glory of God," says Gerard Manley Hopkins, and God is imaged in "all things counter, original, spare, strange."[104] The Christian tradition has narrowed its metaphors and models of God, excluding natural images and focusing on hierarchical, authoritarian, anthropocentric ones. Primitive religions as well as Eastern religions support the mystics and the writers of the Psalms by insisting that experiences of God cannot be so limited, for much of what we feel in worship demands them. Ecstasy and awe cannot be contained in models of God as parent or friend—the ocean, the sky, and the earth express them more fully.

Finally, impersonal models are necessary not only as safeguards against the limits of all images but also as expressions of the depths of our dependence on God. Paul Tillich was right to say that God is "Being-Itself,"[105] for even though, once again, the only kind of "being" we know is creaturely existence and hence "Being-Itself" is a metaphor, still, the phrase points to God as the source and depth of our being. We have no words for this sense of radical and absolute dependence on Another for life itself. We know it is not of our making or doing, that all that is derives from "not itself," that we are something but come from nothing.

Conclusion

I have attempted to chart a course from religious language—the language of images and metaphors—to theological language—the language of models and concepts. This course takes into account two serious issues affecting religious/theological language in our time: the issues of the idolatry of such language (literalism, as seen in various fundamentalist movements) and of the irrelevance of such language to many people (rejection of the Western religious tradition by many women, blacks, and third world people). Hence, the book deals with two problems: How does primary religious language move toward secondary theological language? and How can this be accomplished so as to fall into neither idolatry nor irrelevance?

The answer I suggest to both problems is to understand religious/theological language in terms of metaphors and models. Religious language is largely metaphorical, while theological language is composed principally of models. Insights on the nature and function of models from philosophy of science are helpful for understanding the similarities and differences between models in science and in theology. Models are dominant, comprehensive metaphors with organizing, structural potential. Thus, there is an intrinsic relationship between religious language and theological language suggested in the notion of model, since models have characteristics of both imagistic and conceptual language. Moreover, since models are derived from metaphors, they continue the basic characteristics of metaphors and two of these characteristics—indirection and partiality—are especially important for addressing the issues of idolatry and irrelevance. Models can never be taken literally since they are not descriptions but indirect attempts to express the unfamiliar in terms of the familiar. Moreover, many models are necessary, since all are partial; thus, those who have found the traditional models of God and human life irrelevant are encouraged to work out new models.

The overall intent of the work, then, is a "thought experiment" in what

I have called "metaphorical theology," an attempt to understand religious/theological language on the basis of "metaphor" and its characteristics as distinct from the traditional basis of religious language understood as "symbol" and its characteristics. The metaphorical perspective is not only appropriate to Christianity in that Jesus' parables are metaphors and Jesus himself can be seen as parable of God, but it is also appropriate to the contemporary sensibility in that it allows for a sense of discontinuity, skepticism, and relativity between our language and its reference to God and the world. As an illustration of how a metaphorical theology addresses the issues of idolatry and irrelevance, the model of God as father is considered—a model which many feminists claim is idolatrous and irrelevant to them. A complementary model, that of God as friend, suggests itself as both significant to our time and appropriate to Christian faith.

The thread that has knit together the fabric of this "thought experiment" is the insight—evident in the covenant between God and Israel, in the parables of the kingdom, in contemporary scientific and philosophical epistemology, and in our emerging ecological sensitivity—that we exist only in *relationship*. Our lives and actions take place in networks of relationships. To the extent that we know ourselves, our world, and our God, that knowledge is profoundly relational and, hence, interdependent, relative, situational, and limited. The implication for models of God is obvious: we must use the relationships nearest and dearest to us as metaphors of that which finally cannot be named. Aware that we exist only in relationship and aware, therefore, that all our language about God is but metaphors of experiences of relating to God, we are free to use many models of God. Aware, however, that the relationship with God cannot be named, we are prohibited from absolutizing any models of God.

The last word as well as the first word in theology is surrounded by silence. We know with Simone Weil that when we try to speak of God there is nothing which resembles what we can conceive when we say that word.

Notes

CHAPTER 1

1. Simone Weil, *Waiting for God* (New York: Harper & Row, 1973), p. 32.
2. See Frank Kermode, *The Classic: Literary Images of Permanence and Change* (New York: Viking Press, 1975).
3. James Hillman in *Re-Visioning Psychology* (New York: Harper & Row, 1977) claims Protestantism denied the imagination and myth and killed off fantasy. See the article by Lucy Bregman, "Religious Imagination: Polytheistic Psychology Confronts Calvin," *Soundings* 63 (1980): 36–60. Bregman also suggests an intriguing list that includes the "left" and "right" brains, equating literalism with the left and symbolism with the right.

Rational	Imaginative
Technology	Art
Literal	Symbolic
History	Myth
Western	Eastern, primitive
Masculine	Feminine
Left-brain	Right-brain
Reformation	Renaissance
Repressive	Liberating
Sacred text	Myth
Work ethic	Spontaneous pleasure

4. Clifford Geertz, "Religion as a Cultural System," in *Reader in Comparative Religion*, 2d ed. rev., ed. William Lessa and Evon Vogt (New York: Harper & Row, 1965), p. 209.
5. Ian T. Ramsey, *Religious Language* (New York: Macmillan Co., 1963), p. 107.
6. Phyllis Trible, *God and the Rhetoric of Sexuality*, Overtures to Biblical Theology (Philadelphia: Fortress Press, 1978), p. 16.
7. The following quotation by Carol Christ and Judith Plaskow is an excellent summary of the feminist critique of language and the importance of naming.

> Consciousness-raising . . . leads to a critique of culture and to the tasks of transforming or recreating it. Feminists have called their task a "new nam-

ing" of self and world. It is through naming that humans progress from childhood to adulthood and learn to understand and shape the world about them. Under patriarchy, men have reserved to themselves the right to name, keeping women in a state of intellectual and spiritual dependency. Mary Daly suggests that the Genesis creation story, in which Adam names the animals and woman, is the paradigm of false naming in Western culture. If the world has been named by Adam without Eve's consultation, then the world has been named from the male point of view. As women begin to name the world for themselves, they will upset the order that has been taken for granted throughout history. They will call themselves and the world into new being. Naming women's experience thus becomes the model not only for personal liberation and growth, but for the feminist transformation of culture and religion (Carol Christ and Judith Plaskow, eds., *Womanspirit Rising: A Feminist Reader in Religion* [New York: Harper & Row, 1979], p. 7).

8. The reasons for patriarchy undoubtedly derive in part from the fact that as Elaine Pagels, along with many other scholars, points out, the God of Israel, unlike most other deities in the ancient Near East, shared his power with no female divinity. She writes,

he scarcely can be characterized in any but masculine epithets: King, Lord, Master, Judge, and Father. Indeed, the absence of feminine symbolism of God marks Judaism, Christianity, and Islam in striking contrast to the world's other religious traditions, whether in Egypt, Babylonia, Greece, and Rome, or Africa, Polynesia, India, and North America. Jewish, Christian, and Islamic theologians, however, are quick to point out that God is not to be considered in sexual terms at all. Yet the actual language they use in worship and prayer conveys a different message and gives the distinct impression that God is thought of in exclusively *masculine* terms ("What Became of God the Mother? Conflicting Images of God in Early Christianity," in *Womanspirit Rising*, ed. Christ and Plaskow, p. 107).

9. This point is made at length in the classic study by Peter Berger, *The Social Reality of Religion* (London: Faber & Faber, 1969).

10. See, for example, Rita M. Gross, ed., *Beyond Androcentrism: New Essays on Women and Religion* (Missoula, Mont.: Scholars Press, 1977).

11. Incarnational theology, based on "the Word became flesh," eventuated in the orthodox christology which has always been cryptically Docetic. In spite of the formula, "fully God and fully man," the human partnership was never taken with full seriousness, for again and again the church has been unwilling to deal with such matters as growth and change in Jesus of Nazareth as evidenced by its uneasiness about admitting the possibility of sin in him. An incarnational christology is inevitably static and nature-oriented, rather than dynamic and human-oriented. A thoughtful debate on incarnational christology can be found in John Hick, ed., *The Myth of God Incarnate* (Philadelphia: Westminster Press; London: SCM Press, 1977).

12. There are of course many fine studies of sacramentalism and it is not

necessary or appropriate here to list them. A particularly interesting one, however, is Mary Douglas's *Natural Symbols* (New York: Pantheon Books, 1970) because she sees a direct connection both in primitive and advanced cultures between attitudes toward the body and the ability to think sacramentally. She finds Protestantism especially alienated in this regard, for its stress on inner experience, denigration of ritual, and rejection of mediating institutions make it impossible to see the body and hence the world from a symbolic perspective. I find her analysis of our problematic situation—one in which all connections have been broken—illuminating, but her solution—a return to organic sacramentalism with the full paraphernalia of medieval orthodox incarnationalism—insupportable.

13. The medieval doctrine of analogical predication rests on the analogy of being. We can predicate human characteristics of God (goodness, wisdom, etc.) because our being was created by and is dependent upon God's being. In the order of knowing, we proceed from the creature to the creator for we must start from the concrete and empirical; in the order of being we proceed from the creator to the creature, for God possesses the characteristics we attribute absolutely and truly, though we do not know the *mode* in which they are realized in the divine being. The two prominent types of analogical predication in medieval philosophy were analogy of attribution and of proper proportionality. Both are necessary for one provides the *content*, the other the *form*, of predication. The analogy of attribution allows that we can attribute certain qualities to God because God is the ground of being and hence everything that is participates in God—*what* we say, therefore, is based on the creature as caused by, dependent upon, the creator. The analogy of proper proportionality insists that we do not know *how* such qualities are realized in God and hence this form of analogy serves as a negation of all forms of literalism and idolatry. Another way of expressing the necessity and relationship of the two types is to say that analogies of attribution are "models" licensing certain language for God and analogies of proper proportionality are "qualifiers" insisting on the necessary distance in all talk of God. In order to say *anything* we must use models from concrete, human experience, but in order to say anything *appropriately*, we must qualify our language for we do not know how these terms refer to God. For a fuller elaboration of models and qualifiers see the works of Ian T. Ramsey.

14. The Neoplatonic background of this synthesis is obvious, but so is the Aristotelian. The stress on the independence of each particular thing and the insistence that each glorifies God *only* as it seeks its own rightful end is the contribution of Aristotle; the stress on the relationship of the many to the One as an emanation and a return is from Neoplatonism via Augustine. The issue here (and the interpretation of *analogia entis*) is very complex; my suggestions are meant not as a contribution to that debate but solely to depict in a general way some of the characteristics of a sacramental mentality. For a careful interpretation along the above lines, see Etienne Gilson, *The Christian Philosophy of St. Thomas Aquinas* (New York: Random House, 1956).

15. For a fine discussion and elaboration of this point see Erich Heller, *The*

Disinherited Mind: Essays in Modern German Literature and Thought (Cleveland: World Publishing, 1961), pp. 261–68.

16. David Tracy's impressive new work, *The Analogical Imagination: Christian Theology and the Culture of Pluralism* (New York: Crossroad; London: SCM Press, 1981), presents a contemporary interpretation of the analogical sensibility that in no way falls into either heavy sacramentalism or easy harmonies oblivious of the negativities. In fact, his view of the analogical imagination is in many ways identical with my understanding of the metaphorical sensibility. At one point he quotes Aristotle on *metaphor* as support for the analogical imagination:

> The power of the analogical imagination was honored by Aristotle in his famous dictum "to spot the similar in the dissimilar is the mark of poetic genius." That same power—at once participatory in the originating event of wonder, trust, disclosure and concealment by the whole, and positively distancing itself from that event by its own self-constituting demands of critical reflection—releases the analogical imagination of the systematic theologian to note the profound similarities-in-difference in all reality (p. 410).

As Tracy notes, all post-Enlightenment attempts to revive analogy as a basic Christian sensibility must take with absolute seriousness the skepticism, relativity, negativities, and indeed chaos that characterize contemporary life at intellectual, personal, and political levels. Nonetheless, I believe there is a difference between even Tracy's analogical imagination and what I am calling the metaphorical sensibility: the former, as Tracy says, is in the tradition of "manifestation," a tradition in which a sense of trust, wonder, grace is primary even when profoundly aware of the suffering, evil, and discontinuity that pervade that basic harmony. The other two traditions which he notes as comprising Christianity—"proclamation" and "prophetic action"—are less conscious of that underlying grace, more conscious of the distance between the human and the divine and of the negativities of existence. It is my contention that while all three perspectives are necessary for a full Christian theology, the proclamation/prophetic is not only a necessity for many people in our time but is also an authentic Christian perspective. The different perspectives, as Tracy notes, need to be intensified and articulated in their concrete particularity, as long as such intensification and articulation are carried on in conversation and openness to the other perspectives.

Another case in point is the work of David Burrell who, in his book *Analogy and Philosophical Language* (New Haven, Conn.: Yale Univ. Press, 1973) comes out in favor of metaphor as lying behind analogy and serving as the justification for analogy. His main thesis is to show with the help of Wittgenstein that ordinary language is deeply metaphorical; hence, the use of analogy in predicating of God is not a medieval, esoteric exercise but an extension of ordinary usage. What lies behind analogical predication for Burrell, then, is not *analogia entis* or the analogy of attribution but the metaphorical character of ordinary language—its dialectical, multi-faceted nature in which borrowings and cross-sortings, judgments of aptness and appropriateness are all common characteristics. Analogical predication of God is, says Burrell, the same *kind* of language.

17. Leander Keck voices the position of many New Testament exegetes in the following statement: "The whole network of words, deeds, and death which we call 'Jesus' was pulled into a pattern by the magnetic power of the kingdom and hence reflected the impingement of that kingdom on his life and work. This was not simply a matter of Jesus working out the implications of a root idea. Rather, it was a matter of being grasped by a perception in such a way that the whole career became a celebration of the kingdom's coming and thereby its vanguard as well" (*A Future for the Historical Jesus: The Place of Jesus in Preaching and Theology* [Philadelphia: Fortress Press, 1981], pp. 218–19).

18. Jean Piaget's pattern of "assimilation" and "accommodation" to define the character of learning is similar to what we have presented. Hugh Petrie writes of Piaget's theory, "during assimilation, we learn by changing experience to fit our concepts and modes of understanding. During accommodation, we learn by changing our concepts and modes of understanding to fit our experience" ("Metaphor and Learning," in *Metaphor and Thought*, ed. Andrew Ortony [New York and Cambridge: Cambridge Univ. Press, 1979], p. 440). In assimilation, we stay with existing frameworks, with the familiar; but in accommodation, we pass from the known to the unknown—we change our concepts —and this process is accomplished by means of metaphor: "The crucial use of metaphor is our moving from one conceptual scheme with its associated way of knowing to another conceptual scheme with *its* associated way of knowing" (p. 460). Thus, metaphor is not just heuristic or illustrative, but epistemologically necessary if new learning is to take place. What we discover is an anomaly: the old framework no longer can encompass our experience and only metaphor— which connects both with what we already know *and* with what we are groping to know—provides the movement that is the distinctive mark of learning.

19. See Kenneth Burke, *Permanence and Change: An Anatomy of Purpose* (New York: New Republic, 1935).

20. I am indebted to F. W. Dillistone for his distinction between analogical and metaphorical thinking. Of analogy he writes: "In any organic system the single member is related to the whole according to some pattern of order and proportion; no figure of speech is more fitted to express this relation than analogy" (*Christianity and Symbolism* [London: William Collins, 1955], p. 152). He notes that one can move from the known to the unknown because the part participates in the whole and is similar to it. Analogical thought is positive, comprehensive, and systematic. Analogy has links with the simile, metaphor with the contrast. Metaphor focuses attention on variety and the openness of reality, and on dissimilarity rather than similarity. Metaphor holds together similarity and dissimilarity in a resolution:

> The resolution is not final, for there are ever wider areas of conflict to embrace. But every metaphor which holds together two disparate aspects of reality in creative tension assumes the character of a prophecy of the final reconciliation of all things in the kingdom of God. It is the favorite tool

of all the great poets. . . . Through it the imagination performs its task, the task which Coleridge describes as dissolving, diffusing, dissipating in order to recreate, as reconciling opposite or discordant qualities, as struggling to idealise and to unify. Through it the prophet leaps outside the circle of present experience, the realm of the factual and the commonsense, the typical and the regular. He parts company with those who are travelling the surer and steadier road of analogical comparison. By one act of daring he brings into creative relationship the apparently opposite and contrary and, if his metaphorical adventure proves successful, gains new treasure both for language and for life (Ibid., p. 161).

Finally, Dillistone notes that while analogy tends toward petrification, metaphor moves toward renovation and that Jesus was a metaphorical thinker, disrupting the old by seeing it in a new light.

21. Among the several New Testament critics who see Jesus as a parable of God are Leander Keck and John Donahue. Keck writes: "Jesus concentrated on parabolic speech because he himself was a parabolic event of the kingdom of God" (*A Future for the Historical Jesus*, p. 244). Donahue writes: "Responding to the parable of Jesus in Mark is engagement in the ultimate paradox of the Christian life ("Jesus as the Parable of God in the Gospel of Mark," *Interpretation* 32 [1978]: 386). Both exegetes substantiate their claim by a comparison of Jesus' life with the characteristics of parables: their metaphoricity, mundanity, realism, strangeness, indirection, shocking disclosive power, and existential engagement.

22. Not all parables are of this sort: the kingdom parables of the buried treasure, lost coin, and mustard seed are not, for instance, but as we shall see, relational language, while the dominant model for God, ought to be balanced and is balanced in the Bible by nonrelational, impersonal, naturalistic language.

23. Robert W. Funk, "The Parables: A Fragmentary Agenda," in *Jesus and Man's Hope*, 2 vols., ed. Donald G. Miller and Dikran Y. Hadidian (Pittsburgh: Pittsburgh Theological Seminary, 1971), vol. 2, pp. 287–303.

24. One thoroughgoing version of such a theology is in Sigmund Freud's *Moses and Monotheism* (New York: Alfred A. Knopf, 1947) where the Judeo-Christian tradition is reduced to an exercise in which adherents attempt to rid themselves of latent guilt from the tribal horde's murder of the father of the clan. The Oedipus complex is the individual's version, while Western religion deals with the same issue of coming to terms with guilt from the childhood of the race. But one does not need to accept Freud's somewhat esoteric views on the subject, for there are many examples of mainline Christian theologies where the dominant categories are familiar ones derived from the structural possibilities of patriarchy. The imagistic language in both the trinitarian and christological controversies is principally "Father" and "Son" with the relationships between God and Jesus of Nazareth largely determined by the potential of these images.

25. See Max Black's fine chapters 3 and 13 in his *Models and Metaphors* (Ithaca, N.Y.: Cornell Univ. Press, 1962).

26. Paul Ricoeur, "Biblical Hermeneutics," *Semeia* 4 (1975): 138.

27. The term "root-metaphor" is Stephen Pepper's from his book *World Hypotheses* (Berkeley and Los Angeles: Univ. of California Press, 1942). The quotation is from Earl R. MacCormac, *Metaphor and Myth in Science and Religion* (Durham, N.C.: Duke Univ. Press, 1976), p. 93.

28. I have used the term "metaphorical theology" rather than "parabolic theology" because the latter limits theological discourse to the primary level. I have tried to show that, to varying degrees, all constructive thought is implicitly or explicitly metaphorical (which is not to say that "everything is metaphor," for much philosophical as well as most scientific and ordinary language is at most mainly dead metaphor and does not function as alive metaphorical language). Hence, metaphorical theology can refer to the entire spectrum from parable to concept, though by using this term stress is put on the foundational, primary language that I believe is appropriate and necessary to theology. Moreover, by retaining the term "metaphorical," the characteristics of metaphor that I find critical to a theology in keeping with the Protestant sensibility, are constantly called to mind—tentativeness, open-endedness, secularity, projected rather than realized unity, tension, transformation, revolution, skepticism, and so on.

29. Ursula K. LeGuin, *The Language of the Night: Essays on Fantasy and Science Fiction*, ed. Susan Wood (New York: G. P. Putnam's Sons, 1979), p. 159.

CHAPTER 2

1. John Middleton Murry, *Countries of the Mind: Essays in Literary Criticism*, 2d series (London: Oxford Univ. Press, 1931), pp. 1–2.

2. The literature supporting this point is vast; to date, the most comprehensive bibliography on metaphor is by Warren A. Shibles, *Metaphor: An Annotated Bibliography and History* (Whitewater, Wis.: Language Press, 1971). It consists of 400 pages of entries; however, it is less comprehensive on models in science than on metaphor in other fields. A sprinkling of quotations from its frontispiece will give, in brief, both the passion with which the centrality of metaphor is supported and the breadth of fields from which such support comes. "Both philosophers and poets live by metaphor," S. Pepper; "All thinking is metaphorical," R. Frost; "The history of philosophy should be written as that of seven or eight metaphors," T. Hulme; "The most profound social creativity consists in the invention and imposition of new, radical metaphors," R. Kaufman; "Something like a paradigm is prerequisite to perception itself. . . . Paradigms prove to be constitutive of the research activity," T. Kuhn; "All our truth, or all but a few fragments, is won by metaphor," C. S. Lewis; "To know is merely to work with one's favorite metaphors," F. Nietzsche; "The conduct of even the plainest, most 'direct' untechnical prose is a ceaseless exercise in metaphor," I. A. Richards.

3. David Burrell's argument stretches throughout his book, *Analogy and Philosophical Language* (New Haven, Conn.: Yale Univ. Press, 1973). He contrasts the metaphorical pattern for human knowing with another perspective

which sees metaphor as merely decorative and rhetorical. Such a perspective, he says, implies that we can know the world directly and can describe it adequately, given time and effort. The paragraph is worth quoting:

> The more we are led to recognize the ubiquity of metaphor in ordinary speech, the less plausible is the Renaissance account of its role as decorating a skeleton of expository prose or rational argument. In fact, the contrary seems to be the case: metaphor plays a unique and irreplaceable part in human discourse, from poetry to ordinary conversation to scientific models. Nor is this merely a thesis about language. For as the decorative theory reflected a world view—that of the Age of Reason—so does the contrary inherent theory. And the implications of the contrasting world view are extraordinarily far-reaching. The nub of the Renaissance theory about metaphor was an assumption about the nature of the universe, and one shared in many ways by latter-day positivism. Counting metaphor as a replaceable rhetorical device presumes that we must always be able, sooner or later, to hit upon a proper and unambiguous description. But this presumption reaches to the very structure of the world. It assumes that the world is of such a piece with our language that (in principle) nothing prohibits our giving a complete description of it. The uncertainties of our ordinary language may have to be corrected, and much ingenuity shown in constructing a language equal to the task, but an unambiguous picture of the world is renderable in principle. Hence it is but a matter of time and effort (pp. 258–59).

4. Kenneth Burke, *Permanence and Change: An Anatomy of Purpose* (New York: New Republic, 1935), pp. 137ff.

5. Ibid., p. 141.

6. W. H. Leatherdale, *The Role of Analogy, Model and Metaphor in Science* (Amsterdam: North-Holland Publishing Co., 1974), pp. 28–29.

7. Mary B. Hesse, "Models in Physics," *British Journal for the Philosophy of Science* 4 (1953): 203.

8. Jacob Bronowski, *The Visionary Eye: Essays in the Arts, Literature and Science*, ed. Piero E. Ariotti (Cambridge, Mass.: M. I. T. Press, 1978), p. 28.

9. Roy Dreistadt, "An Analysis of the Use of Analogies and Metaphors in Science," *Journal of Psychology* 68 (1968): 112–13.

10. Arthur Koestler, *The Act of Creation* (New York: Macmillan Co., 1964), pp. 119–121.

11. Ibid., pp. 199–200.

12. Paul Ricoeur suggests, similarly, a nonmetaphorical base for metaphor in his distinction between symbol and metaphor. Symbols are rooted in reality at a cosmic, prelinguistic level, while metaphors are the linguistic innovation of symbols, interpreting and reinterpreting them. Symbol is at "the dividing line between *bios* and *logos*," while metaphor is at the level of articulation. However, they are in a symbiotic relationship, for symbols give roots in the cosmos and lived world to metaphor, while metaphors bring symbols to language, clarify symbols, and display the endless associations and connections of symbols. Thus, "stain" is a symbol; metaphors of guilt and evil build upon

and interpret stain. Ricoeur's fullest discussion of this relationship is in the essay, "Metaphor and Symbol," in his *Interpretation Theory: Discourse and the Surplus of Meaning* (Fort Worth, Tex.: Texas Christian Univ. Press, 1976), pp. 45–69.

13. I. A. Richards, *The Philosophy of Rhetoric* (New York and London: Oxford Univ. Press, 1965), p. 89.

14. Ibid., p. 93.

15. Max Black, "More About Metaphor," in *Metaphor and Thought*, ed. Andrew Ortony (New York and Cambridge: Cambridge Univ. Press, 1979), p. 31.

16. Walter J. Ong, "Metaphor and the Twinned Vision," in his *The Barbarian Within and Other Fugitive Essays and Studies* (New York: Macmillan Co., 1962), pp. 42–43.

17. Ricoeur, *Interpretation Theory*, p. 50.

18. Nelson Goodman, *Languages of Art: An Approach to a Theory of Symbols* (Indianapolis: Bobbs-Merrill, 1968), p. 69.

19. Ibid., p. 73.

20. Goodman, *Languages of Art*, p. 68.

21. Metaphor is not a different way of perceiving reality, but only a heightening of the ordinary way. As John Hick points out, perception involves "seeing-as"; things do not simply register on the retina but an act of perception involves recognition, seeing something *as* something. This basic process is repeated at different levels in all our interpreting; hence, Hick calls faith "experiencing-as," the interpretation of experience *as* living in the presence of God. The point is that metaphor raises the "seeing-as" which occurs at *all* levels in an explicit way and makes us aware that we are always interpreting. See Hick, "Religious Faith as Experiencing-As," in *Talk of God*, Royal Institute of Philosophy Lectures, vol. 2, 1967–68 (New York: St. Martin's Press, 1969), pp. 20–35.

22. Goodman, *Languages of Art*, pp. 79, 80.

23. Ibid., p. 264.

24. Franz Kafka, "Leopard in the Temple," in *Parables and Paradoxes* (New York: Schocken Books, 1962), p. 93.

25. Colin M. Turbayne, *The Myth of Metaphor* (New Haven, Conn.: Yale Univ. Press, 1962), pp. 24–25.

26. Douglas Berggren, "The Use and Abuse of Metaphor," *Review of Metaphysics* 16 (1963): 456.

27. C. S. Lewis makes a somewhat similar point in a most engaging way when he insists that in order to avoid fossilized metaphors, one must use several metaphors as well as new ones. "If a man has seen ships and the sea, he may abandon the metaphor of a *sea-stallion* and call a boat a boat. But suppose a man has never seen the sea, or ships, yet who knows of them just as much as he can glean, say from the following list of Kenningar—sea-stallions, winged logs, wave riders, ocean trains. If he keeps all these together in his mind, and knows them for the metaphors they are, he will be able to think of ships, very imperfectly indeed, and under strict limits, but not wholly in vain. But if in-

stead of this he pins his faith on the particular kenning, *ocean trains*, because that kenning with its comfortable air of machinery, seems to him somehow more safely prosaic, less flighty and dangerous than its fellows, and if, contracting that to the form *oshtrans*, he proceeds to forget that it was a metaphor, then, while he talks grammatically, he has ceased to think of anything. It will not avail him to stamp his feet and swear that he is literal; to say 'An oshtran is an oshtran and there's an end!' " See "Bluspels and Flalansferes," in *The Importance of Language*, ed. Max Black (Englewood Cliffs, N.J.: Prentice-Hall, 1962), p. 47.

29. George B. Caird, *The Language and Imagery of the Bible* (Philadelphia: Westminster Press; London: Gerald Duckworth & Co., 1980), p. 18.

30. Ibid., p. 144.

31. Quotation by R. H. Kennet, ibid., p. 150.

32. Ibid., p. 177.

33. Ricoeur makes this point in a very telling fashion in the following statement: "It is not enough to say that the Parables say nothing directly concerning the Kingdom of God. We must say in more positive terms, that taken *all together, they say more than any rational theology*. At the very moment that they call for theological clarification, they start shattering the theological simplifications which we attempt to put in their place" ("Listening to the Parables of Jesus," *Criterion* 13 [1974]: 20).

34. The analysis of parables and Jesus as a parable that follows in the text is not intended as a thorough or original interpretation. It is a summary of the positions on these matters by Paul Ricoeur, John Dominic Crossan, Leander Keck, and John Donahue. For the purposes of our study what is essential is to establish parable as metaphor and a basic kerygmatic genre central to the Christian tradition, not to engage in detailed exegetical study. The latter task is for New Testament scholars and upon their work theology builds.

35. The move is by no means an absolute one, for John's concepts are usually images (light, life, love), but images with comprehensive, ordering potential. In other words, they come close to being models, that is, dominant metaphors with interpretive powers over a wide range of reality. Any one of the above Johannine metaphors can serve as a grid or screen through which to interpret the new existence brought about by the Word made flesh; each is not just a passing metaphor providing momentary illumination, but a model of the new divine-human relationship introduced by the Christ. The same can be said of Paul's major metaphors; for instance, the Second Adam, justification by faith, the vine and the branches, law and gospel: they are what could be called "conceptual metaphors" or emerging models.

36. Paul Ricoeur, "Biblical Hermeneutics," *Semeia* 4 (1975): 94–112.

37. C. H. Dodd, *The Parables of the Kingdom* (New York: Charles Scribner's Sons, 1961), p. 16.

38. The widespread agreement on this point by contemporary biblical scholars marks a significant change from earlier parable criticism that focused on the conceptual or moral qualities of parables. C. H. Dodd, Norman Perrin, Amos Wilder, Robert Funk, John Dominic Crossan, John Donahue, among

others, see radicality, superabundance, or extravagance as the note that sets the parables off as different from poetic metaphors. Their extremity moves them into the religious dimension.

39. Robert W. Funk, *Language, Hermeneutic and Word of God: The Problem of Language in the New Testament and Contemporary Theology* (New York: Harper & Row, 1966), pp. 193–96.

40. Ricoeur, "Biblical Hermeneutics," pp. 122–128.

41. John Dominic Crossan, *The Dark Interval: Towards a Theology of Story* (Niles, Ill.: Argus Communications, 1975), p. 56.

42. Ibid., p. 61.

43. Ibid., pp. 56, 57.

44. Ricoeur, "Biblical Hermeneutics," p. 126.

45. William A. Beardslee, "Uses of the Proverb in the Synoptic Gospels," *Interpretation* 24 (1970): 69. See also his *Literary Criticism of the New Testament*, Guides to Biblical Scholarship (Philadelphia: Fortress Press, 1970), pp. 30–41.

46. John Dominic Crossan, *In Parables: The Challenge of the Historical Jesus* (New York: Harper & Row, 1973), p. xiv. Ricoeur suggests how the movement from the parables of Jesus to Jesus as parable occurred:

As soon as the preaching of Jesus as the "Crucified" is interwoven with the narratives of his "deeds" and his "sayings," a *specific possibility* of interpretation is opened up, by what I call here the establishment of a "space" of intersignification: by a *specific possibility*, I mean the suggestion to read the proclamation of Jesus as "the parable of God" *into* the proclamation by Jesus of God "in parables." To entirely disregard this possibility would require that we disconnect the parables from the Gospel ("Biblical Hermeneutics," p. 105).

47. Leander E. Keck, *A Future for the Historical Jesus: The Place of Jesus in Preaching and Theology* (Philadelphia: Fortress Press, 1981), p. 244.

48. Ibid., p. 213. See also the essays in John Hick, ed., *The Myth of God Incarnate* (Philadelphia: Westminster Press; London: SCM Press, 1977).

49. Keck, *A Future for the Historical Jesus*, p. 213.

50. Ibid., p. 219.

51. Ibid., p. 246.

52. John Donahue, "Jesus as the Parable of God in the Gospel of Mark," *Interpretation* 32 (1978): 380.

53. Keck, *A Future for the Historical Jesus*, p. 222.

54. Maurice Wiles, *Faith and the Mystery of God* (Philadelphia: Fortress Press; London: SCM Press, 1982), p. 72.

55. Donahue, "Jesus as the Parable of God," p. 386.

56. Goodman, *Languages of Art*, pp. 7–8.

57. Kenneth Burke, *A Grammar of Motives* (Berkeley and Los Angeles: Univ. of California Press, 1969), p. 503.

58. Hans-Georg Gadamer's major work, *Truth and Method* (New York: Crossroad, 1982), considers this issue in depth; his smaller work, *Philosophical*

Hermeneutics, Eng. trans. and ed. David Linge (Berkeley and Los Angeles: Univ. of California Press, 1977) is also helpful, and the introduction by Linge is an excellent brief essay on Gadamer's basic perspective.

59. Gadamer, *Truth and Method*, p. 264.

60. Gadamer, *Philosophical Hermeneutics*, p. 15.

61. Burke, *A Grammar of Motives*, p. 504.

62. Ricoeur puts it this way:

Poetic language also speaks of reality, but it does so at another level than does scientific language. It does not show us a world already there, as does descriptive or didactic language. In effect, as we have seen, the ordinary reference of language is abolished by the natural strategy of poetic discourse. But in the very measure that the first-order reference is abolished, another power of speaking the world is liberated, although at another level of reality. This level is that which Husserlian phenomenology has designated as the *Lebenswelt* and which Heidegger has called "being-in-the-world." It is an eclipsing of the objective manipulable world, an illumining of the life-world, which seems to me to be the fundamental ontological import of poetic language ("Biblical Hermeneutics," p. 89).

63. The view of the Bible as a poetic classic suggested here varies considerably from that of Austin Farrer in his impressive work, *The Glass of Vision* (London: Dacre Press, 1948). In his view the images in Scripture are divinely inspired and while his understanding of inspiration is closer to poetic inspiration than to simplistic views of divine control, still his view results in an absolutism of images and a profound ahistoricism. Since for him "divine truth is supernaturally communicated to men in an act of inspired thinking which falls into the shape of certain images" (p. 57), these images, regardless of their cultural relativism, are raised to the level of divine truth and hence are immutable. The implications for feminist theology, to suggest just one difficulty with this position, are obvious.

64. Frank Kermode, *The Classic: Literary Images of Permanence and Change* (New York: Viking Press, 1975), pp. 117, 121.

65. David Tracy, *The Analogical Imagination: Christian Theology and the Culture of Pluralism* (New York: Crossroad; London, SCM Press, 1981), p. 154.

66. James Barr, *The Bible in the Modern World* (New York: Harper & Row; London: SCM Press, 1973), p. 115.

67. Ibid., p. 119.

68. Tracy, *The Analogical Imagination*, p. 108.

69. The issue of whether the Bible has authority or is "revealed" is, finally, as has been suggested, a matter intrinsic to the text: as classic it speaks its authority and it reveals itself as relevant. Ricoeur puts it well in the following remarks: "If the Bible can be said to be revealed, this ought to be said of the 'issue' that it speaks of—the new being which is displayed there. I would go so far as to say that the Bible is revealed to the extent that the new being unfolded there is itself revelatory with respect to the world, to all of reality,

including my existence and my history. In other words, revelation, if the expression is meaningful, is a trait of the biblical world" ("Philosophy and Religious Language," *Journal of Religion* 56 [1974]: 81).

70. For discussion of these phrases see Ricoeur's *Freud and Philosophy: An Essay in Interpretation* (New Haven, Conn.: Yale Univ. Press, 1970).

71. Gadamer allows the general point that prejudices can become hidden and dogmatic, but it appears to make little difference in his openhanded acceptance of a language tradition: "The basic prejudices are not easily dislodged and protect themselves by claiming self-evident certainty for themselves, or even by posing as supposed freedom from all prejudice and thereby securing their acceptance. We are familiar with the form of language that such self-securing of prejudices takes: namely the unyielding repetitiousness characteristic of all dogmatism" (*Philosophical Hermeneutics*, p. 92).

72. Gadamer, *Truth and Method*, p. 250.

73. Jürgen Habermas, "A Review of Gadamer's Truth and Method," in *Understanding and Social Inquiry*, ed. Fred R. Dallmayr and Thomas A. McCarthy (Notre Dame, Ind.: Univ. of Notre Dame Press, 1977), pp. 335–63.

74. Ricoeur, "Biblical Hermeneutics," pp. 135–36.

CHAPTER 3

1. Aristotle, *Rhetoric*, III, 141b.

2. John S. Dunne, *A Search for God in Time and Memory: An Exploration Traced in the Lives of Individuals from Augustine to Sartre and Camus* (London: Macmillan & Co., 1969).

3. Abraham J. Heschel, *Who Is Man?* (Stanford, Calif.: Stanford Univ. Press, 1965), p. 7.

4. Weller Embler, "Metaphor and Social Belief," in *Language, Meaning and Maturity*, ed. S. I. Hayakawa (New York: Harper & Row, 1954), p. 127.

5. Ibid., p. 126.

6. Scott F. Gilbert, "The Metaphorical Structuring of Social Perceptions," *Soundings* 62 (1979): 166–68.

7. J. David Sapir, "The Anatomy of Metaphor," in *The Social Use of Metaphor: Essays on the Anthropology of Rhetoric*, ed. J. David Sapir and Christopher Crocker (Philadelphia: Univ. of Pennsylvania Press, 1977), p. 10.

8. Victor W. Turner, *Dramas, Fields, and Metaphors: Symbolic Action in Human Society* (Ithaca, N.Y.: Cornell University Press, 1974), p. 36.

9. Turner outlines the passage of new paradigms to conventional ones in the following way:

These first formulations will be multi-vocal symbols and metaphors—each susceptible of many meanings, but with the core meanings linked analogically to the basic human problems of the epoch which may be pictured in biological, or mechanistic, or some other terms—these multi-vocals will yield to the action of the thought technicians who clear intellectual jungles, and organized systems of univocal concepts and signs will replace them. The change will begin, prophetically, "with metaphor, and end, instrumentally, with algebra." The danger is, of course, that the more persuasive the root metaphor or archetype, the more chance it has of becoming a self-certifying myth, sealed off from empirical disproof. It remains as a fascinating metaphysics (Ibid., p. 29).

10. Martin Landau, "On the Use of Metaphor in Political Analysis," *Social Research* 28 (1961): 353.

11. As quoted in Ibid., p. 339.

12. As quoted in W. H. Leatherdale, *The Role of Analogy, Model and Metaphor in Science* (Amsterdam: North-Holland Pub. Co., 1974), p. 202.

13. Ralph M. Stogdill gives a typical example of such use of models in the book he edited, *The Process of Model-Building in the Behavioral Sciences* (Columbus, Ohio: Ohio State Univ. Press, 1970): "Each year in the United States a large number of high school seniors decide to apply to a college (or colleges) of their choice. The U.S. Commissioner of Education would like to be able to (a) predict, and (b) influence these application decisions. How would you develop a reasonable model for him to use? What kinds of additional information would be useful to you? What problems would you foresee?" (pp. 141–42).

14. The full statement is worth quoting:

> The obvious fact is that machines are like men for the simple reason that man made the machine, as far as he could, *in his image.* It would be un-pleasing to some ears to have it said that man left out a soul when he made the machine, but that, or something very like that, is precisely what happened . . . that we should be unaware of the simple fact that men are only in a few unimportant respects like machines, but that machines are, *as far as they go,* in all respects like men is the supreme misunderstanding of our time and accounts exclusively for our lack, just when we need it most, of a real humanistic philosophy (Embler, "Metaphor and Social Belief," p. 137).

15. The company of scientists and philosophers of science who support this view is legion; we will be quoting from many of them, but a preliminary and partial list may be helpful: Albert Einstein, A. N. Whitehead, Michael Polonyi, Thomas Kuhn, Niels Bohr, Werner Heisenberg, E. H. Hutten, Rom Harré, Stephen Toulmin, Stephen Pepper, Ian Barbour, Peter Achinstein, Max Planck.

16. As quoted in Arthur Koestler, *The Act of Creation* (New York: Macmillan Co., 1964), p. 147.

17. Max Black, *Models and Metaphors* (Ithaca, N.Y.: Cornell Univ. Press, 1962), p. 243.

18. I am indebted to Mary B. Hesse's excellent book, *Science and the Human Imagination: Aspects of the History and Logic of Physical Science* (London: SCM Press, 1954) for the outlines of the following argument.

19. See especially ibid., pp. 55ff.

20. Ibid., p. 69.

21. Ian Barbour's description is helpful to the layperson: "The atomic world is not only inaccessible to direct observation, and inexpressible in terms of the

senses; we are unable even to imagine it. There is a radical disjunction between the way things behave and every way in which we try to visualize them. . . . For example, in some experiments we may picture electrons as waves and in others as particles, but there seems no consistent way of imagining what an electron is like in itself" (*Myths, Models and Paradigms: A Comparative Study in Science and Religion* [New York: Harper & Row; London: SCM Press, 1974], p. 158).

22. John Lukacs quoting Heisenberg in "Quantum Mechanics and the End of Scientism," in *Science as Metaphor: The Historical Role of Scientific Theories in Forming Western Culture*, ed. Richard Olson (Belmont, Calif.: Wadsworth Publishing Co., 1971), pp. 296, 297.

23. E. H. Hutten's summary of the results of relativity and quantum theory is precise and clear: "Relativity made the concept of field, and quantisation made the concept of particle, more abstract. Instead of isolated, solid, though invisible, bits of matter we have new energy quanta as the ultimate constituents. Mechanism—the view of the world as a collection of solid particles moving in space-time—was abolished by relativity" (*The Ideas of Physics* [Edinburgh: Oliver & Boyd, 1967], p. 144).

24. See Hesse, *Science and the Human Imagination*, pp. 69ff.

25. Ian Barbour puts it this way: "Our primitive awareness is of being in a world, not of constructing one. Whitehead speaks of 'a consciousness of ourselves as arising out of rapport, interconnection and participation in processes reaching beyond ourselves' " (*Issues in Science and Religion* [Englewood Cliffs, N.J.: Prentice-Hall; London: SCM Press, 1966], p. 171).

26. Ibid., p. 157.

27. Koestler, *The Act of Creation*, p. 242.

28. Ibid., p. 252.

29. The literature on this topic is now substantial, but the basic works include several writings by Thomas Kuhn: *The Structure of Scientific Revolutions* (Chicago: Univ. of Chicago Press, 1962); idem, "The Function of Dogma in Scientific Research," in *Scientific Change*, ed. A. C. Crombie (New York: Basic Books, 1963), pp. 347–69; idem, "Second Thoughts on Paradigms," in *The Structure of Scientific Theories*, ed. Frederick Suppe (Urbana, Ill.: Univ. of Illinois Press, 1977), pp. 459–82. Also, a major critical work on Kuhn's theories is Imre Lakatos and A. Musgrave, eds., *Criticism and the Growth of Knowledge* (New York and Cambridge: Cambridge Univ. Press, 1970).

30. See Kuhn, "Second Thoughts on Paradigms," where these terms are explained more fully.

31. See Margaret Masterman, "The Nature of a Paradigm," in *Criticism and Growth of Knowledge*, ed. Lakatos and Musgrave, pp. 59–89.

32. Earl R. MacCormac, *Metaphor and Myth in Science and Religion* (Durham, N.C.: Duke Univ. Press, 1976), p. 22.

33. Barbour, *Issues in Science and Religion*, p. 154.

34. Kuhn, *The Structure of Scientific Revolutions*, p. 113.

35. Ibid., pp. 24–37.

36. Black, *Models and Metaphors*, p. 229.

37. Ibid., p. 222.

38. Barbour, *Issues in Science and Religion*, p. 158.

39. It is impossible to divide all scientists and philosophers of science who have written on models into two neat camps; however, such well-known commentators as Russell, Braithwaite, Nagel, Toulmin, Achinstein, and Brodbeck fall into the "low" view since they all basically see models as useful but with qualifications, while Nash, Barbour, Ferré, Hesse, Hutten, and Harré see them as essential but with qualifications. Hence these latter people I would call "high" view. The listing of names, however, is not very helpful because the commentators differ on various issues and have sufficiently different proposals to make so that the lines between the two "schools" is at most a fuzzy one.

40. From E. Mach, "On the Principle of Comparison in Physics," in *Popular Scientific Lectures*, pp. 240f, quoted in Leatherdale, *The Role of Analogy, Model and Metaphor in Science*, p. 63.

41. Peter Achinstein, "Theoretical Models," *British Journal for Philosophy of Science* 16 (1965): 102.

42. E. H. Hutten, "The Role of Models in Physics," *British Journal for Philosophy of Science* 4 (1954): 294.

43. Ibid., p. 295.

44. Barbour, *Myths, Models and Paradigms*, p. 76.

45. In Roy Dreistadt, "An Analysis of the Use of Analogies and Metaphors in Science," *Journal of Psychology* 68 (1968): 100.

46. Sir James Jeans, *Physics and Philosophy* (New York: Macmillan Co., 1943), p. 176.

47. C. S. Lewis, "Bluspels and Flalansferes," in *The Importance of Language*, ed. Max Black (Englewood Cliffs, N.J.: Prentice-Hall, 1962), pp. 38–39.

48. Donald Schon, *The Displacement of Concepts* (London: Tavistock Publications, 1963), p. 105.

49. See chapter 2, pp. 32–33.

50. Achinstein, "Theoretical Models," p. 104.

51. Niels Bohr, frontispiece in Robert Rogers, *Metaphor: A Psychoanalytic Approach* (Berkeley and Los Angeles: Univ. of California Press, 1978).

52. Schon, *The Displacement of Concepts*, p. 18.

53. Leatherdale, *The Role of Analogy, Model and Metaphor in Science*, pp. 56–57.

54. See chapter 3, pp. 67–70.

55. Barbour, *Myths, Models and Paradigms*, pp. 47–48.

56. Ibid., p. 6.

57. Hutten, *The Ideas of Physics*, pp. 80–81.

58. Frederick Ferré provides another fine example of the explanatory function of models as giving connections between laws, coherence, and conceptual unity: "Thus a model is doing its most important task when it helps those who are thinking 'through' it to find new connections among previously discovered laws, or to appreciate an otherwise baffling phenomenon as a special case of

what is already familiar, or to see analogies between new data and what is already known, or to gain an intuitive 'grasp' of the subject matter through a fresh encounter with the familiar" ("Metaphors, Models and Religion," *Soundings* 51 [1968]: 336).

59. Hutten, *The Ideas of Physics*, p. 149.

60. Mary B. Hesse, *Models and Analogies in Science* (Notre Dame, Ind.: Univ. of Notre Dame Press, 1966), p. 170. N. R. Hanson makes a similar point: "Models suggest to us ranges of possible explanations—routes to the unsurprising. . . . Full knowledge of anything consists in expecting every feature of that thing 'as a matter of course' " (*Observation and Explanation: A Guide to Philosophy of Science* [New York: Harper & Row, 1971], p. 78).

61. Hesse, *Models and Analogies*, p. 169.

62. Frederick Ferré, "Mapping the Logic of Models in Science and Theology," in *Philosophy and Religion: Some Contemporary Perspectives*, ed. Jerry H. Gill (Minneapolis: Burgess Publishing Co., 1968), p. 289.

63. Ibid.

64. Hutten, *The Ideas of Physics*, pp. 80–81.

65. Gordon D. Kaufman, *God the Problem* (Cambridge, Mass.: Harvard Univ. Press, 1979), p. 113.

66. Hutten, "The Role of Models in Physics," p. 298.

67. As quoted in Barbour, *Myths, Models and Paradigms*, p. 37.

68. Paul Ricoeur, "Listening to the Parables of Jesus," *Criterion* 13 (1974): 20.

69. Black, *Models and Metaphors*, pp. 228–29.

70. Mary B. Hesse, "Models and Analogy in Science," in *Encyclopedia of Philosophy*, ed. P. Edwards (London: Macmillan & Co., 1967), vol. 5, p. 355.

71. Rom Harré, *The Principles of Scientific Thinking* (Chicago: Univ. of Chicago Press, 1970), p. 52.

72. Ibid., pp. 52–59.

73. Hesse, *Science and the Human Imagination*, p. 13.

CHAPTER 4

1. Frederick Ferré puts the issue clearly when he says, "the role of theological models with respect to understanding, unlike that of scientific models, is to help construct a completely comprehensive conceptual scheme in which every possible event can be interpreted as exemplifying it" ("Metaphors, Models and Religion," *Soundings* 51 [1968]: 341).

2. Frederick Ferré, "Mapping the Logic of Models in Science and Theology," in *Philosophy and Religion: Some Contemporary Perspectives*, ed. Jerry H. Gill (Minneapolis: Burgess Publishing Co., 1968), pp. 290–91.

3. Ibid., p. 283.

4. I hesitate to posit the relationship between theory and model as it appears here, for it suggests that models are illustrations of theory, providing flesh for the skeleton or vividness for abstraction. While models can be used in this way, it is not, in my view, their major function, and in fact, skews the

basic relationship between models and concepts, which, I believe, is one where models *fund* concepts and concepts *order* models. Nonetheless, the point needs to be made that theologians cannot move from theory to observation, bypassing models as scientists may do, albeit limiting the explanatory potential of their theories as a consequence.

5. Ferré, "Mapping the Logic of Models," p. 284.

6. Ian Ramsey, *Models and Mystery* (New York and London: Oxford Univ. Press, 1964), p. 60.

7. Earl R. MacCormac, *Metaphor and Myth in Science and Religion* (Durham, N.C.: Duke Univ. Press, 1976), p. 138.

8. Ferré, "Metaphors, Models and Religion," p. 331.

9. Ian G. Barbour, *Myths, Models and Paradigms: A Comparative Study in Science and Religion* (New York: Harper & Row, 1974), p. 124.

10. David Tracy, "Metaphor and Religion: The Test Case of Christian Texts," in *On Metaphor*, ed. Sheldon Sacks (Chicago: Univ. of Chicago Press, 1978), p. 106.

11. Paul Ricoeur, *Interpretation Theory: Discourse and the Surplus of Meaning* (Fort Worth, Tex.: Texas Christian Univ. Press, 1976), p. 64.

12. David Tracy, who finds the theological language of John and Paul to be in continuity with the parables, sums up the point persuasively: "No more than the religious discourse of the parables does the theological discourse of John (or Paul) presume to describe literally either God or that Christian mode of being-in-the-world called *agapic* love. If one removes the tensive character of the metaphors, at any level (word, statement, or text), one imposes—through substitution—various descriptive and prescriptive candidates for the 'real' meaning of these redescriptive metaphorical statements." "Metaphor and Religion," pp. 105–106.

13. Amos Wilder, *The Language of the Gospel: Early Christian Rhetoric* (Cambridge, Mass.: Harvard Univ. Press, 1971), p. 64.

14. Barbour, *Myths, Models and Paradigms*, p. 151.

15. Frederick Ferré, *Language, Logic and God* (New York: Harper & Row, 1961; London: Eyre & Spottiswoode, 1962), p. 164.

16. Earl MacCormac expresses the influence of the creeds on attitudes as follows:

> When the Christian repeatedly utters the opening lines of the Apostles' Creed—"I believe in God the Father almighty, maker of heaven and earth . . ."—he fixes in his mind certain associations that may be used to describe and interpret his own religious feelings. The metaphoric association of God with the function of a cosmic father finds the reinforcement in the Nicene Creed as part of the Trinity. The image of God as a creator father forms one of the major concepts of Christian theology and both personal experiences and the events of scripture are interpreted in light of it. . . . Creeds . . . provide the very concepts used to express and reflect upon religious experience (*Metaphor and Myth in Science and Religion*, p. 69).

17. The monarchial model is closely associated with the patriarchal in the

Christian tradition and one finds that the models of king, lord, father, husband, and judge mutually affect one another, so that "father," which *can* be interpreted in the direction of person-to-person reconciliation, is more often seen in hierarchical terms as dominance and control by the divine in relation to the human.

18. Ian T. Ramsey, *Religious Language: An Empirical Placing of Theological Phrases* (New York: Macmillan Co., 1967), pp. 184–85.

19. J. F. Bethune-Baker, *Introduction to the Early History of Christian Doctrine*, 9th ed. (London: Metheun & Co., 1957) p. 160.

20. Arthur Koestler, *The Act of Creation* (New York: Macmillan Co., 1964), pp. 323–24.

21. John MacQuarrie, *God-Talk: An Examination of the Language and Logic of Theology* (New York: Harper & Row; London: SCM Press, 1967), p. 209.

22. MacCormac, *Metaphor and Myth in Science and Religion*, p. 64.

23. Paul Ricoeur relates and distinguishes symbol and metaphor in the following way. Symbols exist at the level of *bios*, metaphors at the level of *logos*: symbols bind us to the cosmos while metaphors are the linguistic play that interprets symbols and brings them to expressive availability. Symbols unite us harmoniously to our roots in the world while metaphors redescribe reality, creating *tension* between oneness with existence and alternative ways of being in the world. They are, therefore, on a continuum, with metaphor the interpretive aspect of symbol: "Everything indicates that symbolic experience calls for a work of meaning from metaphor, a work which it partially provides through its organizational network and its hierarchical levels. Everything indicates that symbol systems constitute a reservoir of meaning whose metaphoric potential is yet to be spoken" (*Interpretation Theory*, p. 65).

24. Paul Ricoeur, "Biblical Hermeneutics," *Semeia* 4 (1975): 36.

25. These hints of Ricoeur's appear principally in three studies, one of which has already been mentioned: "Biblical Hermeneutics." The others are *The Symbolism of Evil*, Eng. trans. Emerson Buchanan (Boston: Beacon Press, 1967), especially the introduction and conclusion; and *The Rule of Metaphor: Multi-Disciplinary Studies of the Creation of Meaning in Language*, Eng. trans. Robert Czerny (Toronto: Univ. of Toronto Press, 1977), especially Study no. 8, "Metaphor and Philosophical Discourse." My brief analysis does not pretend to be a thorough presentation of the intricacies of Ricoeur's various arguments, but rather a gathering together of some of his more provocative insights on the relations between the two forms of language that might be especially helpful to theology.

26. Ricoeur, *The Symbolism of Evil*, p. 15.

27. Ricoeur, *The Rule of Metaphor*, pp. 296, 297.

28. Ibid., p. 303.

29. Ricoeur, "Biblical Hermeneutics," p. 135.

30. Ibid., p. 138.

31. Ricoeur's cryptic remarks on this point in the closing pages of "Biblical Hermeneutics" are more frustrating than illuminating. He calls there for a

"post-Hegelian return to Kant," by which he seems to imply that Hegelian-type systems are not the goal of conceptual thought. However, Kant's refusal to deal with transcendence—his placing of limit-concepts against it—while a healthy rebuttal to Hegelian pretensions, might have been less negative had Kant been more aware of a kind of language between empirical and metaphysical, i.e., poetic language and its potential for "indirect presentation of the Unconditioned" (p. 143). But Ricoeur leaves the matter there.

32. Ibid., pp. 95, 125.

33. Ian T. Ramsey, *Models for Divine Activity* (London: SCM Press, 1973), p. 1. Ramsey's position on models appears in many of his books, but perhaps most clearly in *Religious Language, Models for Divine Activity,* and *Models and Mystery.*

34. Jerry H. Gill, *Ian Ramsey: To Speak Responsibly of God* (London: George Allen & Unwin, 1976), p. 88.

35. See chapter 3, pp. 83–85 for the previous discussion of this point.

36. Karl Barth, *Church Dogmatics,* II. 2, ed. G. W. Bromiley and T. F. Torrance (Edinburgh: T. & T. Clark, 1961) for Barth's treatment of the model of election.

37. It is not our task here to defend in any detail "critical realism" as an epistemological position. An excellent defense of it, however, can be found in Dorothy Emmet, *The Nature of Metaphysical Thinking* (London: Macmillan & Co., 1961). Her position, *in nuce,* is that a critical realist assumes that we find ourselves in an environment to which we respond. As such we are always in relationships (even perception is such a relationship in which we respond to "things"). Because we are responsive to an environment rather than at one with it, all our contacts with reality are necessarily indirect rather than direct, i.e., metaphorical or analogical. Reality impinges upon us and we respond indirectly to it; hence, our analogies and metaphors appear to us both as discoveries coming to us as well as creations going out from us.

38. Max Wartofsky, *Models: Representation and the Scientific Understanding* (Boston and Dordrecht, Neth.: D. Reidel Pub. Co., 1979), pp. 38–39.

39. Max Born, quoted in Barbour, *Myths, Models and Paradigms,* p. 47.

40. Ibid., pp. 34–38.

41. Ibid., p. 42.

42. Ibid., p. 37.

43. See Ricoeur, *The Rule of Metaphor,* pp. 243–46.

44. Ibid., p. 244.

45. Ibid., Study no. 7, for a thorough discussion. A passage on the paradoxical character of metaphorical truth, its "is and is not" nature, is worth quoting:

> The paradox consists in the fact that there is no other way to do justice to the notion of metaphorical truth than to include the critical incision of the (literal) "is not" within the ontological vehemence of the (metaphorical) "is." In doing so, the thesis merely draws the most extreme consequences of the theory of tension. In the same way that logical distance is preserved in metaphorical proximity, and in the same way as the impossible literal interpretation is not simply abolished by the metaphorical interpre-

tation but submits to it while resisting, so the ontological affirmation obeys the principle of tension and the law of "stereo-scopic vision." It is this tensional constitution of the verb *to be* that receives its grammatical mark in the "to be like" of metaphor elaborated into simile, at the same time as the tension between *same* and *other* is marked in the relational copula (pp. 255–56).

46. Ibid., p. 154.
47. Ibid., p. 239.
48. Barbour, *Myths, Models and Paradigms*, p. 124.
49. Ian G. Barbour, *Issues in Science and Religion* (Englewood Cliffs, N.J.: Prentice-Hall, 1966), pp. 253–54.
50. See Ian T. Ramsey, *Christian Empiricism*, ed. Jerry H. Gill (London: Sheldon Press, 1974) for further discussion of these criteria.
51. The term is Jerry Gill's in his discussion of Ramsey's notion of "empirical fit." See Gill, *Ian Ramsey*, pp. 113ff.
52. Barbour, *Myths, Models and Paradigms*, pp. 49, 52.
53. Ferré, *Language, Logic and God*, pp. 164–65.
54. Ferré, "Metaphors, Models and Religion," pp. 341–42.
55. The latest in a long stream of books starting with the death-of-God literature of the 1960s (or perhaps one should go back to Feuerbach) is Don Cupitt's *Taking Leave of God* (New York: Crossroad, 1981; London: SCM Press, 1980). He argues for an internalization of God as "the mythical embodiment of all that one is concerned with in the spiritual life."

CHAPTER 5

1. The literature criticizing the model of God as father is large and growing. A few well-known and readily available studies include the following: Carol P. Christ and Judith Plaskow, eds., *Womanspirit Rising: A Feminist Reader in Religion* (New York: Harper & Row, 1979); Sheila D. Collins, *A Different Heaven and Earth: A Feminist Perspective on Religion* (Valley Forge, Pa.: Judson Press, 1974); Mary Daly, *Beyond God the Father: Toward a Philosophy of Women's Liberation* (Boston: Beacon Press, 1973) and idem, *Gyn/Ecology: The Metaphysics of Radical Feminism* (Boston: Beacon Press, 1978); Naomi R. Goldenberg, *Changing of the Gods: Feminism and the End of Traditional Religions* (Boston: Beacon Press, 1979); Rita Gross, ed., *Beyond Androcentricism: New Essays on Women and Religion* (Missoula, Mont.: Scholars Press, 1977); Robert Hamerton-Kelly, *God the Father: Theology and Patriarchy in the Teaching of Jesus*, Overtures to Biblical Theology (Philadelphia: Fortress Press, 1979); Rosemary Ruether, ed., *Religion and Sexism: Images of Women in the Jewish and Christian Traditions* (New York: Simon & Schuster, 1974) and idem, *New Woman-New Earth: Sexist Ideologies and Human Liberation* (New York: Crossroad, 1975); Phyllis Trible, *God and the Rhetoric of Sexuality*, Overtures to Biblical Theology (Philadelphia: Fortress Press, 1978).
2. David Tracy, "Metaphor and Religion: The Test Case of Christian

Texts," in *On Metaphor*, ed. Sheldon Sacks (Chicago: Univ. of Chicago Press, 1978), p. 106.

3. Daly, *Beyond God the Father*, p. 19.

4. Donald Schon, *The Displacement of Concepts* (London: Tavistock Publications, 1963), pp. 194–96.

5. Collins, *A Different Heaven and Earth*, p. 52.

6. Ibid., p. 51.

7. For different but related analyses of this dualism, see Collins, *A Different Heaven and Earth* and Ruether, *New Woman-New Earth*.

8. Ruether, *New Woman-New Earth*, p. 74.

9. Collins, *A Different Heaven and Earth*, p. 67.

10. Ruether, *New Woman-New Earth*, pp. 74–75.

11. Ruether, "Motherearth and the Megamachine: A Theology of Liberation in a Feminine, Somatic and Ecological Perspective," in *Womanspirit Rising*, ed. Christ and Plaskow, p. 51.

12. It is noteworthy that Sigmund Freud's interpretation of both Judaism and Christianity is entirely in terms of fathers and sons, from the primal horde of brothers who kill the father and suffer under the guilt (Judaism) to the sacrificial death of one of the brothers to free the others from the burden of guilt (Christianity). "The Mosaic religion had been a Father religion; Christianity became a Son religion. The old God, the Father, took second place; Christ, the Son, stood in His stead, just as in those dark times every son had longed to do" (*Moses and Monotheism* [New York: Alfred A. Knopf, 1947], p. 141). What is interesting about this analysis is that it sketches the rise of Western religion as a drama played out in masculine imagery entirely for and by men. Women presumably enter the picture only as prizes awarded to dominant males. It is a religion for "brothers" against the "father" with women as the booty (the Oedipus myth mirrors the primal crime on an individual level—one murders the father in order to possess one's mother). Freudianism, in its complete neglect of women as *subjects*, is impressive witness to the thoroughness with which the patriarchal model has pervaded Western culture.

13. Dorothy Emmet, *The Nature of Metaphysical Thinking* (London: Macmillan & Co., 1961), p. 184.

14. George Caird, *The Language and Imagery of the Bible* (Philadelphia: Westminster Press; London: Gerald Duckworth & Co., 1980), p. 178.

15. Rosemary Ruether interprets Mary as a symbol of humanity's absolute dependence on God. She represents the "feminine" aspect of man as passive before God and as such is a sadomasochistic symbol, allowing men to experience their passive, feminine side in relation to God but remain as dominant masculine selves in relation to women. Ruether claims that Mary can be a liberating symbol for women only when she is seen as the representative of the original and eschatological humanity freed from patriarchal domination: "She is the reconciled wholeness of women and men, nature and humans, creation and God in the new heaven and the new earth" (*New Woman-New Earth*, p. 59). But, claims Ruether, this Mary is not the mother of Jesus but Mary

Magdalene—not the one who gives birth, but the one who keeps the word of God.

16. See Peter Berger, *The Social Reality of Religion* (London: Faber & Faber, 1969) for elaboration of this point.

17. Ibid., p. 33.

18. Austin Farrer, *The Glass of Vision* (London: Dacre Press, 1948), pp. 100–101.

19. Robert Hamerton-Kelly, in his book *God the Father*, makes an exorbitant claim along these lines for Jesus' restructuring of the patriarchal family. He insists that the new family of adoption by the compassionate, heavenly father undercuts the repressive, earthly family (pp. 101–102). Phyllis Trible in a trenchant critique of the book notes that "to the extent that Jesus disavowed the earthly father in the name of the heavenly father, as Hamerton-Kelly proposes, to that extent Jesus reenforced patriarchy by absolutizing the rule of the father. To transfer male dominance from earth to heaven is not to eliminate but to exacerbate it" (*Theology Today* 37 (1980): 116–19).

20. Ruether, *New Woman-New Earth*, pp. 66.

21. See the excellent introduction to *Womanspirit Rising* by its editors Christ and Plaskow for a sensitive analysis of the varied positions in feminist theology.

22. Marcia Keller, quoted in ibid., p. 13

23. Earl R. MacCormac, *Metaphor and Myth in Science and Religion* (Durham, N.C.: Duke Univ. Press, 1976), p. 138.

24. Victor W. Turner, *Dramas, Fields, and Metaphors: Symbolic Action in Human Society* (Ithaca, N.Y.: Cornell Univ. Press, 1974), pp. 28–29.

25. A case can be made that all enduring theological doctrines, regardless of how abstract and nonexperiential they may appear, are grounded in profound religious experiences. Ewert H. Cousins notes, for instance, that Anselm's doctrine of the atonement, which is expressed in the model of satisfaction and the terminology of feudalism, is based in his profound consciousness of the mystery of sin: "The specific experiential model in Anselm's case was the overpowering burden of guilt. At its center is a grasp of the infinite dimension of evil which causes the burden of guilt to weigh down on man with such force that he is unable to remove it and needs the Infinite itself to lift the burden. It is this depth of religious experience that Anselm conveys by sketching the outlines of the feudal lord to whom satisfaction is due because of his offended honor" (Ewert H. Cousins, "Models and the Future of Theology," *Continuum* 7 [1969]: 85).

26. Christ and Plaskow, *Womanspirit Rising*, p. 6.

27. Ibid., p. 8.

28. Valerie Saiving, "The Human Situation: A Feminine View," in *Womanspirit Rising*, ed. Christ and Plaskow, pp. 25–42.

29. Daly, *Beyond God the Father*, p. 8. It is for this reason that sex-inclusive language, in liturgy and theology as well as in ordinary conversation, has become such an issue to all feminists. They see—and they would be supported by such luminaries as Wittgenstein and Heidegger—that language is not a

superficial coating human beings merely "use" but *is* the human world. What is not named is not thought; symbol and concept go together and hence the form of the naming dictates the nature of the thought.

30. E. O. James, *The Cult of the Mother-Goddess: An Archeological and Documentary Study* (New York: Barnes & Noble, 1961; London: Thames & Hudson, 1959), p. 11.

31. Ruether, *New Woman-New Earth*, p. 13.

32. Goldenberg, *Changing of the Gods*, pp. 103ff.

33. Ibid., p. 93.

34. Ibid., p. 89.

35. Starhawk (Miriam Simos), "Witchcraft and Women's Culture," *Womanspirit Rising*, ed. Christ and Plaskow, p. 263.

36. Carol Christ, "Why Women Need the Goddess: Phenomenological, Psychological, and Political Reflections," in *Womanspirit Rising*, ed. Christ and Plaskow, p. 277.

37. Daly, *Gyn/Ecology*, pp. 10–11.

38. Denise Carmody says that even in the Goddess religions the stress was always on the procreation role of women: "It is true that archaic women regularly are full economic partners. It is true that many shamanize, divinize, and, especially in prehistoric groups, even rule. The base line of women's role, however, has been potential motherhood" (*Women and World Religions* [Nashville: Abingdon Press, 1979], p. 37).

39. Robert Scholes, *Structural Fabulation: An Essay in Fiction of the Future* (Notre Dame, Ind.: Univ. of Notre Dame Press, 1975), p. 29.

40. Leander Keck, *A Future for the Historical Jesus: The Place of Jesus in Preaching and Theology* (Philadelphia: Fortress Press, 1981), p. 227.

41. C. S. Lewis as quoted in "Priestesses in the Church?" in *God in the Dock: Essays on Theology and Ethics*, ed. Walter Hooper (Grand Rapids: William B. Eerdmans, 1970), p. 237.

42. Arthur Koestler, *The Act of Creation* (New York: Macmillan Co., 1964), p. 216.

43. Ibid., p. 7.

44. Ursula LeGuin, *The Language of the Night: Essays on Fantasy and Science Fiction*, ed. Susan Wood (New York: G. P. Putnam's Sons, 1979), p. 163.

45. Ibid., p. 168.

46. LeGuin, *The Left Hand of Darkness* (New York: Ace Books, 1969), pp. 202–203.

47. Ibid., p. 234.

48. LeGuin, *The Language of the Night*, p. 158

49. Rosemary Ruether, "A Religion for Women: Sources and Strategies," *Christianity and Crisis* (December 10, 1979): 309.

50. Ibid.

51. The claim that the experience of relating to God rather than describing divine characteristics is the point of models such as "father" is by no means a novel assertion in the Christian tradition. George Tavard, for instance, says

that the fatherhood of God in Catholic theology is an analogy of proper proportionality and hence does not refer to qualities of fatherhood in God but to the experience of human filiation:

> It is negative since it negates that human fathers are images of God in their fatherhood; it is positive since it affirms that the human experience of fatherhood—at its best, not in the sorry instances of too many individuals—helps us to understand our relationship to God and therefore God as the originating and dominant term of this relationship. . . . The human term of the fatherhood analogy is not human fathers: it is the experience of human persons, women as well as men, of relating to a human father in love, gratitude, and obedience. The point of comparison for the divine Fatherhood is not human fatherhood: this would imply a point by point comparison which proportionality denies radically. It is human filiation ("Sexist Language in Theology," *Theological Studies* 36 [1975]: 717).

52. Phyllis Trible, *God and the Rhetoric of Sexuality*, p. 202.

53. Phyllis Trible, "Depatriarchialism in Biblical Interpretation," *Journal of the American Academy of Religion* 41 (1973): 34. The entire paragraph is worth quoting:

> To summarize: although the Old Testament often pictures Yahweh as a man, it also uses gynomorphic language for the Deity. At the same time, Israel repudiated the idea of sexuality in God. Unlike fertility gods, Yahweh is neither male nor female, neither he nor she. Consequently, modern assertions that God is masculine, even when they are qualified, are misleading and detrimental, if not altogether inaccurate. Cultural and grammatical limitations (the use of masculine pronouns for God) need not limit theological understanding. As Creator and Lord, Yahweh embraces and transcends both sexes. To translate for our immediate concerns: the nature of the God of Israel defies sexism.

54. Trible, *God and the Rhetoric of Sexuality*, p. 19.
55. Ibid., pp. 16, 21.
56. Ibid., p. 21.
57. Ibid., pp. 31–59.
58. Ibid., p. 38.
59. Caird, *The Language and Imagery of the Bible*, p. 154.
60. Elisabeth Schüssler Fiorenza, "Feminist Spirituality, Christian Identity, and Catholic Vision," in *Womanspirit Rising*, ed. Christ and Plaskow, p. 138.
61. Hamerton-Kelly, *God the Father*, p. 81.
62. Edward Schillebeeckx, *Jesus: An Experiment in Christology* (New York: Crossroad, 1979), pp. 262–63.
63. Ibid., p. 268.
64. See Elaine Pagels, *The Gnostic Gospels* (New York: Random House, 1970) and "What Became of God the Mother? Conflicting Images of God in Early Christianity," in *Womanspirit Rising*, ed. Christ and Plaskow, pp. 107–119.
65. Pagels, "What Became of God the Mother?" p. 110.

66. Ibid.

67. Ibid.

68. Jürgen Moltmann, "The Motherly Father. Is Trinitarian Patripassionism Replacing Theological Patriarchalism?" in *God as Father?* ed. Johannes-Baptist Metz and Edward Schillebeeckx (New York: Seabury Press, 1981), p. 53.

69. Eleanor McLaughlin, "The Christian Past: Does it Hold a Future for Women?" *Anglican Theological Review* 57 (1975): 36–56.

70. McLaughlin, " 'Christ My Mother': Feminine Naming and Metaphors in Medieval Spirituality," *St. Lukes Journal of Theology* 18 (1975): 371.

71. Ibid., p. 374.

72. Ibid., p. 375.

73. Ibid., p. 372.

74. Ibid., p. 383.

75. "In all this nuptial imagery the Phrygian cradleland in which it arose is clearly in the background. Behind it lies that of the Goddess cult in Asia Minor interpreted in terms of the mystical thought and language of the motherhood of the Virgin Church conceiving children spiritually through the natural process of parturition with its attendant labour and travail. The female principle, originally personified in the Magna Mater, became the Magna Ecclesia, at once the Bride and Body of Christ, the Mother of the faithful proceeding towards perfection, in whom the Bride is merged" (E. O. James, *The Cult of the Mother-Goddess*, p. 200).

76. Ibid., pp. 224–25.

77. Ruether, *New Woman-New Earth*, p. 56.

78. It is therefore appropriate, I believe, to address God as "she" as well as "he." As Rita Gross notes, the nature of theism in Judaism (and the same holds for Christianity) demands the use of personal pronouns for addressing God, both in prayer and in theology. Unless one uses the feminine personal pronoun, says Gross, one hides behind implicit sexism. She notes further that throughout theological tradition, the *via negativa* has been applied to all human characteristics predicated of God, except the male pronoun. She believes this stems from the profound androcentricism of our culture, revealed in the fact that atheists may deny God's existence but do not question the use of the male pronoun for the nonexistent deity! "Why has this single designation escaped unscathed even in a theological tradition that tries to question all positive and therefore inaccurate God language? Shouldn't 'He' and all variants of it be as circumscribed as any other positive attributes of God—or more circumscribed since they are more misleading?" ("Female God Language in a Jewish Context," in *Womanspirit Rising*, ed. Christ and Plaskow, p. 170).

79. The quotation, given in full below, is by Yorick Spiegel:

A theology (and this is something that political theology understands) located in the family situation, which nowadays is characterised by need-satisfaction and wish-fulfilment, must necessarily unilaterally favour the illusionary nature of belief to the disadvantage of its concern to banish political repression and economic exploitation. . . . Only if theological research succeeds in incorporating family symbolism into the contemporary world-wide struggle for the humanisation and self-assertion of the masses, is it possible for the religious symbolism of the family to become a truly guiding image ("God the Father in the Fatherless Society," in *God as Father?*, ed. Metz and Schillebeeckx, pp. 8–9).

80. Ruether, *New Woman-New Earth*, p. 26.

81. LeGuin, *The Language of the Night*, p. 162.

82. LeGuin, *The Left Hand of Darkness*, p. 235.

83. See Joachim Jeremias, *New Testament Theology* (New York: Charles Scribner's Sons, 1971), vol. 1, pp. 115–16, 121; Günther Bornkamm, *Jesus of Nazareth*, Eng. trans. Irene and Fraser McLuskey with James Robinson (New York: Harper & Row, 1960), pp. 80–81; Norman Perrin, *Rediscovering the Teaching of Jesus* (New York: Harper & Row, 1967), pp. 102, 107. I am indebted to Mary Ann Tolbert for directing me to this material.

84. Bornkamm, *Jesus of Nazareth*, p. 81; Perrin, *Rediscovering the Teaching of Jesus*, p. 102.

85. Jeremias, *New Testament Theology*, p. 121; see also Perrin, *Rediscovering the Teaching of Jesus*, p. 102.

86. Bornkamm, *Jesus of Nazareth*, p. 81.

87. Jeremias, *New Testament Theology*, pp. 115–16; Bornkamm, *Jesus of Nazareth*, p. 81; Perrin, *Rediscovering the Teaching of Jesus*, p. 107.

88. Raymond E. Brown, *The Gospel of John*, Anchor Bible Commentaries (New York: Doubleday & Co., 1970), vol. 29a, p. 682.

89. Moltmann, "The Motherly Father," in *God as Father?*, ed. Metz and Schillebeeckx, p. 55.

90. I am indebted to Ronald Olson and Robin Mattison, both doctoral students in the Department of Religion at Vanderbilt University, for this insight.

91. Ruth Page, "Human Liberation and Divine Transcendence," *Theology* 85 (1982): 184–190.

92. Ibid., p. 188.

93. Ibid., p. 189.

94. Ibid.

95. The model of God as friend has obvious connections with process theology; in fact, the appropriate metaphysics accompanying this model— were it to be seen as a root-metaphor (which I am not suggesting be done)— would be process thought.

96. Page, "Human Liberation and Divine Transcendence," p. 190.

97. "The reader of medieval piety is constantly assailed with images of God and God's relationship to the soul which break out of the sexual/familial range of experiences. A most obvious category is friendship with God: God as Friend to the soul and vice versa is a recurring theme, especially in the later middle ages" (McLaughlin, "Christ My Mother," p. 381).

98. A good source for other contemporary nonsexist models is the article, "Changing Language and the Church," by Letty M. Russell in her edited book, *The Liberating Word: A Guide to Non-Sexist Interpretation of the*

Bible (Philadelphia: Westminster Press, 1976). Many Protestant denominations have issued statements on language about God. The one by the United Presbyterian Church, U.S.A. has a fine paragraph:

> Given that God does act in our (Israel's) midst, the whole realm of language and association, feminine as well as masculine, is available for the describing and confessing of God's activity, though the tradition has made little use of the full range. This is the crux: as metaphor, everything is admissible which does not demean or confine. Nevertheless, as long as the female and the feminine are assumed in our culture to be limiting, defective or evil, feminine language for the naming of God's acts is excluded. The theological problem of language about God derives from anthropological assumptions about human possibility—in Old Testament times as well as today (UPCUSA. "Language About God: 'Opening the Door,'" adopted by the 187th General Assembly, 1975).

99. Letty M. Russell, *The Future of Partnership* (Philadelphia: Westminster Press, 1979), p. 18.

100. Ibid., p. 35.

101. Ibid., pp. 34–35.

102. McLaughlin, "Christ My Mother," p. 381.

103. Ibid.

104. *Poems and Prose of Gerard Manley Hopkins*, ed. W. H. Gardner (Harmondsworth, Eng.: Penguin Bks., 1953), pp. 27, 31.

105. Paul Tillich, *Systematic Theology*, (Chicago: Univ. of Chicago Press, 1959), vol. 1, pp. 238–39.

Index of Authors

Achinstein, Peter, 88, 208 n.15, 210 n.39, 210 n.41
Anselm of Canterbury, 131, 174
Aquinas, Thomas, 27, 124–26, 130
Aristotle, 32, 37, 67, 134, 198 n.16
Arius, 115
Auden, W. H., 23
Augustine, 1, 2, 6, 27, 71, 113, 126, 130–31, 149

Barbour, Ian, 78, 80, 83, 90–92, 109, 111, 132–33, 137–38, 141, 208 n.15, 208 n.21, 209 n.25, 210 n.39, 211 n.67
Barr, James, 61
Barth, Karl, 13, 27–28, 82, 129–30, 140
Beardslee, William A., 48
Berger, Peter, 150–51, 158, 196 n.9
Berggren, Douglas, 37, 41, 136
Bernard of Clairvaux, 174
Bethune-Baker, J. F., 115
Birgitta of Sweden, Saint, 174
Black, Max, 23–24, 37–38, 76, 83, 100, 122, 133, 182
Bohr, Niels, 86, 88, 208 n.15
Bonhoeffer, Dietrich, 186
Born, Max, 132
Bornkamm, Günther, 180–81
Braithwaite, R. P., 72, 133, 210 n.39
Bregman, Lucy, 195 n.3
Brodbeck, Mae, 210 n.39
Bronowski, Jacob, 35
Brown, Raymond E., 181
Burke, Kenneth, 34, 56, 59, 199 n.19

Burrell, David, 33, 198–99 n.16, 201–2 n.3

Caird, George B., 42, 149–50, 170
Calvin, John, 13, 126, 140
Carmody, Denise, 218 n.38
Christ, Carol, 154, 156–59, 195 n.7, 215 n.1, 217 n.21
Christina of Markgate, 174
Coleridge, Samuel, 35, 37, 200 n.20
Collins, Sheila D., 148, 215 n.1
Cousins, Ewert H., 217 n.25
Crossan, John Dominic, 47–48, 109, 204 n.34, 204–5 n.38
Cupitt, Don, 215 n.55

Daly, Mary, 3, 147, 155–59, 215 n.1
Dante, 6, 179, 189
Darwin, Charles, 16, 70
Descartes, René, 34
Dillistone, F. W., 199–200 n.20
Dilthey, Wilhelm, 56
Dodd, C. H., 46, 204–5 n.38
Donahue, John, 50, 52–53, 200 n.21, 204 n.34, 204–5 n.38
Dostoyevsky, Fyodor, 60
Douglas, Mary, 195–96 n.12
Dreistadt, Roy, 202 n.9, 210 n.45
Dunne, John S., 68

Einstein, Albert, 70, 208 n.15
Eliot, T. S., 23, 59
Embler, Weller, 73, 207 n.4, 207 n.5
Emmet, Dorothy, 149, 214 n.37

223

Farrer, Austin, 151, 206 n.63
Ferré, Frederick, 90, 95, 104, 106–7, 111, 142–43, 210 n.39, 210–11 n.58, 211 n.1, 211 n.3
Feuerbach, Ludwig, 6
Fiorenza, Elisabeth Schüssler, 170
Freud, Sigmund, 70, 114, 200 n.24, 216 n.12
Frost, Robert, 201 n.2
Funk, Robert W., ix, 22, 46, 103, 204–5 n.38

Gadamer, Hans-Georg, 56–59, 63–64, 207 n.71
Galileo, 70
Geertz, Clifford, 6–7, 158
Gilbert, Scott F., 207 n.6
Gill, Jerry H., 214 n.34, 215 n.51
Gilson, Etienne, 197 n.14
Goldenberg, Naomi R., 156–59
Goodman, Nelson, 37, 39–40, 55
Gross, Rita, 196 n.10, 215 n.1, 220 n.78

Habermas, Jürgen, 64
Hamerton-Kelly, Robert, 170–71, 215 n.1, 217 n.19
Hamilton, Alexander, 71
Hanson, N. R., 90, 211 n.60
Harré, Rom, 90, 100, 208 n.15, 210 n.39
Hartshorne, Charles, 96
Heidegger, Martin, 8, 34, 63, 96, 118, 120
Heisenberg, Werner, 208 n.15, 209 n.22
Heller, Erich, 197–98 n.15
Heschel, Abraham J., 68
Hesse, Mary B., 35, 90, 93–94, 100–101, 208 n.18, 208 n.19, 208 n.20, 209 n.24, 210 n.39
Hick, John, 195 n.11, 203 n.21, 205 n.48
Hillman, James, 195 n.3
Hobbes, Thomas, 71
Hopkins, Gerard Manley, 11

Hulme, T., 201 n.2
Husserl, Edmund, 96
Hutten, E. H., 85, 90, 92–93, 95, 98, 208 n.15, 209 n.23, 210 n.39

James, E. O., 156, 159, 176, 220 n.75
Jeans, Sir Thomas, 87
Jeremias, Joachim, 170, 180–81
Julian of Norwich, 3, 174–75

Kafka, Franz, 41
Kant, Immanuel, 34
Kaufman, Gordon D., 97
Kaufman, R., 201 n.2
Keck, Leander, 48–50, 52–53, 160–61, 199 n.17, 200 n.21, 204 n.34
Keller, Marcia, 152
Kennet, R. H., 204 n.31
Kermode, Frank, 60, 195 n.2
Koestler, Arthur, 36, 75–76, 79, 117, 161
Kuhn, Thomas, 75, 79–83, 201 n.2, 208 n.15, 209 n.34

Landau, Martin, 71
Leatherdale, W. H., 202 n.6, 210 n.53
LeGuin, Ursula K., 29, 162–64, 175, 179
Lewis, C. S., 87–88, 161, 201 n.2, 203–4 n.27
Linge, David, 205–6 n.58
Luther, Martin, 12–13, 82, 126, 154

MacCormac, Earl R., 107, 119, 153, 209 n.32, 212 n.16
McLaughlin, Eleanor, 174–76, 192, 221 n.97
Mach, E., 85
Macquarrie, John, 118
Masterman, Margaret, 209 n.31
Mechthild of Hackeborn, 174
Merleau-Ponty, Maurice, 96
Moltmann, Jürgen, 173, 181, 188
Murry, John Middleton, 32

Nagel, Ernest, 210 n.39

Nash, Leonard, 210 n.39
Niebuhr, Reinhold, 3
Nietzsche, Friedrich, 201 n.2

Ong, Walter J., 37–39
Orwell, George, 115

Page, Ruth, 183–84, 188
Pagels, Elaine, 172–73, 196 n.8
Pepper, Stephen, 201 n.27, 201 n.2, 208 n.15
Perrin, Norman, 180–81, 204–5 n.38
Petrie, Hugh, 199 n.18
Piaget, Jean, 199 n.18
Planck, Max, 75, 208 n.15
Plaskow, Judith, 154, 195 n.7, 217 n.21
Plato, 33, 70–71
Polonyi, Michael, 208 n.15

Rahner, Karl, 115
Ramsen, Ian T., 7, 106, 115, 122–25, 131–32, 141, 154, 197 n.13, 215 n.50
Richards, I. A., 37–38, 201 n.2
Ricoeur, Paul, 27, 34, 37–40, 45–47, 59, 63–65, 96, 99–100, 110, 119–22, 124, 131–32, 134–36, 154, 202–3 n.12, 204 n.33, 204 n.34, 205 n.46, 206 n.62, 206–7 n.69, 213 n.23, 213 n.31, 214–15 n.45
Ritschl, Albrecht, 133
Ruether, Rosemary, 148–49, 151, 156, 159, 165–66, 176–77, 179, 215 n.1, 216 n.7, 216 n.8, 216–17 n.15
Russell, Bertrand, 210 n.39
Russell, Letty M., 190–91, 221–22 n.98

Saiving, Valerie, 154
Sapir, J. David, 207 n.7
Schillebeeckx, Edward, 171–72
Schleiermacher, Friedrich, 27, 56, 82, 126, 133
Scholes, Robert, 160–61
Schon, Donald, 88, 147, 210 n.52
Shakespeare, William, 38, 59
Shibles, Warren A., 201 n.2
Spiegel, Yorick, 220–21 n.79
Spinoza, Baruch, 34
Starhawk (Miriam Simos), 157
Stogdill, Ralph M., 208 n.13

Tavard, George, 218–19 n.51
Tillich, Paul, 13, 96–97, 126, 192
Toulmin, Stephen, 133, 208 n.15, 210 n.39
Tracy, David, ix–x, 14, 61–62, 109–10, 146, 198 n.16, 212 n.12
Trible, Phyllis, 7, 168–70, 215 n.1, 217 n.19, 219 n.53
Turbayne, Colin M., 41–42
Turner, Victor W., 70, 207–8 n.9, 217 n.24

Vico, G., 37

Wartofsky, Max, 132
Weil, Simone, 1, 2, 131, 194
Wesley, John, 82
Whitehead, A. N., 34, 96, 105, 176, 208 n.15
Wilder, Amos, 111, 204–5 n.38
Wiles, Maurice, 53
Wittgenstein, Ludwig, 8, 34

Zwingli, H., 12–13